Place
IN AMERICAN FICTION

$\mathcal{Place}$ IN

UNIVERSITY OF MISSOURI PRESS · COLUMBIA AND LONDON

AMERICAN FICTION

Excursions and Explorations

Edited by H. L. Weatherby and George Core

In Honor of Walter Sullivan

Photo by John Sullivan

Copyright © 2004 by
The Curators of the University of Missouri
University of Missouri Press, Columbia, Missouri 65201
Printed and bound in the United States of America
All rights reserved
5 4 3 2 1   08 07 06 05 04

Library of Congress Cataloging-in-Publication Data

Place in American fiction : excursions and explorations / edited by
H. L. Weatherby and George Core.
       p.   cm.
    Includes bibliographical references and index.
    ISBN 0-8262-1563-7 (alk. paper)
    1. American fiction—20th century—History and criticism.
2. Setting (Literature)   3. Place (Philosophy) in literature.
4. Regionalism in literature.   5. Local color in literature.
I. Weatherby, Harold L., 1934–   II. Sullivan, Walter, 1924–
III. Core, George.
    PS374.S45P57 2004

But where's the man, who counsel can bestow,
Still pleased to teach, and yet not proud to know?
Unbiased, or by favor, or by spite;
Not dully prepossessed, nor blindly right;
Though learned, well-bred; and though well-bred, sincere;
Modestly bold, and humanly severe;
Who to a friend his faults can freely show,
And gladly praise the merit of a foe?
Blest with a taste exact, yet unconfined;
A knowledge both of books and human kind;
Gen'rous converse; a soul exempt from pride;
And love to praise, with reason on his side?
—ALEXANDER POPE, ESSAY ON CRITICISM

♾™ This paper meets the requirements of the
American National Standard for Permanence of Paper
for Printed Library Materials, Z39.48, 1984.

DESIGNER: KRISTIE LEE
TYPESETTER: PHOENIX TYPE, INC.
PRINTER AND BINDER: THE MAPLE-VAIL BOOK
    MANUFACTURING GROUP
TYPEFACES: MINION AND LTZAPFINO

The University of Missouri Press offers its grateful acknowl-
edgment to Vanderbilt University for a generous contribution
in support of the publication of this volume.

Latecomer

for Walter Sullivan

He stands outside unwontedly alone,
The door muffling the ebullient social natter
Of voices he's known forever: Lon
And Mr. Ransom, Jean's bright, unnerving chatter,
And Allen, of course there's Allen, and Davidson
And Peter, Cal and Cleanth, Caroline
And chuckling Red. He names them one by one.
Auld lang syne. *Eternity's auld lang syne.*

The talk is fugal music whose themes he knows
Thoughts of a literary renaissance,
Intricacies of intellectual lives.
He enters, takes his accustomed place, and bows
To the pleased party his genial recognizance—
But will wait his toddy until Jane arrives.
—FRED CHAPPELL

Contents

Preface

The essays in this collection—which consist both of personal pieces written by fiction writers working chiefly in the vein of reminiscence and of essays in criticism principally devoted to the works of individual writers such as Faulkner, Fitzgerald, J. F. Powers, and, most especially, Eudora Welty—have been commissioned by the editors to celebrate the career of Walter Sullivan as a teacher and a writer. The collection was not conceived as the usual festschrift, a book of scholarly articles (often random) written along the lines of old or new literary history and buttressed by thickets of footnotes. Walter Sullivan is a fiction writer and a critic. The work presented in *Place in American Fiction*, as the reader will find, is written in the same modes as his literary criticism and his informal essays of various kinds. No one was instructed to write an article taking account of every item ever written on, say, place in Fitzgerald's stories laid in St. Paul; or place as revealed in Faulkner's stories about the big woods; or the many places (particularly in the South) that appear in Robert Penn Warren's novels; or place as seen in Updike's many stories and novels, especially those located in New England. Instead each author was given free rein to range as he or she thought best in considering representative fictions.

Indeed, no one involved in this celebration has endeavored to mention all the possibilities of place as it is brought to bear in fiction in general—or in any one writer. There is, for instance, place as afforded by the natural world; and some of the best writers considered here, particularly Faulkner, are masters at creating that world: "one of the most impressive features of Faulkner's work is the vivid realization of the natural background," as Warren has written in his classic essay on Faulkner that appears in *Selected Essays* (1958). We have many examples here of places in fiction that are not natural or topographical but that occur in towns or houses or rooms or other enclosed or otherwise defined spaces.

Place is not only attached to scene and therefore to the characters appearing within various scenes occurring in fiction; it also involves memory—the memories of the author who is creating the scenes and of his characters who are living within the unfolding action of the given story or novel. So, as George Garrett says in "Places We Have Come From, Places We Have Been," "memory and place are hopelessly entangled." Place provides the setting for the action, and it is seen through the lens of memory. Or, to frame these issues a little differently, we can quote Eudora Welty, the presiding spirit for this occasion: "place," she says, "has the most delicate control over character too: by confining character, it defines it."

Relatively little of enduring value has been written about the role of place in American fiction, a fact that becomes evident if you read such a study as Floyd C. Watkins's *In Time and Place: Origins of American Fiction* (1977) and scan the many references therein, especially those for the two chapters devoted to Willa Cather, a writer for whom place plays a pivotal role. The paucity of material published about place in American fiction has provided the contributors with the occasion to explore a central aspect of fiction as well as to celebrate the life and work of Walter Sullivan.

Acknowledgments

We wish to thank Professor John H. Venable, former dean of the College of Arts and Science at Vanderbilt University, for setting aside money in the college's budget to honor Professor Walter Sullivan upon his retirement. With this thoughtful and generous gesture Dean Venable launched the project that has eventuated in *Place in American Fiction.*

We are also grateful to Professor Ward Allen and to Professor R. L. Arrington for reading the page proof of this book.

To Professor Fred Chappell we extend our thanks for the superb dedicatory poem that graces this volume of essays—"Latecomer."

We would be remiss not to record our special appreciation to Professor Louis D. Rubin, Jr., who not only contributed an essay but at the outset struck the theme pursued by everyone involved in this occasion—place in modern American fiction.

We are most indebted to Professor Robert Benson for unflagging work on this book, which extends far beyond his writing the essay on J. F. Powers and *Morte D'Urban.* Mr. Benson's augean labors are such that he should be shown as our coeditor.

Part

I

Introduction
A Ball of Golden Thread

George Core

It is the sense of place going with us
still that is the ball of golden thread
to carry us there and back and in every
sense of the word to bring us home.
. . . Place is forever illustrative:
it is a picture of what man has done and imagined.
—EUDORA WELTY, "PLACE IN FICTION"

When Robert Benchley was caught in the vise of writer's block, he sat down at his typewriter and pecked out the word *The*, thinking it "as safe a start as any." Then he "left for a cheerful hour or so" with some friends of the Algonquin Round Table. Later, after returning to his room and finding that solitary word "on the expanse of yellow paper," he finished the inchoate sentence so it read "The hell with it." Then, conscience assuaged, he "went out happily for the evening." We owe this story to Nathaniel Benchley, who tells it in his biography of his father.[1]

Few American writers have written about Hell, which Benchley did not investigate but merely invoked. Jean-Paul Sartre wrote his most famous play, *No Exit,* about four characters who are trapped in their own Hell by being confined to their own company. And William Faulkner, in a famous passage in his Snopes trilogy, has Flem descend into Hell. After Flem confronts Satan and outwits him,

---

1. Nathaniel Benchley's life of his father was published in 1955. This anecdote appears in *The Oxford Book of American Literary Anecdotes,* ed. Donald Hall (New York: Oxford University Press, 1981), 233.

he tells his lieutenants to expel Flem from Hell's precincts. "'Take Paradise!' the Prince screams. 'Take it. Take it.'"[2] This is one of the great moments in Faulkner's fiction.

When we think of place in Faulkner, we do not recall this remarkable scene: instead we remember the Yoknapatawpha country, including the great wilderness that H. L. Weatherby considers in his essay. In Faulkner, as Robert Penn Warren observes, "nature . . . is more than a backdrop." This "mastery of place in fiction," as Eudora Welty calls it,[3] is what often makes the difference in fiction, the difference in its being humdrum or mediocre and its being at least good and its sometimes (as in Faulkner, Warren, Welty) achieving greatness. That case also applies to other modern southern writers such as Katherine Anne Porter, Elizabeth Spencer, and Wendell Berry; it applies just as well to such midwestern writers as F. Scott Fitzgerald and J. F. Powers and such western writers as Wallace Stegner and such New England writers as John Updike. These modern American writers, our own for this occasion, do not exemplify Frederick Hoffman's observation that "much modern literature is a literature without place." That dubious distinction belongs to Kafka, Sartre, Beckett, Pirandello, and others.

"Much of the psychic imbalance described in modern literature occurs in an abstracted setting; it is not identified with a place, a culture, or a family," Hoffman goes on to say in "The Sense of Place." "It is only when scene is identified with place that the full powers of the literary imagination are challenged and used."[4] His essay, while not so central to our book as Eudora Welty's "Place in Fiction," is nevertheless exceptionally useful, especially in his remarks about the relation of place and scene, which, as he says, often are connected by metaphor.

Any fiction writer worth his or her salt shapes the narrative and plot in terms of scene. The scene, as Henry James makes plain throughout his prefaces and his criticism of fiction in general, is the sine qua non of fiction—its essential component. "The *scenic* method is my absolute, my imperative, my *only* salvation," James tells us in his notebooks, explaining that "the scenic scheme is the only one I can trust . . . to stick to the march of an action."[5] For the scene to work best, it must be placed in a recognizable milieu, which can be as large as a town

2. Faulkner, *The Hamlet* (New York: Random House, 1940), 155.

3. Warren, *Selected Essays* (New York: Random House, 1958), 68; Welty, *The Eye of the Story: Selected Essays and Reviews* (New York: Random House, 1978), 116. Subsequent parenthetical references to Welty's essays are to this edition.

4. Louis D. Rubin Jr. and Robert D. Jacobs, eds., *South: Modern Southern Literature in Its Cultural Setting* (Garden City: Doubleday, 1961), 60–61.

5. *The Notebooks of Henry James*, ed. F. O. Matthiessen and Kenneth B. Murdock (New York: Oxford University Press, 1947), 263.

or country or as confined spatially as a house or even a room within a house. In her essay Martha Hall says how essential to her short fiction is the house, which she presents from within and without in such stories as "Privacy" and "The Snakeshooter." Scene comes to life against the massed details that emerge from and through the depiction of place. We get a sharp sense of the landscape abutting the house, and at the same time we learn something about the neighborhood and the town where it is (especially in "Privacy"), so that the microcosm of the scene and the succession of scenes lead us to the macrocosm of the world beyond—what Eudora Welty calls "the test of the outside world" in her "Writing and Analyzing a Story" (109), in which she examines her own story "No Place for You, My Love."

This story has been chosen by both Lewis Simpson and Denis Donoghue in their essays devoted to Welty and the fiction of place. It is the kind of story that no good teacher of fiction writing, such as Wallace Stegner or Walter Sullivan, would ever encourage a student, regardless of how brilliant, to pursue. There are but two characters, strangers to each other as the action begins and hardly more than acquaintances when it ends less than a day later; they remain nameless; there is no conflict; and the plot is limited to a journey they take together south of New Orleans, "south from South" (111). It is an automobile trip along the south pass of the Mississippi River toward Burrville and Pilot Town and through Venice.

"They were strangers to each other, both fairly well strangers to the place," it begins. In the course of the action we learn as little about them as they learn about each other. The plot is provided by their almost eventless journey together down the narrow road, the "road ahead of you and following you," as the author says in her essay on river country (291); and the action concludes when they return to New Orleans from the café Baba's Place near land's end. Seldom will one encounter a simpler plot.

Our two distinguished critics glance at two stories similar to "No Place for You, My Love." Simpson comments briefly on "The Bride of the Innisfallen," and Donoghue quickly considers "A Worn Path." Each fiction is based on a journey. The longer and more complicated story of course unfolds in "The Bride of the Innisfallen." In it we follow the progress of the boat train from Paddington station in London to Fishguard in Wales to Cork in Ireland. (It seems probable that Eudora Welty took the same trip when she visited Elizabeth Bowen in Ireland, who said of her guest: "She's like me in preferring places to people."[6]) None of

6. Quoted in Victoria Glendinning, *Elizabeth Bowen: A Biography* (New York: Knopf, 1978), 262.

the characters, except a little boy with a minor role, is named. The protagonist is an American woman whose short marriage is in jeopardy. Most of the action occurs in a single compartment of the train, and the journey provides the plot. As with "No Place for You, My Love," the author does not let us inside the mind of any character, including the unhappy woman who seems to be fleeing not only her confining circumstances in London but also herself. "A Worn Path" is a much simpler and far shorter tale of a courageous elderly woman making her way along the worn path in the winter landscape. That path is not only the locus of the action but also the controlling image so that place and scene are conjoined. "Her persisting in her landscape was the real thing," Welty declares of this account of "life's uncertainty" (161). The journey, unlike those in the other stories, has been made regularly and will continue to be made so long as Phoenix Jackson lives. In contrast the other journeys are unique.

Donoghue's and Simpson's accounts of "No Place for You, My Love" complement and fortify each other. Donoghue stresses Welty's imagery through considering W. B. Yeats and Guy Davenport, stressing the occasional and emblematic nature of the local image: "One's sense of life is amplified without losing the immediate force of the image." And, he concludes, "she makes space and place subsume the historical time in which her people, houses, and habitats have become what they are." (Here place and time become a seamless whole.) In following the logic of his reflections Donoghue decides that Welty's focus on place constitutes "a theory of pastoral." This is a moment worthy of William Empson at his best.

In contrast, Simpson, while also stressing the importance of place as the essential element in the same story and discussing the mysterious relationship between the two unnamed principals, shows the importance of time in fiction, especially the novel; and he reveals the linkage that connects time to memory, specifically to what he deems "the culture of memory" in Faulkner and Welty. What is portrayed, in considerably different ways, in the fiction of these writers, as Simpson shrewdly demonstrates, is "a vision of place and time that reveals the mystery of 'the living relationship' between what is going on and our selves." He mounts his argument partly through considering Welty's work as a photographer and her efforts to freeze significant moments in human experience through perfect snapshots.

I have lingered on these superb essays because Eudora Welty is the pivotal figure in this book, and her "Place in Fiction" is the crucial critical essay that is considered in this collection time and again by many of the contributors. The strong essays on place in fiction written by Frederick Hoffman, Wallace Stegner, Blair Rowse, and others pale in comparison. "Place, then, has the most delicate control over character . . . : by confining character, it defines it," she tells us. "Place in fiction is the named, identified, concrete, exact and exacting, and therefore credible, gathering spot of all that has been felt, is about to be experienced." Now she clinches her argument: "Location pertains to feeling; feeling profoundly pertains to place; place in history partakes of feeling, as feeling about history partakes of place. Every story would be another story, and unrecognizable as art, if it took up its characters and plot and happened somewhere else" (122).

Perhaps the most representative critical essay in this collection is the one written on Wallace Stegner's fiction by Thomas Bontly. Stegner, who has declared that "in fiction . . . we should have no agenda except to be truthful," has also observed this: "No place, not even a wild place, is a place until it has . . . that human attention that at its highest reach we call poetry." This is one of several essential passages from Stegner's criticism that Bontly quotes. Place, as Stegner shows us, is fundamental to the whole person, not merely to the writer: "Some are born in their place, some find it, some realize after long searching that the place they left is the one they have been searching for." He concludes "The Sense of Place" with these words: "Only in the act of submission is the sense of place realized and a sustainable relationship between people and earth established."[7]

It is this lesson—the importance not only of a person securing his or her place but of an author's doing so as well—that Bontly explains the ordinary student of writing cannot understand and then seize the implications of that understanding. The minimalist, as he says, conveys the absurd notion that in the given work of fiction the vaguer the setting the more universal it may therefore become. But anywhere, including Hell, is more believable than nowhere. The more details and the more definite and concrete the place, whether it is ordinary (the Delta) or exotic (Trieste or Florence), the more the author will establish and secure a believable and seamless interrelationship among what Eudora Welty calls "setting, characters, mood, and method of writing," which all work "as parts of the same thing and subject to related laws" (114). The crucial element—place—enables the circumstantiality and realism of her stories and the same dimension in Stegner's fiction, what Bontly calls lyrical realism.

This term *lyrical realism* can also be applied to the fiction of John Updike, especially to his stories, as Pat Hoy shows. You can encounter poetic language almost anywhere in Updike's fiction: "You allow this black skirt to slide off your raised knees down your thighs, slide *up* your thighs in your body's absolute geography"

7. Stegner, *Where the Bluebird Sings to the Lemonade Springs: Living and Writing in the West* (New York: Random House, 1992), 222, 201–6 passim.

("Wife-wooing"). Hoy, in considering Updike's recurring themes and iterative imagery, measures them by various places and spaces, especially the geography of the female body; and he reveals the significance of Updike's remark about one of his couples, the Maples, a remark that has a far larger application: "The musical pattern, the advance and retreat, of the Maples' duet, is repeated over and over, ever more harshly transposed."[8] Technically, as our critic shows, this virtuoso works in a general way: "As place recedes into the background, . . . his vision comes into the foreground, and we see instead of place the dramatic action of the scene itself." James, in his preface to *What Maisie Knew,* joins the matter: "The treatment by 'scene,' regularly, quite rhythmically recurs . . . ; each of the agents, true to its function, taking up the theme from the other very much as the fiddles, in an orchestra, may take it up from the cornets and flutes, or the wind-instruments take it up from the violins."[9] Pat Hoy, like Denis Donoghue, is especially apt in considering the connection of place and scene that is supplied and revealed by and through metaphor.

Once the author learns the importance of place in fiction—often the hard way, as Elizabeth Spencer tells us (and as Thomas Bontly has already warned)— he or she can write convincingly about a place, as Spencer states as she recounts her own experience in forging *The Light in the Piazza,* which is set in Florence, Italy, not in Mississippi. (Later she would place a novel in Canada.) She began writing *The Light in the Piazza* during a snowstorm in Montreal as she thought of her controlling image in Florence—the "radiant light." "Ideally," she observes, "the feelings the fiction writer finds in the characters arise out of a known place." Spencer mentions the differences between the hill country of north Mississippi, where her family seat is located, and the flat rich land of the Delta, which is Charles East's subject in his essay of the same name. East, a short story writer like Martha Hall, describes this region with dazzling exactness: "Except for green patches of woods and the willows and cypresses that lined old streams . . . the Delta was mostly fields, and as flat as a tabletop. It was a land white with cotton in late summer and brown in winter, a land that stretched from horizon to horizon." Now he mentions his own fiction, the first of the stories collected in two books. "In . . . 'Under the Blue Cup,'" he says, "I saw my characters trapped under 'a canopy of cloud and sky, like a blue cup turned upside down over them.'" Here place is as wide and limitless as the sky and as vast as the flat land between

8. Updike, *Too Far to Go: The Maples Stories* (New York: Fawcett Crest, 1979), 30, 10.
9. James, *The Art of the Novel: Critical Prefaces,* ed. Richard P. Blackmur (New York: Charles Scribner's Sons, 1934), 157–58.

horizons. Even so, it has its own character and nature and distinctiveness, and it is by no means vague and without identity. At once punctuating the land and holding it together is the great Mississippi River: "Behind the levee," he tells us, "beyond the bar pits and blue holes and the *batture* with its cottonwood trees and willows, the river eddied its way south, carrying logs and sometimes dead bodies with it." We also encounter the southern reaches of the Mississippi in "No Place for You, My Love," as it is emptying into the Gulf of Mexico.

West of the Mississippi River is east Texas, which Katherine Anne Porter limns in her Miranda stories in a sequence collected under the title *The Old Order*. East Texas is the native country of her heart, but she writes well of many places, including Mexico, Germany, and Louisiana. These Miranda stories, which are considered by William Pratt in his essay, reveal what he calls "the culture that nurtured her imagination and that is at the center of her best fiction." He also deals in passing with stories such as "Pale Horse, Pale Rider," which is laid in Denver. And he shrewdly quotes Porter on place as providing a sense of form and an equilibrium for fiction.

An entirely different kind of place is considered by Scott Donaldson in his essay "St. Paul Boy." St. Paul, Minnesota, is at the other end of the Mississippi River from the Delta and the other lower reaches of that river which we have seen through the eyes of Eudora Welty, Charles East, and others. Donaldson examines F. Scott Fitzgerald's long, awkward, and complicated relation to his hometown, especially to Summit Avenue, the best street in that town, the high street. As Donaldson shows, Fitzgerald lived on the fringes of this tony neighborhood by which as a boy and, later, as a writer he measured the city as a whole. As our critic says, Fitzgerald drew from his boyhood in St. Paul the basic donnée of his fiction: the situation of the "poor young boy unable to win the love of the beautiful rich girl." It is Summit Avenue, place of "dwellings of the rich" and of the "monumental residential boulevard," that draws Fitzgerald to use it for the setting of his stories of Basil Lee and others. As at least one reader has said in conversation, this essay makes anyone interested in Fitzgerald want to walk slowly through the Summit Avenue neighborhood to understand its magnetism for the impressionable author. Toward the end of this engaging piece Scott Donaldson takes the reader on this walk.

In his essay devoted to J. F. Powers, Robert Benson considers what is finally a much less secular Middle West than the one Fitzgerald wrote about. In his fiction, chiefly given to the Catholic Church and its priestly community, Powers ordinarily confines his characters to boardrooms, hotels, and country clubs; to churches, rectories, and monasteries. Benson reveals how the thematic movement of the action in *Morte D'Urban*—from vice to virtue in the life of the protagonist—is reflected in the movement from the city to the country. This comic novel of Christian redemption is thus also a version of pastoral as the scene moves from Chicago to the monastery in the country. It is instructive to compare the sacramental elements in the religious fiction of Powers with the secular fiction of John Updike, who celebrates carnal, not divine, love. (Walter Sullivan's latest story, "Bare Ruined Choirs," published in *Sewanee Review* in the fall of 2003 and written in the vein of Powers, explores the domestic and spiritual life of the priesthood.)

Robert Penn Warren is the most gifted and various of the writers making their appearances in this book, and it is no surprise that he has written persuasively about more places, with the exception of George Garrett, than any other author involved here. Warren has laid good novels in piedmont Kentucky and Tennessee, as Joseph Blotner points out; and his greatest novel, *All the King's Men*, is set in Louisiana. His poetry is often placed elsewhere—particularly in Vermont and Italy. The opening scene in *All the King's Men* contains some of Warren's most hypnotic prose: "Way off ahead of you, at the horizon where the cotton fields are blurred into the light, the slab will glitter and gleam like water, as though the road were flooded. You'll go whipping toward it, but it will always be ahead of you, that bright, flooded place, like a mirage."[10] This reminds us of the Delta as Charles East paints it.

In working on his superb biography of R. P. Warren, Blotner visited most of the places important to Warren, including spots in and around Nashville with Jane and Walter Sullivan. Some of these occur in Warren's last novel, *A Place to Come To*. Warren wanted to settle in Middle Tennessee, which he also wrote about in *At Heaven's Gate*. "The place I wanted to live, the place I thought was heaven to me, after my years of wandering, was middle Tennessee, which is a beautiful country. . . . When I went back to teach for three years there, I enjoyed living in the country. . . . But I was let out of Vanderbilt. . . . I went to Louisiana State University, which was quite fortunately a very exciting place," he said in an interview.[11]

So, too, have many of the places in which George Garrett has set his fiction been exciting to him—Trieste, for example, where the action of *Which Ones Are the Enemy* unfolds. Garrett speaks of this and many other matters in his lively

E.g. dialogue (internal)

10. Warren, *All the King's Men* (New York: Modern Library, 1953), 3–4.
11. *Talking with Robert Penn Warren*, ed. Floyd C. Watkins, John T. Hiers, and Mary Louise Weaks (Athens: University of Georgia Press, 1990), 272.

essay on place. He discusses military service (which is essentially the same every-where)—in his case in the U.S. Army—as a form of place. And in this same piece he writes: "Memory and place are hopelessly entangled." He continues by speaking of "family memory," explaining: "Almost always a family farm stood as a real place and a place that stood for something." The farm is the locus of family memory and at least until recently has been the special place for most Americans, especially in the South.

Louis Rubin, in his "Thoughts on Fictional Places," comments: "In the best fiction, place is not only geography and history; it is a way of looking at the world." Here is one of the most acute remarks about the nature of fiction that appears in this book. Rubin, like Garrett, is a novelist. Of such a writer he observes: "By definition the writing of fiction requires the novelist to come to terms with the documentation of the world." Place supplies much of that documentation, whether the writer is Dreiser or Joyce or Hemingway.

As she carefully surveys the developing use of place in Walter Sullivan's novels, all laid in middle Tennessee, Martha Cook reveals the truth of Blair Rowse's insight into how place ideally works in fiction: "Both time and place, especially place, are so presented they are completely integrated factors in the inner artistic structure of the work." He says of *All the King's Men:* "place becomes completely integrated into the very structure of the work and is clearly so necessary an element for comprehending all that one must know and realize about the characters, that place in this novel is truly an 'actor' in the drama." Rowse is also revealing about Faulkner and place (as is H. L. Weatherby in this book): "The woodland of 'The Bear' and the great beast himself are significant because they are meaningful for the human beings with whom they are involved; thus they assume spiritual stature and a significance far greater than as simple elements of an action or a scene."[12]

Place, whether the interior of a house or the exterior aspects of the outer world (especially landscape or cityscape), is the vehicle through which action, the driving motion of the plot, is revealed. Place is not mere setting in the sense of a static background but an essential constituent in what Andrew Lytle deems enveloping action. The enveloping action in fiction reveals not raw geography but the whole culture out of which the action proper emerges. Hence the family, as both Lytle and Garrett have observed—and as the novels of Sullivan

12. Rowse, "Time and Place in Southern Fiction," in *Southern Renascence: The Literature of the Modern South,* ed. Louis D. Rubin Jr. and Robert D. Jacobs (Baltimore: Johns Hopkins Press, 1953), 139, 143.

demonstrate—tends to be of central importance in fiction; and out of the family connection, especially one long rooted in a particular place, derives family memory that can yield dozens of stories and plots. In writing of Sullivan's *Sojourn of a Stranger* and novels by Peter Taylor and Howard Nemerov, Lytle declares: "Land keeps the family intact.... The parts of the family make a whole by their diversity."[13] Such diversity will be seen in the stories, spoken and written, that result.

Wendell Berry, the last of the Agrarians, reveals the importance of place in his own life as a farmer and as a writer. He provides a unique insight into our subject, writing from the standpoint of a man who knows how the small farm is properly run and maintained—and who also understands how landscape can become essential in the fictive scene. In both his essays and his fiction Berry has extended and deepened the Agrarian ideal developed by Andrew Lytle, John Crowe Ransom, and others into new realms of enduring significance.

In our beginning is our end, and so we return to Eudora Welty, and we think of the close connection of family and place in her fiction, especially *The Ponder Heart, Losing Battles,* and *The Optimist's Daughter.* "One element," she says, "that connects all the arts" is place. "Where does the mystery lie? Is it in the fact that place has a more lasting identity than we have, and we unswervingly tend to attach ourselves to identity?" "Being shown how to locate, to place, any account is what does most toward *making* us believe it" (119), she concludes.

13. Lytle, *Southerners and Europeans: Essays in a Time of Disorder* (Baton Rouge: Louisiana State University Press, 1988), 119.

Thoughts on Fictional Places

Louis D. Rubin, Jr.

We tend to see the world in terms of what artists, literary and otherwise, have shown us about it. Lewis Simpson and I were driving once from Oxford to Greenville, Mississippi. When we reached Greenwood and the cantilever bridge over the Yazoo River, painters were at work. At the entrance was a sign:

> BRIDGE BEING PAINTED. STOP ON OTHER SIDE
> TO HAVE PAINT SPOTS REMOVED FROM YOUR CAR

There is no doubt about who taught us to identify the comedy in that: the same author who noticed the sign outside the McLain Bijou theater:

> DEPOSIT REQUIRED FOR GOING IN TO TALK

Would we have thought of the wording of the sign as comic if we had encountered it in Ohio or Vermont? Hard to say, but doubtless we would not have seen it in quite the same way. It was not the wording of the sign alone, but the mode of looking at people in their time and place that enabled us to view it in other than strictly practical terms. (I don't recall whether any paint was found and removed from the car.)

Elsewhere, one of Eudora Welty's characters remarks that Edna Earle Ponder was the kind of person who could sit for hours wondering how the tail of the first *C* got through the second one in Coca-Cola. Until then I'd never so much as noticed the calligraphy, never thought to speculate that there might be anything to it other than a brand name.

Thomas Wolfe writes of the far-wandering W. O. Gant riding a streetcar home from the train station in Altamont: "There was a warm electric smell and one of hot burnt steel." Growing up in Charleston, South Carolina, I rode a trolley car downtown and back six days a week, but not until I encountered *Look Homeward, Angel* did I recognize the experience as visually and sensorily remarkable. I have since written about the looks and odors of trolley cars and trains; Wolfe showed me how to observe them emotionally—or, more accurately, made me realize that I did observe them emotionally.

Emotional experience is three-dimensional; all places in fiction are potentially sensory. Wolfe used lots of adjectives to re-create his feelings; Ernest Hemingway, very few. When young, in my first writing class, I was once pontificating about the supposed lack of physical descriptiveness in Hemingway's prose. One of my students, John Barth, disagreed. "The yellow overcoats in 'The Killers' are the only ones I can remember in fiction," he said.

Hemingway agreed with Mark Twain on the deployment of the adjective: "when in doubt, strike it out." William Faulkner did not; early in the unfolding first sentence of *Absalom, Absalom!* he depicts Quentin Compson listening to Miss Rosa Coldfield as she drones away about events that happened long before he was born. The time is a "long still hot weary dead September afternoon"; the place is the parlor of Miss Rosa's long-unpainted house. The adjectives describe the climate, tell us how Quentin feels about the place and the occasion, and begin to suggest what kind of person young Quentin is.

Neither Hemingway nor Clemens could have written anything so emotionally intricate as *Absalom, Absalom!* Neither would have wished to. "Well, you better not think about it," Nick Adams is advised at the end of "The Killers." But Faulkner could not have written about his native place without thinking about the complexity of Quentin's emotions concerning it.

Clemens wrote about the South during the heyday of local color, the later nineteenth century. Reading local-color fiction got him to depicting his early days in a town fronting on the Mississippi River: "After all these years I can picture that old time to myself now, just as it was then." What he did not do was stop at the level of descriptive portraiture that his magazine contemporaries did, with the surface oddities and quaintnesses of the place of his birth and rearing. Sam Clemens had strong, sometimes contradictory feelings about the country of his early experience; his literary gift compelled him, inevitably if sporadically, to ferret them out. Physical description deepened into moral vision.

Back before television destroyed the market for magazine fiction, the publications for would-be writers used to run advertisements for decks of cards showing plot situations. The faces of the cards were divided into three sections, each with the segment of a plot. You shuffled the deck, dealt yourself three cards, and by combining the top section of one, the middle section of another, and the bottom section of a third, you had yourself the beginning, middle, and end of a story for writing. All you needed to do was fill in the details—that is, provide some texture for the story's structure, such as the place where it would happen. Vladimir Propp would very likely have agreed with the approach.

Anthony Powell's magnificent *A Dance to the Music of Time* takes place for the most part in and around London. There is comparatively little physical description of the place itself, yet the comic quartet, each made up of three novels, seems not merely English but inescapably Londonish in nature. One can scarcely imagine Powell's narrator—or for that matter Powell himself—living in Westchester County or the West Side of Manhattan Island, not to say Nashville.

Obviously it is not the particulars of the metropolitan geography but the way the characters comport themselves in it and what the author thinks is significant about their behavior and what is not that establish the place and its moral identity. I say this without the local knowledge to spot any of the real-life models. But any British litterateur could—which is to the point; for the fiction grows out of, though it does not depend for readability upon, just that kind of familiarity.

The nearest equivalent in this country is, I suppose, New York City. Alfred Kazin once quoted the response of Philip Rahv when told that one of the habitual contributors to the *Partisan Review* had published a novel: "Who's in it?" But American novelists for the most part don't write *about* New York City to anything like the extent to which British novelists do about Oxford, London, and their environs. For one thing, it isn't necessary to live or die there; an occasional professional visit will suffice.

The Great Theme of Henry James, the contrast of cultures inherent in the American presence in Europe, is predicated upon the emotional dimensions of place. In London, Paris, Venice, Rome are the institutions of history and high culture that make possible the full and ample exercise of the artistic imagination. Accompanying them, seemingly inseparable from them, are the fixed restrictions of rank and class. Enter Christopher Lambert Adam, the New Man, innocent of those stratifications, having come into his adult strength and in pursuit of the fruits of European culture. Can he put on that knowledge with his power?

If that American arriviste is a materialist, a sensualist, a cad, or else if he is so morally frozen as to be hopelessly rigid, nothing will happen beyond the exchange of money for the superficial trappings of culture. But if, when tested in the European social crucible, that American, while remaining morally incorruptible, proves receptive toward new experiences, he (or she) can win through to genuine artistic enlightenment and henceforth be One of Those Upon Whom Nothing Is Lost. So the European place is the proving ground for aesthetic and moral vision—as in that early Jamesian parable of the American artist, "Daisy Miller," Winterbourne is the one who flunks the test, even as Lambert Strether later passes it in *The Ambassadors*.

One would be hard put, in James's international fiction, to turn up much evidence for the possibility of the artistic vision being fulfilled while in residence in the United States. His famous catalog of the institutions customarily used in the exercise of that vision, but unavailable to the American literary sensibility—"no sovereign, no court, no personal loyalty, no aristocracy," and so forth—was developed to explain the poverty of social texture in Hawthorne's fiction. The assumption on which James proceeds is that artistic life in America will be at worst crass and materialistic and at best thin and undernourished. "American humor" (he places the term within quotation marks), based as it is on the chasm between reality and aspiration, alone may flourish there.

The outrage among the intellectual set on either side of the Charles River that followed publication of *The Bostonians,* in which James satirized the frazzled remnants of New England Transcendentalism—reformers, do-gooders, spirit rappers, simpletons in general—may well have been perceived by him as validation of the wisdom of his own decision to depart the American scene for Europe. Yet James's view of Europe, as is often pointed out, is not really of Paris, London, Venice, Rome, but of Americans visiting in those cities.

Late in his life, after long years of self-induced exile, he comes home to survey the American scene and is appalled by the vulgarity and the commercialism. The despoilment of the continent is producing an abiding ugliness. When there is vitality, as in immigrant-crowded New York City, it is alien to the older America of his childhood. What elegance exists is essentially that of a commercial hotel. *The American Scene* may be said to adumbrate Pudd'nhead Wilson's aphorism: "*October 12, the Discovery*. It was wonderful to find America, but it would have been even more wonderful to miss it."

When I reread James's chapters on New York City recently, I thought of Alfred Kazin's memoir *A Walker in the City*. From James's standpoint, that it could have ever been written would be almost inconceivable. Yet between James's despairing visit and the childhood in Brownsville that Kazin describes so beautifully, scarcely twenty-five years intervened.

. . .

At the opposite extreme from Henry James on the American urban scene is the description of Fitzgerald and Moy's in *Sister Carrie:* "It was a truly swell saloon." I doubt that James had read Dreiser's first novel at the time, but the adverb and adjective alone would have confirmed all of his apprehensions about what dire things were happening to the English language in the turn-of-the-century United States. Certainly, when James was a boy living in Washington Square in the pre–Civil War years, nobody who was writing novels would have chosen to describe a tavern—it would not have been called a saloon—in just this way. By the early 1900s much had changed; the scope of the American novel had been broadened to include varieties of experience, some of them unpleasant, and attitudes toward it that even a professional realist such as William Dean Howells considered too crude to be written about. Yet the true vulgarian of the day was not Theodore Dreiser, a great literary artist in his own right; it was William Sidney Porter (O. Henry).

Sister Carrie was published in 1900; *The Ambassadors,* in 1903. A century later, and who is now the champion active vulgarian? What are the top ten paperback novels currently on sale at the Raleigh-Durham airport?

The use of locale in a best-selling "blockbuster" novel such as James Michener's *Hawaii* differs from the presence of place in Eudora Welty's Mississippi or, to choose a more recent example, Lee Smith's Appalachia, in that Michener's people are imposed upon the place from without, while Welty's and Smith's people grow out of an emotional relationship to the place and are manifestations of the imaginative experience of the locales in their creators' own lives.

In the best fiction, place is not only geography and history; it is a way of looking at the world. In that sense, the imagination that created "The Killers" is as surely a product of the city of Chicago as is that of *Sister Carrie,* even though Dreiser set out consciously to write about the geographical and historical entity of the place in its time, while Hemingway had no such objective.

In the early decades of the nineteenth century it was considered appropriate to have actual historical characters play prominent parts in the plots of period romances. We have since become more scrupulous about keeping the documentary record and the fictional action separate. The contemporary historical novel customarily portrays historical figures, but it does not let them participate importantly in the fictional plot.

The exception would be novels such as *Ragtime,* which dissolve fact into fiction in order to play games with "reality." These succeed as fiction, however, only for so long as we remember that what is going on *is* the deliberate blurring of known history and novelistic fantasy. So-called metafiction can be sustained only *as* illusion. Without a generally agreed upon reality that can be violated, it would make little sense. Barth's *Sot-Weed Factor* rings the changes on appearances versus reality, with the illusions securely grounded in (and afloat upon) the geography and early history of the Chesapeake Bay country.

Writers of "metafiction" are not the only authors who sometimes enjoy playing games with time and place. In *The Last Gentleman,* Walker Percy has Will Barrett remember being introduced as a child to Senator Oscar W. Underwood of Alabama. Later Barrett discovers that the senator died before he was born. The youthful introduction could well have happened to Barrett's creator, however, and very likely did.

Hamilton Basso, in *The View from Pompey's Head,* opens with a man aboard a Pullman car, arriving home in the southern coastal city of his birth and raising. The train backs into the station, from which the man is conveyed to a downtown hotel. When I first read it I was sure that the author was describing the advent of the morning Palmetto Limited at Union Station in Charleston, South Carolina. The geographical arrangements seemed to fit. Reviewers of Basso's novel, however, located it variously in Savannah, Jacksonville, and New Orleans, where the author grew up. With the reader as willing collaborator, seemingly specific details could be made to suggest all of those places.

A little readerly empathy is a treacherous thing. As Stephen Dedalus said, "Local color. Work in all you know. Make them accomplices."

The novelist might be said to be in the position of the little boy found standing at the corner. "I'm running away from home," he explained, "but my mother won't let me cross the street by myself." However faithfully—or sketchily—a work of fiction may draw upon the material of geography and history, it is based upon illusion. Depending upon attitudes, objectives, and assumptions about the needs of life and art, novelists labor to imitate "reality": that is, to re-create it in language. A novel that doesn't happen somewhere is a contradiction in terms. It needn't, of course, be a known geographical entity; the interior of a spaceship will do. The novelist can leave it up to the reader to furnish almost all the trapping and fixings. But to adopt the punch line of another, less decorous joke, "Well, everybody's got to be somewhere."

· · ·

There are novelists—to a degree John Barth is one, James Joyce another—for whom fiction must not only happen in a known, bounded place, but the details of the place itself must be authentic. From there it may soar into the empyrean or the occult, but there must be a place to come back to. There is the letter that Joyce wrote to his aunt back home in Dublin, asking her to verify that the iron fencing in front of No. 7 Eccles Street was low enough to be climbed over by a man of average height and strength. Leopold Bloom, who was doing the fictional climbing, is an almost totally imagined character. Why, then, could not Joyce also have simply adjusted the fence to fit the needs of the story? Joyce even made Bloom the possessor of a muscle-building manual, for no apparent reason other than to make sure that his scaling of the iron fence would be credible.

What prompts this kind of insistence upon authenticity of detail is something beyond an effort to ensure a continued suspension of disbelief on the reader's part. At least as important, in writing fiction the novelist is engaged in doing an audacious thing: creating fictional life out of language, inventing entire characters, endowing them with *consciousness*—and doing this in a very precisely delineated setting, against which the authenticity of the fictional characters can be readily measured. It is not enough that Leopold Bloom, Stephen Dedalus, Molly Bloom, and the others be made to live in Dublin; they must be *of* Dublin. It is something like building a bridge, or creating a platform that will reach out from a recognizable substantial place into what until then has been empty air. To undergird the span as it extends into the void, the novelist needs the moral support of pilings that will help to stabilize his projection in the here and now—needs it for his own self-confidence perhaps most of all.

Joyce had actually watched a friend lift himself over the iron fence at No. 7 Eccles and let himself into the house by the backdoor, just as Bloom does; but, he explained to his aunt, the man who did it was rather athletic in build, while his fictional character was not. Still, he had arranged things so that Bloom had been following Eugene Sandow's exercise regimen and had increased his chest expansion by one and one-fourth inches. So the query to his aunt back in Dublin may not really have been a check on the accuracy of his memory, but a reflexive response on the part of an increasingly anxious author whose gigantic project is nearing completion. He is reassuring himself that the model for this intricately imagined representation of two men's wanderings through a place and time, in which No. 7 Eccles Street has been chosen to be Ithaca, is still in place, and that he remains in contact with it.

. . .

Desmond McCarthy had a story about someone visiting Joyce's apartment in Paris. On one wall was a print showing Nora Joyce's home city of Cork. When the guest looked at it closely, he realized that the frame was constructed of cork. You have no idea how difficult it was to secure that frame, Joyce remarked, adding that of course it was essential to find it. His prodigious imagination required buttressing on more than one level of authenticity.

This was the author who, when *Finnegans Wake* was criticized as being trivial, replied that it was not only trivial but quadrivial.

It would be interesting to know the books of reference, maps, and other such material that various novelists kept close at hand when they wrote certain books. Joyce no doubt kept a goodly supply of Dubliniana, including city directories, almanacs, rail and trolley car schedules, street maps, programs of fairs and bazaars, church registers, and the like. By contrast, I doubt that William Faulkner required a great deal of local documentation; he was the kind of writer who could have Quentin Compson commit suicide by jumping into the Charles River in June 1910 in one novel, and in another have him leave Mississippi for Harvard the next September. But he knew where everything was, and had been, in his little "postage-stamp's worth" of north Mississippi.

Cleanth Brooks and I once decided to try to retrace the route of the Bundren family from Frenchmen's Bend to Jefferson in *As I Lay Dying*. We found the place where the bridge had washed away, forcing the family to make a lengthy detour. Then we followed the road westward to Water Valley. Logically it must be the Mottstown of the novel. When we drove into town almost the first thing we came upon was a large sign on a building: MOTT PACKING COMPANY.

Sometimes it helps for readers to see the originals of the places of fiction. What is striking about Rowan Oak, Faulkner's home in Oxford, Mississippi, is that the exterior, with its columns and portico, looks like the abode of a General Compson, but the interior seems more that of a Flem Snopes.

I wrote my own three forgettable novels with a city map and a chart of Charleston harbor close by. Apparently what I should have used instead was a stethoscope.

It has been my experience that novelists tend to be able to appreciate and to admire work composed out of very different artistic assumptions than their own. Poets generally do not. This may be because by definition the writing of fiction requires the novelist to come to terms with the documentation of the world. Poets, by contrast, seem to be engaged in a war with it; they wish to intensify it beyond its particularities, "like gold to airy thinnesse beat," and each poem is a field of action. All other contemporary poets are either allies or enemies; there are no neutrals.

It is useful and valuable training for would-be novelists to try a hand at writing poems. It is also appropriate for most of them to give it up after a time. Thomas Hardy is the—or maybe *an*—exception that tests the rule.

Just as in answer to the advent of photography the French Impressionists concentrated on portraying the nuances and emphases of light, which the photographic plate couldn't capture, so one response of the novelist to movies and television has been to explore the subtleties of consciousness. There are intricacies of characterization in *The Golden Apples,* infused into fictional locale and reinforced by myth, that go far beyond what any photographic lens, however sensitive, can reproduce. Language may not be "reality" itself, as some claim, but it is as close as we can come to identifying and embodying its workings in time and place, and the tension between the apparent and the real is the terrain where the literary artist works. "October rain on Mississippi fields, maybe on the whole South, for all she knew on the everywhere. She stared into its magnitude." That is Virgie Rainey at the close of Eudora Welty's best book of all. What her comic vision notices is what we can thereafter recognize for ourselves. And that, I believe, is where we came in.

Part

II

EXCURSIONS

Places We Have Come From,
Places We Have Been

George Garrett

The last time I was in Orlando, Florida, the home place where I was born and (more or less) raised, I got lost. I wanted to show my grandchildren the house my father had built, a house near a lake, where I grew up. The grandchildren were, of course, bored, but polite enough to hide it. Our real destination was Disney World. They could tolerate a brief delay. I knew exactly where the old house was, yet . . . But the intricate network formed by the interstate highway, I-4, and interconnected expressways, with their elaborate cloverleaf architecture and all the pulsing noise and shine of continuous city traffic, made it difficult, almost impossible it seemed, simply to get there. Briefly from an expressway I could see the dark blue-green of the lake itself, Lake Copeland, but that was as close as we got.

As we drove on, aiming for the Magic Kingdom and all that, I found myself wondering how many other Americans returning to a home place, say after twenty or thirty or fifty years, suddenly find themselves lost, the power of memory over-whelmed by what is new and strange? It is memory I must depend on to tell me what Orlando was before it became what it is. My "real" memory extends for my lifetime, more than seventy years, but at the far edges it must include also the memories of others, parents and grandparents, uncles and aunts and cousins, whose stories became part of my own. On one side of the family I am a fifth-generation Floridian. On the other side, my father's side, I am a third-generation arrival. My grandfather Leigh Osborn Garrett and his brother, Hardy Greeley Garrett, came to live in Orlando in November 1884. Hardy kept notes in his journal. Here is an observation about the attitude of "natives" toward "settlers." By "natives" he meant early settlers, not the Seminoles who had possessed the land until driven from it during the Seminole Wars. He wrote: "The natives had lived lives of seclusion and seriously resented any and all invasions. It was their country, and they did not welcome outsiders. Judge Spear, who lived about six miles west of Orlando on the south end of Lake Apopka, told me that when he first lived there, his nearest neighbor lived six miles away. He met this neighbor one day and found him so overcast with gloom that he asked him what the trouble was. He answered, 'I'll have to leave this country; they're crowding me.' It turned out that another family had settled where Orlando is now, about six miles from both Judge Spear and his neighbor."

In the early 1840s, there was a U.S. Army post, Fort Gatlin, close to which a settlement grew up. Florida, at least the peninsula (the "Panhandle" had been occupied and settled much earlier), was as much a frontier as the West. The U.S. Army had moved in and built or seized some forts from the Spanish even before the official acquisition of Florida in July 1821. The Florida of the early 1840s was described as the "nation's most fortified state." In a letter to the secretary of war (April 9, 1837), General Thomas Sidney Jessup noted that "we have perhaps as little knowledge of the interior of Florida as of the interior of China." By 1856 the casual settlement close to Fort Gatlin was a town called Jernigan, county seat of Orange County. The next year it was renamed in honor of a soldier, Orlando Reeves, who had been killed there while doing sentry duty in the Seminole Wars.

Young Hardy Greeley Garrett came on the scene late in 1884 and joined his brother in the real estate business in a firm known as "L. O. Garrett & Bro." Later, in the American tradition, he would reinvent himself as a banker and a lawyer. "My reason for going was as follows," he wrote.

> The South Florida Railroad had just been completed. It connected Jacksonville on the Atlantic with Tampa on the Gulf and passed through Orlando. It opened up the central portion of the state for settlement by providing transportation for man and the products of his labor. The resulting land boom lasted several years. . . . People came from all parts of the United States and a great many from England to buy property in Florida. It was so easy for them to believe that they could make money raising oranges that it became a craze. . . . There had not been a killing frost since 1837. We could show small groups of orange trees around native houses to prove our point. Then came the question, "If so much is to be made out of raising oranges, why hasn't somebody already done it?" Our answer was that it could not have been done before the railroad was completed. A reasonable yield is two to four carloads to the acre. It would have been the wildest folly to plant and cultivate groves of orange trees in advance of rail transportation.

People bought land to grow oranges, acres of piney woods for "naval stores"—resin, turpentine, and tar—and swampland where huge, ancient cypress trees grew in profusion. "In 1887 we had a killing frost and the boom slowed down to normal." A year later, yellow fever raged in Jacksonville and Tampa and all around Orlando. "There were many pathetic cases. A minister in Orlando became terribly frightened and got out of the state as quickly as possible, going to Alabama. We never had a case of the fever in Orlando, but this poor frightened minister came in contact with it somewhere en route and died of yellow fever in Alabama, spreading the dread disease there."

Hardy took up politics and read for the law. "In 1891, I was admitted to the bar and went into practice in Orlando." He tells stories, which might as well have come out of the Old West, of murders, train robberies, curious quirks of trial by jury, and a certain amount of courtroom comedy: "A woman living some three miles east of Orlando haled several men and boys into court for bathing in the nude in a lake upon the shore of which she lived. The magistrate asked her about the size of the lake, the location of her house, and the spot at which she had seen the bathers. He then asked her how she could tell whether they were naked or not at so great a distance. She said she used her field glasses. The case was dismissed."

Most of the important things about the place of place in fiction have been said before and said better by my betters. And so it is probably outrageous, bad form all around, to write about place again, to try to recapitulate the persuasive arguments so ably advanced that they are by now our unspoken assumptions, matters of faith and belief. Yet, precisely because one so seldom examines or even questions one's unspoken assumptions, it might be useful to reconsider my own life and work, how my private practice coincides and connects with the public assumptions that I accept and honor without thinking much about them.

For my own good reasons I have tried to avoid too much self-consciousness as a writer, thinking, superstitiously perhaps, that I might somehow inhibit or at least limit myself and my work by too much self-study. That's a proposition that might well prove to be true; but here I am in my seventies, someone whose past is a good deal longer and stronger than any imaginable (or maybe even desirable) future. From this point of view it would seem to be a more serious inhibition not to be able freely to look back and consider the road behind me, the road already taken. It is not necessary to stake claims or to make claims about that work. The work will simply have to speak for itself.

Over the years I have written novels, short stories, poems, and some other things (plays, movies, biography, essays, criticism, and journalism). Not that it makes that much difference; because, beyond my tacit acceptance of the working rules of the road and some safe driving tips for each of these forms, I think of them all, large or small, lighthearted or heavy, as chips off the same block. Which is to say that I think that the writers I most envy and admire and honor leave their signs on all they touch, and that, as Auden says somewhere and I here have to paraphrase: even a limerick ought to be something a man facing a firing squad or death from cancer could read without contempt.

There is something that, enjoying the pleasures of hindsight, I had not noticed before because I was not looking for it. Looking back now, it seems to me that I took advantage of the variety of work I was doing to play off one form against another. For example, when I was writing more or less realistic fiction, stories, and several early novels, colloquial in style and matter-of-fact in mundane detail, I was, at one and the same time, composing verses that were more or less formal, metrical, and rhymed. Later, when I was deeply engaged, for thirty-odd years, in creating an Elizabethan trilogy and searching to understand the language of that time and then to echo and to translate that slightly more elevated, even elegant level of speech, all through those days, while not completely abandoning my other habits (in either fiction or poetry), I wrote looser if not "freer" verses focused on less "poetic" subjects and sources. These things seem to have depended on each other.

Just so, one cannot escape from the good and bad habits of the age, its customs, conventions, and stereotypes. One acts and reacts within the literary context of a real world with real values, though many of these values, over a lifetime, prove to be as transient and insignificant as the height of hemlines and the length of haircuts.

Places matter greatly in the art and craft of making. I said places plural, because I think now, after stumbling through the twentieth century and into this one, that plurality in and of itself is something that tends to separate us from the world of our parents, grandparents, and ancestors. Most of us in those days were born in one place, lived our lives in that place, and came at last to be buried there. Other places were mostly imaginary, though our imaginations were fueled and sometimes fired by the tall tales of drifters and passing strangers, the reports of some few travelers who had left behind this place only to return later with the good news or bad news of a wider world and all its various and sundry places. And there were always the wars, close by or often very far away, that gathered up our young men and took them off to alien places where many died and from which many, often maimed beyond repair or recovery, hobbled home to take up (gratefully) their old lives in the home place. These veterans could have told us a tale or two, but most often they didn't. What had happened to them was beyond their power to describe or evoke. Silence was the golden rule. Later, as with, say, the aged veterans of the Civil War or World War II, they mellowed enough to begin to share some of their memories, memories colored and distorted by nostalgia and blessed forgetfulness.

Of course, for me and all Americans there is always the great leap sideways, that long voyage over from old countries to the newfound land, a migration that continues, for better and for worse, to this day. But for those of us whose people came here earliest, it was an enormous change of place, beginning with the dangerous passage across the wide sea and, for the lucky survivors of those voyages, arrival at and then living and dying in bleak, hardscrabble settlements on the edges of a vast, dark, brooding wilderness.

Would we now be witness to the overwhelming migrations of today, from all directions from ancient and distant civilizations, if that were the inevitable end of today's journey? Who knows? But I kind of doubt it.

Recently I read an accounting, synoptic to be sure, of the amazing travels and travails of an English sailor, Davy Ingrams, in the middle of the sixteenth century. Left behind on a beach in Yucatán by Sir John Hawkins (Sir John had some men ashore but had to flee for his life to save his ship and crew from superior Spanish forces that suddenly appeared on the scene), this fellow escaped the clutches of Spaniards and Indians alike and set off, briskly at first one likes to imagine, in a generally northeast direction, hoping to get to Newfoundland just as soon as possible. He had sailed on fishing vessels to Newfoundland and knew that fishermen and other adventurers congregated there in the high summertime. He had no idea how far away from Yucatán Newfoundland might be. A few years later, after walking all the way across the continent, he arrived at Newfoundland, found a vessel that would take him aboard, and eventually returned to his home place in the west of England. There, after a while, some authorities (in the modern terminology) "debriefed" him. He told them all that he knew and could remember—the basic problem being that anybody tough enough to walk across the whole American continent for several years, all by himself, though he was often given hospitality by Indians . . . and sometimes not, anybody who could do that might not, most probably wouldn't, be a highly sensitive observer. He climbed big mountains, he crossed the wide rivers, he lived through hard seasons. He came home. It was soon apparent to his official questioners that the fellow had very little to add to their knowledge of the secrets of darkest America. When they began to look sidewise, to shrug to each other, and to yawn in his face, Davy began to make up things that might arouse their interest: multicolored sheep and monstrous rabbits, miracle plants and crops, tribes of two-headed Indians, buckets of silver and great lumps of gold—the usual things. They eagerly copied down his testimony, and some people even elected to believe it.

Imaginary places, emerald cities at the ends of yellow brick roads, have always been part of our sense of place.

Sometimes imaginary history, and at its heart an imaginary sense of place, not only haunts our lives with ghostly voices and echoes but is, finally, stronger, even more accurate than the cut, shuffled, and dealt world of hard facts. Having lived long enough, I have inevitably witnessed things, experienced them, that later, in the hands of others, as past history, were rearranged to suit the pleasure and purposes of "objective" observers, historians who, never deviating from factual "accuracy," nevertheless have turned the truth completely upside down. It is in this sense that narrative history, even fictional history, can be as important as factual history. Born to one place, for generations we almost always lived and died there. Our ghosts spoke to us in the common language of presences, with the common logic of poetry. We knew our past, chiefly by word of mouth, in our skin and bones, though our knowledge of the facts might be more than a little sketchy. We could love it or we could hate it or both at once; but we could not easily leave it. Or, if we did manage to move on, as many did, we left our hearts behind in the home place, often feeling a little ashamed of ourselves as if we had failed in our bounden duty.

All that changes in a mere historical blink of an eye. Complex forces set us Americans off a-wandering to many places. Meantime our home places changed radically before our very eyes—many shriveling and shrinking into a shabby insignificance, others growing, "developing" into huge, crowded, disorderly suburban and city places that share not much more than a name with the original place and its vanished inhabitants.

Among writers, the first great generation of modern American masters— Faulkner, Hemingway, Fitzgerald, and their contemporaries—had to contend with this. Many moved on and about for the rest of their lives. Others, particularly the southerners, stayed or regularly returned where, even amid the shrinking and shriveling, or the lunatic expansion, they could feel at home. That was the last literary generation of Americans that truly enjoyed that choice. We who followed after are close enough to them to feel a nostalgia for the lost (or fading) place they once and for all summoned up for us. We tend to be sentimental about it. They were not. Nostalgia and sentiment are not true love. No *caritas* there. To do their work, Faulkner and Welty and Warren and Foote and Settle and all the rest had to love the place. Deeply.

I doubt seriously that we will again see that kind of love shining through American writing, not exactly in the same form, anyway. We will live to see something else, something different, maybe even some things quite wonderful, but never that true, unconditional love again.

One of the many drastic changes in the late American twentieth century has been the association and affiliation of our writers with our academic institutions. For the first time since the great years of the monasteries, a large number of serious writers are kept by colleges and universities as teachers and performers. This began just before World War II but accelerated and expanded rapidly in the 1950s. It follows that the writers went to the places where the jobs were. Some found homes and tenure. Most of the others became academic nomads. Many, myself among them, imagined this to be a kind of temporary condition, one we would shed as soon as possible for careers as full-time writers. Failing that, in fact as well as imagination, I have only recently retired from thirty-odd years of full-time teaching, broken occasionally by free or study years here and there. Thus I have lived (never mind considering short or long visits) in Middletown, Connecticut; Rome, Italy; Houston, Texas; Charlottesville, Virginia; York Harbor, Maine; Miami, Florida; Charleston, West Virginia; Lexington, Virginia; Ann Arbor, Michigan (twice); Charlottesville (again); Tuscaloosa, Alabama; not counting some early times logged in New York City, first in the Village, then on 115th Street. A fairly typical record, I reckon, for a writer of my generation.

And so it is that, in my lifetime, place has become plural. We have "places" real and imaginary. We have those places where we have worked well and whose qualities, as we know and understand them, seem to bring out the best in us.

For example, I have not written a single word of fiction set on the coast of Maine. Where I lived year-round for several years. Where I still return yearly. Where I wrote more than half of my novels and collections of stories. Wrote them mostly in one particular place—at a zinc-covered worktable, set by a couple of small windows in a long, narrow boathouse, itself fixed on a rock and earthen pier, jutting out into the York River. It is a place that has been, first in my wife's family, now in ours, for five generations. Behind the boathouse, set on a little slope, the old house (1780) faces the river, too. Tidal, the river is always moving, and the boats moored out there, the fishing boats of lobstermen and, in summertime, the yachts and pleasure boats of summer people, move in and out also. Gulls fish, cry out, roost, and fly.

And one writer managed to get a good deal of work done there without writing a word of fiction about it. Others there have worked well too: Mark Twain upriver half a mile; Sidney Lanier, Thomas Nelson Page, William Dean

Howells, May Sarton, and now Ann Beattie, among others, in the area, in the neighborhood.

What I have said, though, needs to be slightly modified. If I have written no fiction about the place, I have in fact done a play *(Enchanted Ground),* for readers' theater and for local performance, about the place and some of its history. And, I now notice, I have done any number of short poems whose setting, firmly in that place, is as much the subject as anything else.

An obvious example is this little poem, what I would call "a watercolor":

Maine Morning

Where clear air blew off the land,
wind turns around and the sky changes.
Where there was burning blue is pale gray now,
heavy and salty from the cold open sea.
And the long groaning of the foghorn
saying *change... change... change...*
like a sleeper dreaming and breathing.

Tide turning, too, with the weather.
The lobster boats swing about to pull
against moorings like large dogs on chains.
Gulls cry like hurt children and disappear.
And I think, surely it is a magician,
bitter and clever, who has pulled this trick

That old magician is laughing in the fog,
and the cries of wounded children fade away
while the bellbuoy sounds *farewell... farewell...*
daring the dead to rise up from dreaming,
to hold their lives like water in their hands.

Some years ago, speaking to the North Carolina Historical Society (the talk was entitled "Why They Left Home and What They Were Looking For"), I touched on the kinship of that place and my work. I said to them that much of the work, almost all of the writing of my trilogy of Elizabethan novels, was done in that rickety boathouse set on an earth-and-rock pier jutting out into the York River in York, Maine. This place was once the site of the first town pier with its warehouse and with the village marketplace conveniently and directly behind it between the boathouse and where my house stands. There I sat in my boathouse on the place of the first pier in the first village that was settled in what was then called the Palatinate of Maine, governed, from a great distance, by Sir Ferdinando Gorges. Who was, as these things happen, a cousin of Sir Walter Ralegh.

We know that for one reason and another Europeans had been coming to the coast of Maine, most often to the offshore islands but sometimes inland as well, for a much longer time than anyone has yet reckoned. Certainly the English were coming here in the early years of the sixteenth century for the sake of the seasonal fishing and to set up fishing camps, some of them quite elaborate and as solid as little settlements; also for the sake of exploring and for some trading with the local Indians. Sir Ferdinando, owner of the Palatinate, decided on what became York as the appropriate site for the first permanent, year-round settlement in Maine. It had already been cleared and somewhat tamed. There had been a village there inhabited by some agricultural Indians. Sometime around the end of the sixteenth century and the beginning of the seventeenth, more or less coincident with the end of the reign of Queen Elizabeth, they simply vanished. It was speculated that they had died from disease or during one of the innumerable and unquenchable tribal wars.

It was a likely place, then, clear and empty of its people when, in the early seventeenth century, Captain Christopher Levett sailed the *York Bonaventure* through the tricky, rocky mouth and safely into the calm harbor of the York River (in those days called the Agamenticas) looking for an appropriate place to plant a settlement. He recommended this one: "There I think a good plantation may be settled, for there is a good harbor for ships, good ground and much already cleared, fit for the planting of corn and other fruits, having heretofore been planted by the Savages who are all dead. There is good timber and likely to be good fishing."

And so they came here and have been here ever since, the original families — the Bragdons and Blaisdells and Moultons and Sewalls and Stovers and so forth. My boathouse is insured by Bob Bragdon, himself directly descended from Arthur Bragdon, who came to York in middle age from the English town of Stratford-upon-Avon, where it is quite implausible to imagine that he did not have at least some memories of that place's second most honored and famous citizen at that time — William Shakespeare.

The history of York is not entirely uneventful. On the day after Candlemas in 1692 a large band of Abenaki warriors attacked the village at dawn, killed many men, women, and children, and carried off more than half the inhabitants. Two garrison houses withstood the attack. One of them, Captain Alcocks's, was located roughly one hundred yards downriver from my boathouse. Captain Alcocks reported as follows to Captain John Floyd, who brought some troops (too late) to the rescue from nearby Portsmouth: "All gone. Everything we built and planted, every mark we made on this place is gone. There is nothing left but bloody corpses and cold ashes."

For the next decade or so the survivors all slept for safety in garrison houses. And they planted crops and rebuilt their village. A lot of their work stands there to this day.

By the way, the first encounter with the Abenaki war party occurred at first light when a young boy, checking a line of traps, came upon a great pile of their snowshoes. He was shortly captured but lived to tell about it. He was the third Arthur Bragdon of York, Maine.

Also an aside. I remember that the old women of my family, keepers of tribal lore, sometimes spoke of ancestors of ours who came in the seventeenth century to live in Portland, Maine, just up the coast a ways from York Harbor. These people, they said, were seamen and their families. One of them, captain of a vessel, drowned at sea when the ship was lost. Sometime in the eighteenth century they moved away, to the South as it happens. I do not know the name of my Portland forefathers. The women who could tell me are long gone. But I think that they were named Holmes. In any case, the memory that some of my family had been here in Maine from earliest days helped to make Maine a kind of home place for me.

I mention these things to make the point that after all my reading and research, all my travels and sightseeing in England and Scotland, I ended up writing my Elizabethan novels in as good a place as any I can think of for the summoning up of old ghosts. It was not, is not, a haunted place, really; but it surely is a kind of enchanted ground. And there were bright moments for me when I felt the bristling energy of that enchantment, moments when I felt the presence of others as close as my elbow, ghostly presences as palpable as any shadow, including my own, moments when, out of the shadows, I seemed to hear voices speaking to me.

As for those Elizabethan novels of the old country, the story is fairly simple. Except for a look at the white cliffs of Dover from the crowded deck of a troop ship and later a few days' holiday, I was never in England (in fact) until after I had brought out the first book of the trilogy—*Death of the Fox*. For *The Succession*, which followed, I spent a good deal of time, by car and on foot, following in the footsteps of my characters, looking not so much at the houses and buildings and artifacts, though I certainly looked at them where I could, as feeling the ground under my feet, walking and wondering how this may have felt for those for whom (the times as well as the places) it was home. It was a foreign place, to be sure, but it was my foreign place.

I was stationed in Trieste, courtesy of the U.S. Army, and I have lived in Italy, once for more than a year in Rome, and have visited there whenever I could, logging more time and mileage than I have in England, Scotland, and Ireland. Out of the Italian experience has come one novel, *Which Ones Are the Enemy* (1961), an army story set in Trieste (written in Middletown, Connecticut), a couple or three short stories, and a scattering of poems. While living in Rome, courtesy of the American Academy in Rome, I wrote my first novel, *The Finished Man,* set in central Florida, my home and birthplace. Like many other American writers, I had to leave home for Rome (or somewhere) to begin to rediscover my original place in the world. I had to go elsewhere to find out where I had already been.

Here is a "Roman" poem from that time, a quick sketch or candid snapshot of the impact on a visiting (American) stranger.

> ### Night Poem: Rome
>
> When the great gray European dark
> settles on the city like a spell,
> the streetlights haloed, the old people
> huddled in doorways, eyes alert,
> and my heart sags in a net of veins
> like a rock in a sling (for History
> is the giant here, stretches and straddles
> the dark continent), and I walk home
> and would go on tiptoe if I could
> so as not to break anything,
> not to kiss dust from anybody's lips
> or change anything from stone to flesh,
>
> then, by God, I see the lovers,
> the Roman lovers on the walk,
> leaning together, he whispering,
> she listening, laughing, so close
> you can't separate their shadows.
> O Noah's pairs of all creation
> couldn't please me more! I hurl
> my heart against the night
> and hear the astounded giant fall.
> And I rejoice. I fumble with a key

and open doors. I kiss my wife
and hold my children hostage in my arms.

Another word or two about living in Rome. Looking back, I now think that only living there like that, surrounded by that glowing, ruined, immemorial city, would have permitted me the active leisure to imagine (in a state of complete practical ignorance) that I could invent and create, together with some others, an international literary magazine—the *Transatlantic Review*. It was named after Ford Madox Ford's celebrated (and then defunct) magazine, a copy of which none of us had ever so much as seen. Nonetheless, using our own money, such as it was (not much), together with the very generous support of Joseph McCrindle, literary agent and, in the best sense, amateur and entrepreneur, we put out the first issue early in 1959, in and from Rome. We presented it to McCrindle, and he kept the project going well for about twenty years, head-to-head competition with the elegant and slowly fading *Botteghe Oscure* and with George Plimpton's little hobby—the *Paris Review*. For a while, with offices in London and New York, we were the leading English-language literary magazine in the world, widely circulated (and with a magnificent and eclectic list of contributors) everywhere in the world—except the United States, where our circulation was typically modest.

All that is another story for some other time and place.

The reason for doing it in Rome was that we were there and that we had found, out in the high ground of Frascati, overlooking the sunny sprawl of Rome, an Italian doctor who loved English and its literature and who, coincidentally, owned a printing business. His outfit offered us a deal and printed the first couple or three issues.

I would go out to Frascati, hanging on to the back of a motorcycle owned and operated by the Irish poet John Patrick Creagh. We would pick up proof and then settle down at a café table with a view of Rome, armed with pencils and a carafe of the white wine for which that town is justly famous, to proofread. The first two issues are, needless to say, riddled with proofing errors.

Back in the city Fellini was shooting the movie *La Dolce Vita* (or as it was then titled *La Vita Dolce*), and some of our *Transatlantic* people, notably Desmond O'Grady, are in that movie. In "the Steiner sequence," concerning the arty side (and suicide) of the "sweet life," you can see a copy of the *Transatlantic Review* on Steiner's table—if you don't blink.

This recollection is prompted by the notion that, of all the places I have lived, Rome alone demanded some kind of direct and immediate response. I was writing a first novel about politics in Florida. The magazine became for me, as it was, I think, for my comrades in arms, an answer and a salute to the ancient and modern stones of this home place (one of them anyway) of our embattled Western civilization.

As for Trieste, that beautiful port city of the Adriatic, I was a soldier there, stationed near the village of Padriciano upon the Yugoslav border (in those days). My place was the U.S. Army. But there were powerful literary vibrations.

You could not go down into the city to the main PX without passing the Berlitz school where Joyce taught for years and worked on *Ulysses* and other things. His brother, Stanislaus Joyce, was teaching at the University in Trieste while I was there. You could not leave the city, going west along the coast, without passing by Duino Castle where Rilke listened for angels. Two of my favorite Italian/Triestine writers, the poet Umberto Saba and the novelist "Italo Svevo" (Ettore Schmitz), had lived there and had written in the local Italian dialect, which was the first Italian I learned.

In one sense the real subject here is memory. Memory and place are hopelessly entangled. Memory exposed to hard-edged facts that sometimes directly contradict memory. It seems to me that there are at least three kinds of memory—one is private, your own secret word hoard of facts and fiction; the second is public; and somewhere in between, but perhaps more powerful than both, lies family memory, what we can recall from the experience of kinfolk we know and have touched, those we have witnessed.

Thus, for example: as a baby I was held up high by one of my great-grandmothers for a family photograph. She lived as a girl and as a young bride on a very large, remote, and isolated plantation near Apalachicola, Florida, before the Civil War. She well remembered looking out her window over wide flat fields at dawn and seeing scattered tree stumps begin to move around. The stumps were, in fact, Indians, not up to any harm or mischief, just checking out the lay of the land.

That was the Florida frontier six generations ago.

Another example. In my childhood we had a maid who often brought her mother, a very old woman it seemed to me then, with her. This woman had been born in slavery. She told me stories about those slavery days and she taught me, though I have long since forgotten most of them, some songs and games and skip-rope rhymes from that gone time.

All these stories, and others, became a part of memory.

Another time and place, speaking to the Florida Historical Society in Orlando, I described myself as someone for whom the Orlando of the 1930s and '40s is more vividly present than this bright and shiny hotel ballroom and the bright and shiny world outside just beyond the windows where massive towering bank buildings, vaguely brutal and Babylonian, brood over this city by day and by night. . . . There was a time, lasting a decade from the end of the 1920s to the beginning of World War II, when it would have been distinctly disadvantageous to flaunt such prosperity around these parts, when even the (secretly) rich professed and pretended to be members in good standing of the genteel poor. It was a time I hiked and biked and hunted and fished all over what is now this large city and most of Orange County. I would have sworn that I knew every inch of it, but I got lost today trying to find my way to this hotel.

World War II was a time of great change for central Florida. Thousands and thousands of men from the army and the army air force came to train to fight in the war they later won. (See James Gould Cozzens's *Guard of Honor.*) It was a very exciting time for a teenager. I remember the very young RAF pilots, veterans of the Battle of Britain, coming to our house on Phillips Place for Christmas dinner in 1941. They smoked all the time, drank, and laughed a lot. Their eyes had the thousand-yard stare that I had so far seen only in the eyes of uncles who had fought in World War I. They were daredevils, those young pilots, and a surprising number of them crashed and were killed hereabouts just when it seemed that their most dangerous days were behind them.

Here is another sign of the turn of the tide during World War II, the beginning of the end of sleepy old, shady Orlando: My mother was standing at a corner on Orange Avenue, the corner next to Ivey's department store, waiting quietly for the traffic light to change. Next to her, also waiting for the light, was an officer of the army air corps. Suddenly, loudly and directly overhead and very low, there was an airplane, with clouds of smoke pouring out of it, sputtering and staggering (if a plane can be said to stagger).

"Lord have mercy!" my mother exclaimed. "Is that plane going to crash?"

The officer standing beside her had already spoken his reply before she realized that he was Clark Gable. "I don't know, ma'm," he said in the famous, expensive, and throaty voice. "But I sure am glad I'm not on it."

I elect to date the time of great change in central Florida from the arrival, on the scene and in the flesh, of Clark Gable. First came the war, then Gable, then air-conditioning.

Florida has (so far) been the explicit setting of two of my novels— *The Finished Man* (1959) and *The King of Babylon Shall Not Come Against You* (1996), written in Charlottesville, Virginia, and Tuscaloosa, Alabama—and maybe a dozen or two dozen short stories and a few poems.

Explicit setting? More and more in an interchangeable contemporary landscape our writers are rooting their fictions in an indefinite, one might say *implicit,* setting. Partly this is an attempt to avoid the pejorative label of being "a regional writer," as if, at this late stage of our wildly changing culture, that meant anything or made any difference at all. Do these fictions take root, bloom, and flourish? Time will tell, one supposes.

I believe that the summoning up of place from memory is likely to be different from inspection of the place where one is, in fact, standing and looking. Each point of view has its strengths and weaknesses. Memory is all too often flawed and untrustworthy. Just so, close familiarity breeds not contempt but the likelihood of taking too much for granted.

Another place I have written about in poems and stories, and in one novel, *Do, Lord, Remember Me* (1965), written in Houston, Texas, is the mountain country of western North Carolina. This is the home turf of any number of "Appalachian" writers. One thinks of Fred Chappell, Wilma Dykeman, Robert Morgan, and, just over the border in Virginia, people like David Huddle, Lee Smith, Alyson Hagy, and R. H. W. Dillard.

Always a visitor, an outsider there, I spent some of my life, especially my youth, in various seasons and for various years, at my grandfather's farm. It was then and there, under the tutelage of a tall mountain man I always called Uncle Tom, though I have no good reason to think he was any blood kin, that I learned to milk a cow and how to plow a field behind two horses or one mule, what were weeds to hoe and plants to cherish and protect in the kitchen garden, how to kill chickens, with ruthless efficiency and dispatch, for noon dinner, where to find the best wild blackberries, and where the pigs went and could be found when they escaped to a temporary freedom. All those things and more. Now chances are I could not again perform even these rudimentary chores. But I was proud of myself in those days. That childish pride became part of the place. What was up early and soon sweating became in memory, and thus in the camouflage of art, a little glimpse of Eden. Lost and gone. Near the end of his long life, that grandfather sold off the farm place and moved back down to the low country of South Carolina to the village of McClellanville where he had been born and raised (briefly "raised"—for, like so many others in Reconstruction days, he went to work before he was twelve). In his old age, his nineties, he was inspired by his own rage and by the stylish speeches of Adlai Stevenson to go forth and to campaign (a Lost Cause if there ever was one) for him across South Carolina, in person (as they say) and on the radio.

All of the above memory, the whole story, flickers through a single poem I wrote at that time and place, like a reel of movie film running out of control in an empty projection booth:

Main Currents of American Political Thought

Gone then the chipped demitasse cups
at dawn, rich with fresh cream and coffee,
a fire in the hearth, winter and summer,
a silk dandy's bathrobe, the black Havana cigar.

Gone the pet turkey gobbler, the dogs and geese,
a yard full of chickens feeling the shadow of a hawk,
the tall barn with cows and a plough horse, with corn,
with hay spilling out of the loft, festooning the dead Pierce
    Arrow.

Gone the chipped oak sideboards and table,
heavy with aplenty of dented, dusty silverware.
Gone the service pistol and the elephant rifle
and the great bland moose head on the wall.

"Two things," you told me once, "will keep
the democratic spirit of this country alive—
the free public schools and the petit jury."
Both of these things are going, too, now, Grandfather.

You had five sons and three daughters,
and they are all dead or dying slow and sure.
Even the grandchildren are riddled with casualties.
You would not believe these bitter, shiny times.

What became of all our energy and swagger?
At ninety you went out and campaigned for Adlai Stevenson
in South Carolina. And at my age I have to force
myself to vote, choosing among scoundrels.

Most southern writers that I know of, at least the last several generations of them, going back to the days before the Civil War, have been townspeople, not farmers. But the society was, for a long time, predominantly agricultural, and almost always a family farm stood as a real place and a place that stood for something. From before Jefferson until here and now, we have looked on the great cities with a farmer's frisson of illicit awe, contempt, desire, scorn, and humility. Remember how Jefferson (somewhere in the letters) calls the yellow fever a blessing in disguise because it purges the population in the cities. Many of us, at least in my generation, Agrarians and not, gratefully include the family farm as part, if only a ghostly one, of our full sense of a home place. Some of us—I think at once of Madison Jones and Wendell Berry—have returned to farming and to writing directly out of the experience. Others, the poets Henry Taylor and Fred Chappell for example, growing up on farms, have kept the place and the experience alive for all of us. That many of the Agrarians of the 1930s didn't know (in an old rural definition) "which end of a horse to feed sugar to" is not strictly relevant. Many of their points and arguments were, and still are, well taken, if seldom seriously debated.

Would we really call the U.S. Army a place? An *institution,* yes, but a *place*? Why not? Millions and millions of us, especially Americans of the twentieth century, spent years as a part of it. I spent eight years in the Active Reserve, two of those years on active duty overseas with the Twelfth Field Artillery Battery (Separate), part of the 351st Regiment Combat Team (TRUST), stationed in the Free Territory of Trieste, then later up on the Danube at Linz, Austria, where the Twelfth Field was attached to a reconnaissance battalion whose name and number, and even the shoulder patch, I have mercifully forgotten, having only the memory that at its battalion headquarters this unit, originally a Union cavalry outfit, had battle flags from the Civil War and trophies from the Indian wars in the West.

The army, one learns soon enough, is the same place wherever it goes and is located, though it is, or is said to be, a professional army now (read: mercenary) and was still a citizens' army from the beginning until the end of the Vietnam War. It was, is, always will be the same place.

I remember that they often tried to explain things to us in terms of our place in "The Big Picture." Some of my fellow sergeants, good men and true to be sure, believed there really was somewhere an enormous Big Picture, a TV screen as big as the Pentagon or even bigger, where, like crowds of people in a D. W. Griffith movie (*Intolerance*?), we were all to be seen and observed. Someone somewhere out there was in charge and in control, always looking out for our interests, health, and welfare. There was a place (Eden) where the Big Picture was and where everything made perfect sense.

Taking the army as a place (the West Virginia of the American psyche? the Mississippi of the soul?), one also assumed a past. Up close and personal the men of the Twelfth Field in Trieste were sometimes fired on (and sometimes returned fire) by various kinds of terrorists and Yugoslavs. A goodly number served in Korea. Some of the older sergeants had good, clear memories of World War II. One of them was captured at Kasserine Pass, recovered, then later wounded and overrun in the Battle of the Bulge. Their past became your past if you listened and learned.

And there was the much larger, longer past, all the way back to the *Iliad*. All of a piece throughout.

For southerners the army was always a place to be, once in our own army, not for long but long enough to kill or maim one in four of us and a good many of them, too. You might safely say then, and even now with all its cultivated diversity, that the army is a southern place. It is not a Tom Hanks/Steven Spielberg/Tom Brokaw kind of place, full of mellow old men with their weepy memories and neat graveyards.

We have family memories in the middle, between our own and the sad end of Hector, Tamer of Horses. There is, for instance, my Uncle Oliver (my father's side), not himself a southerner, though we incorporated him when he wrote the final shooting script for *Gone with the Wind*. He went early to World War I, spending Christmas of 1917 in the trenches. His unit went into action very early in our part of that war and stayed late; and when, at the end, they were pulled out of the line, they were each and all carefully searched for the possession of any loose cartridges, lest someone should take a notion to shoot General "Black Jack" Pershing when they passed in review in a big parade in their honor. Oliver H. P. Garrett had some good stories to tell and even wrote and published some of them. And he wrote the screenplay for the first talking film version of *A Farewell to Arms,* the one with Gary Cooper and Helen Hayes and maybe the best film adaptation ever of a Hemingway novel. Oliver's stories were authentic veteran talk. They were always oblique, jokey, and usually funny, never dealing directly with the inexplicable experience of mortal combat, just the context of it. He was once asked why he didn't write a "war novel." "What is a war novel?" he answered. "Is that like a *life* novel? The Great War was my whole life."

We served and fought in all the American wars—the earliest soldier of the family that I can track down so far was one Gershom Palmer of Stonington, Connecticut, who was lieutenant of a Stonington company during King Philip's War in 1675. We have been at it ever since. The army was, as yapping and barking sergeants were continually reminding us, our home away from home.

Of course, the Civil War, which killed more of us than all the other American wars taken together (so far), was the worst and the one that mattered most. I had four great-grandfathers and one grandfather who walked (or rode) across those killing fields and experienced the slaughterhouse directly. None of them ever said more than a few words about it. As irony would have it, the only one who put any words on a page—a private diary and journal for his own family—was the one Yankee of the bunch, Colonel Oliver Hazard Palmer, commander of the 108th New York Volunteers.

He saw action ("going to see the elephant" was what they called it) any number of times in desperate places, most notably at the Battle of Antietam and the Battle of Fredericksburg. From his notes on the latter one can learn a good deal about what it was really like. Prior to the passage quoted below he had led his brigade, following direct orders, to attack the Confederate positions on the high ground overlooking the town. To start the assault they had to begin by crossing roughly four hundred yards of open terrain in the face of "a most destructive, accurate and deadly fire.... It was too hot. One third of my Brigade was disabled in twenty minutes and I was compelled to fall back." The brigade was withdrawn into the cover, such as it was, of the town. After which he wrote:

> I remained on the field until nearly dark and until the fighting of the day was mainly over. It was a terribly hot place. The shells were flying in every direction and plowing up the earth all around me, frequently covering me all over as in a whirlwind. The scene was frightful but intensely exciting. New Brigades of fresh troops were forming in line and advancing hoping to be more successful, but I knew they were doomed to disappointment and death. Broken and shattered Companies, Regiments and Brigades were falling back. Dead and wounded officers and men were being borne to the rear, some in blankets, some on the shoulders of their comrades. You would see one here with one arm, another there with one leg trying to get back. Some moaning, some swearing, occasionally a poor fellow trying to save the half not shot away in front would disappear in fragments by a solid shot or amidst the smoke of an exploding shell.... About sundown I made my way to town to gather up fragments of my Brigade not knowing what the next day might require. Out of the 1200 men in my command in the morning I could get together at night only 400. It was a sorry sight.

The place, Fredericksburg; the time and place, the Civil War. You have now been there.

As luck would have it, or maybe it's not luck, but (in Nabokov's sense and term) as *synchronicity* will have it, I am working on this piece on place in my high attic study in Charlottesville, Virginia, a place, the one place, where I have lived, off and on, for more than twenty years. My attic windows overlook the hedge, the handsome toothpick fence, the huge, shady sweetgum tree (in their backyard) separating my place from that of my next-door neighbor for a dozen years and more—the late Peter Taylor. His widow, the poet Eleanor Taylor, lives there still. It is now Monday, July 2, 2001, a cool, bright summer day, with clear breezes blowing. Coming after more than a week of hot and humid days, with the temperature in the high nineties, it is most pleasant weather.

As synchronicity will have it, the daily *New York Times* has an essay by the writer Geraldine Brooks, "You Live Differently in a Small Place." It is part of the *Times*'s ongoing series of star turns—"Writers on Writing."

Brooks's article is pertinent in a number of ways. She identifies herself as having been, until now, a city person at home "in the dense urban tangles of Sydney, New York, Cairo, and London." She has now come to live "in a tiny village of 250 souls in the Blue Ridge foothills of Virginia." A place, whatever its name and wherever it may be, that cannot be far from where I am at work. We are (assuming she is still there at this moment) sharing the same good weather and, to some extent, sharing the same view of the Blue Ridge Mountains lining the western horizon. The central point of her article is to make the case that living in this Virginia village has been an experience that has served to liberate her from some prejudices and preconceptions, and allowed her to write and finish her (then) forthcoming novel—*Year of Wonders*. *Year of Wonders* is a historical novel set in 1666 in Eyam, "a tiny English village of 250 souls in the year the Bubonic Plague struck." In a larger sense, the piece is a defense of historical fiction in general, defending the art of it against the doubts of Henry James, as voiced in a 1901 letter to Sarah Orne Jewett. Brooks disagrees with James's arguments and concludes: "It is human nature to imagine, to put yourself in another's shoes. The past may be another country. But the only passport required is empathy."

The past may be another country. . . . That is, *another place.* At some point in the past (James announced it was fifty years) there is a conflation of time and place; unless we are able to imagine it, the deeper, darker past, inhabited by strangers, is lost to us. Past time becomes an exotic and remote place as far away from and as strange to us as (real or imaginary) China was to Marco Polo.

I spent thirty busy years as an expatriate southerner living, at least part of the time, among Elizabethans and trying to write some news from their time and place to ours. It proved to be at once more pleasure and more challenge than I could have imagined at the outset. One of the most serious problems was to contend with, if not to overcome (impossible), my twentieth-century mind-set. In order to confirm and strengthen our precarious self-esteem and to nurture our hopeful sense of historical superiority, we are ready, willing, and able to distort, even to suppress, any information and likewise to encourage rare or common misconceptions and misunderstandings in order to defend assumptions and preconceived views. We regularly, almost reflexively, do this with current events and issues. Why would we not seek to do so as well with the imagined and imaginary past?

In her article, Brooks takes note of this challenging difficulty, honestly noting that, from her globalized, cosmopolitan point of view, from "the dense urban tangles of Sydney, New York, Cairo and London," it was a very strange experience to move to a village in Virginia, after years of living among friends with "like minds and agreeable opinions," and to make friends with alien others there—"I found it hard to be thrust into relationships with supporters of the death penalty or the N.R.A., of prayer in the schools or unbridled property rights."

There it is, exactly there, that the southern writer, a writer out of the southern tradition, has something else to offer, beyond the ritual celebration of the flora and fauna, the weeds and flowers, the winds and weathers of his (increasingly imaginary) home place. And that something more is not the mere ability, but the habit, of accepting the ragged contradictions of our age: understanding, without a need to justify, that we are all of us bundles of contradictory assumptions, beliefs, superstitions; that we have been wrong about so many things and will surely be wrong again; that our tradition, though it be sorely tested, tried by ordeal, is to question the truth and value of the wisdom of "like minds and agreeable opinions." When we summon up our place in the world we have to call up as well the people who live there.

Finally, however, what can help to save us from the weight and woe of our self-concern is the persistent southern habit of laughter, of skeptical laughter, even at our easy pretensions. I think here of the public service rendered by the avant-garde southern writer R. H. W. Dillard, by his satirical, parodic short story "That's What I Like (About the South)." There, taking as his starting point "the defining characteristics of Southern fiction," as defined by the prominent editor Shannon Ravenel, he holds them, each and all, in the light of pitiless scrutiny. The section under the solemn rubric of "deep involvement in place" is devoted to a richly detailed scene set in (where else?) a 7-Eleven market—"Roy pulls a medium-sized paper cup, red and white with Slurpee written on it in blue, from the torpedo rack of cups by the machine."

The southern place, "real" or remembered and imagined, past and present, is as much haunted by comedy as by tragedy. When we summon up our place and our past, together with a renewed awareness of the ineradicable tears of things, we also hear the sound of ghostly laughter.

The Delta

Charles East

I was one of the last generation to be born at home. There were no hospitals in the small towns then. The doctor was called, and he came. The scene as it was described to me years later was of a young mother terrified of losing her life as the doctor worked to deliver the baby breech first. The time of my arrival is recorded in the silk-covered baby's book that was a gift from my great-grandmother I never knew: 6:05 a.m. My mother, late getting to the book, wrote the wrong year in: December 11, 1925. It was in fact 1924.

Long before I knew there was a place called Mississippi, I was aware that I lived in the Delta. I doubt that I had a very clear idea of what the word meant, though I think I remember being told we were leaving the Delta as we drove up into the hills on our way south to Vicksburg or north to Memphis. Simply, I suppose I thought, our part of the country.

Except for green patches of woods and the willows and cypresses that lined old streams like the Bogue and the Sunflower River, the Delta was mostly fields, and as flat as a tabletop. It was a land white with cotton in the late summer and brown in winter, a land that stretched from horizon to horizon. In my first published story, "Under the Blue Cup," I saw my characters trapped under "a canopy of cloud and sky, like a blue cup turned upside down over them."

The Delta where I grew up was in every way tied to cotton: planting it, hoeing it, picking it, ginning it—cotton gins, cotton houses in the fields where the cotton was stored before being taken to the gins in wagons, cotton compresses, cotton buyers, and cooks and yardmen who failed to show up in your house or yard in cotton-picking time when they could get a dollar a hundred. Who had brought in the first bale? How much a pound was it bringing? Would rain keep the pickers out of the fields? You couldn't escape it.

There were signs on the highway at both ends of our town announcing that Shelby, Mississippi, was the LONG-STAPLE COTTON CAPITAL OF THE WORLD. I

didn't know what long-staple cotton was, just accepted the signs at face value—
played king of the mountain on the piles of cottonseed hulls behind the gins,
played hide-and-seek among the cotton bales in the compress. Never imagined
that one day the pickers would be gone, replaced by machines, and the cotton
mostly replaced by soybeans and rice and catfish farms. Sic transit gloria.

The Delta I was recalling in my fiction was the small-town Delta of the 1930s
and early 1940s. In all of these towns there was of course the depot, which stood
next to the Yazoo and Mississippi Valley Railroad tracks running south to New
Orleans and north to Memphis. There were the silver water tanks where the high-
school boys had left their initials—the tallest things in these towns and the first
things you saw from a distance. Most of the towns had one or two of them; ours
had three, in addition to the squat wooden tank below the depot where the steam
locomotives took on water.

There were two rows of brick stores, one on either side of the railroad. One of
these streets was a highway, in our town U.S. 61, exactly one mile of concrete that
ran out in gravel half a mile above the depot and half a mile below until the highway construction crews came through and paved all of it in the late thirties. The
stores were a mix of drugstores, dry-goods stores, hardware stores, and grocery
stores—frequently sandwiched between banks at each corner. Along one or
the other side of the tracks in these towns was a Ford dealership, its Chevrolet
counterpart, a service station, a two- or sometimes three-story hotel, a barbershop, a café, and a theater that we called the picture show. In Shelby, there was as
late as 1940 a blacksmith shop.

But the focal point of the town was the depot. There we said our good-byes
and were met and embraced on our return. The town set its time by the trains or
by the big railroad clock ticking the seconds and minutes away in the depot. The
train whistle in the night was a comforting sound now lost to us.

The social life as well as the religious life of the town was centered on the
churches. The Baptists were probably the most numerous of the congregations,
followed by the Methodists and then the Catholics, whose communicants were
largely drawn from the Italian population. There was also a small but closely knit
band of Presbyterians. Friendships were often rooted in church membership,
but my Presbyterian family had good friends who were Baptists or Methodists.
Sunday evenings I accompanied my friends the Rogers brothers to their BYPU
meetings.

The schools of these towns did an exceptional job of educating their students,
and they did it in the hard times of the Depression. At the school I first attended,
the dividing line was not the color of your skin—the blacks had their own

school—but whether you lived in town or in the country. The "colored school," as I think we called it, was in the "colored section" of town and as foreign to us as the British Museum or the Eiffel Tower. Our acquaintance with blacks—and by "our" I mean whites'—was generally limited to yardmen and cooks or to town fixtures like Rush, who drove Denton's ice wagon.

The children who attended the white school and who lived on farms within a few miles of town came in on school buses, bringing their lunches in brown paper bags or one-gallon tin syrup buckets. The rest of us walked to school or were driven there by our fathers on their way to work; when the bell rang at noon we walked or rode home to eat dinner with our families. The noon meal was always called dinner; the evening meal, supper.

I don't remember that we called the children from the farms the "country children," but that is the way we thought of them. They tended to sit in the back of the room near the windows and to congregate together on the school grounds at recess or at noontime. We never played with them after school because by then they had been loaded onto the buses and were being dropped off at their homes, where farmwork awaited them. In cotton-picking time they were often absent. The children from the country were generally well behaved. The school bullies were almost always the poorer and meaner of the town children.

Like many of the schools in the Delta, ours had been built in the 1920s and was a two-story brick building with flights of stairs at both ends of the hall running the length of it. The superintendent's office, the "sick room," the teachers' lounge, and the classrooms of the lower grades were on the first floor. There we learned our ABCs and our multiplication tables, got our smallpox vaccinations, and from time to time had our throats sprayed by "Dr. Ded"—Dr. Dedwylder— or his nurse from the county health office in Cleveland.

Except for the superintendent and the coaches our teachers were all women— usually "old maids," as they were considered to be if they were single and over thirty. There was always a pretty young teacher new to the school who retired after a year or two to marry one of the coaches. By and large they were dedicated to the profession they had chosen; there were good and even excellent teachers among them. Discipline was not a problem at a time when punishment was mostly left to the teachers and ranged from standing at the blackboard with your nose pressed to a chalk-drawn circle (my fate in the second grade) to licks across the palm of your hand with a ruler or being sent to the superintendent's office for a paddling. News of paddlings traveled faster than a speeding locomotive, usually by word of mouth from those who had been sent to the office.

The auditorium on the second floor, where we assembled by class for "chapel" and at the end of the school year for graduation exercises, was also a place of public entertainment. Beauty pageants and talent shows were held there, in addition to that favorite of small towns in the 1930s, the womanless wedding. At a time when cross-dressing was something no one talked about, nor indeed had a word for, the biggest and sometimes ugliest of the town's men entertained the audience with a bouncing walk down the aisle as bride and bridesmaids. The more of their hairy legs showing the better!

One talent show I remember all too well because I was a contestant, my mother having thrust me into it even when, at seven or eight, I knew better. And here we came, one at a time, out onto the stage: tap dancers, singers, students of band or piano—the rankest amateurs in the Delta. Backstage we had drawn numbers out of a hat to determine the order. It was my misfortune to draw 1. The emcee, Floyd B. Stratton—never called anything but Floyd B.—announced my coming, as terrifying a moment as I can remember. I walked out to the edge of the stage, looked to my left at my music teacher seated at the upright piano below, and let go with "Is It True What They Say about Dixie?" No doubt this was the day my mother's dream of going to Hollywood with a child star in hand ended!

The minstrel shows held in the school auditorium featured men of the town whose faces had been blackened by an application of burned cork or sometimes by what appeared to be shoe polish, leaving circles or ovals of white skin around their mouths and eyes. The men masquerading as blacks always wore black wigs and white gloves and sounded like Amos 'n' Andy. But there were other minstrel shows of an altogether different character. "Silas Green from New Orleans" was one, the "Orleans" pronounced "Or-*leens*" to make it rhyme with "Green." The Rabbit Foot Minstrel was another. Both were black-owned and had all-black casts of performers.

These shows and the circuses that came to town were the only occasions when white and black alike gathered under one tent, though still separated by seating, with a grassy aisle between them. The star attraction in the traveling minstrels was usually a stout woman in a red satin evening dress who came to the stage and belted out the blues in a voice strong enough to be heard as far as Mound Bayou. The blues singer Bessie Smith, who was with one of these shows, was killed in an automobile accident up the highway near the neighboring town of Clarksdale in 1937. The bands that were a part of the minstrels played jazz and ragtime as well as blues, and at some point in the performance brought the audience to its feet with a rousing rendition of "Dixie."

There were also whites-only dances where black musicians—bands from Clarksdale or Memphis—played at the Firemen's Club hall in Shelby. I was too young to go—I in fact don't recall that I ever saw the inside of the building—but on more than one occasion my father drove past while a dance was in progress. The hall was across the road from the Valley Gin and the Zion Grove Church, one of the town's black Baptist churches. I remember boys in their late teens and men in their twenties standing on the porch of the Firemen's Club smoking with the sound of music coming from inside—nothing at all like the music and the shouting I had heard coming from the Zion Grove Baptists.

Even before the schools built gymnasiums, the other Delta towns had gathering places of one kind or another where they could hold dances. In more than one of these towns, it was the American Legion hall. Cleveland, for instance, had one. So did Merigold. By the mid-1930s the larger towns had country clubs. In the county seats, dances like the ball held on President Roosevelt's birthday were sometimes held in the courthouses.

Several of the local families were known for their horsemanship, and by the late 1920s they had brought horse shows to Shelby. There were also mule races and donkey baseball games that pitted one town's team against another's. Black jockeys rode the mules in the mule races. As farm animals used to plow and to pull cotton wagons, mules occupied a place of special affection in the Delta. Their very commonness and their proverbial stubbornness made them appealing. Mule barns where the animals could be bought at auction were a common sight in the larger towns until the mule population declined and finally disappeared altogether with the coming of mechanization.

One social event that had earlier been a staple of local political campaigns was the fish fry, sometimes held at one of the hunting camps back of the levee. Behind the levee, beyond the bar pits and blue holes and the *batture* with its cottonwood trees and willows, the river eddied its way south, carrying logs and sometimes dead bodies with it. Nobody had to say what river—just "the river." It was of course the Mississippi. There were other rivers and creeks and bayous, like the Bogue, which was never called by its full name, Bogue Phalia (Fa-*li*-ya), and Deer Creek, which meandered its way through the southern part of the Delta. And there were the lakes, many of them once parts of the river—Lake Beulah, Lake Bolivar, Lake Washington, Concordia. On the other side of Clarksdale there was Moon Lake, which Tennessee Williams would use in his plays and stories. Delta men and boys all fished and hunted and early learned to clean the fish and dress the deer and cultivate a taste for squirrel and venison.

And there were Sunday drives. What else was there to do on a Sunday afternoon in the Delta in the 1930s? Sunday dinner out of the way, my father at the
wheel of our Ford, windows open (for there was no air-conditioning then), we
would head west to the river or north on the road to Duncan and Alligator, or
sometimes east to Parchman for a visit with one of my father's friends who
worked at the state prison farm and occupied one of the houses on the grounds,
attended by prisoners who were trusties.

The roads that we traveled those Sunday afternoons were all gravel, at least
until the late 1930s, when that section of U.S. 61 was paved, and even then we
rarely took 61 but instead our old routes of habit, which followed the curves of the
river and took us to the top of the levee, where my father would survey the terrain for the possibility of future coon hunts. Occasionally he would drive down
one of those roads that crossed the levee, descending at a steep angle to the leafy
bower of some fishing spot where he had caught thirty bass or forty-five bream (I
could never understand how he remembered the exact number). The memory
of those Sunday afternoons at the river and of the men caulking their boats and
mending their nets inspired me to write "Fisherman's Wife," one of my early stories.

The roads were full of nails dropped by passing cotton wagons, and not in-
frequently a tire would go flat and require attention unless, as sometimes happened, the driver decided to drive to the next town on the rim. My father was
not one of those. He would immediately stop, jack up the car, remove the tire,
and replace it with the one he carried in the trunk, and we were on our way once
more. Sometimes we would take a friend with us on these drives, usually one of
my grandmother's friends whose husband did not have a car of his own—not
because he couldn't afford one (he was a prosperous merchant) but because the
idea of owning a car simply didn't appeal to him. Deltans, I very soon learned,
had a streak of independence, indeed of perverseness.

I was told my father had once owned a Chevrolet, but the cars I remember
him driving were all Fords—for one thing because Herron Rothrock, who owned
"the Ford place," was an elder in our church and a man well liked in the town.
I'm sure my father would have considered a switch to Chevrolet or some other
make of car an act of betrayal. The town was mostly divided between Chevrolets
and Fords, though I can remember a big dark-blue car driven by Miss Lucille
Wooten that I believe was a Cadillac, one Dodge, and at least two Lincolns. Our
friends the Childs owned a brown Oakland Landau that took the family to the
World's Fair in Chicago. The Oakland sat high and had an imperial splendor
about it.

The Delta that I recalled in my early stories was a self-contained world of small towns where a crank of the phone on the wall brought you the operator— "Central," we called her. She could tell you the time, or where the fire was, or whether the party you were calling had stepped out for a minute or had gone to Memphis on business. *Party* was a word appropriated by the phone company as a substitute for *person.*

The Delta was a charmed world, or so it seems now, perfectly shaped in memory. Even the names of the towns had a kind of magic to them: Midnight, Panther Burn, Indianola, Itta Bena. To the west was the river; to the east, the hills. To the south the Delta ended at the Yazoo River a few miles above Vicksburg or at Yazoo City; to the north, a little below Memphis, the city where our mothers went to do their shopping at Goldsmith's or to buy wedding presents at Brodnax—where we went to be among the first to see *Gone with the Wind* or, as we grew older, simply to be seen in the lobby of the Peabody.

The Delta was small towns like Shelby, where I was born, and Cleveland, where my family went to live when I was twelve, and larger towns like Greenwood and Greenville. Greenwood was the last stopping-off place before the hills to the east of us. Greenville was on the river. Greenville was familiar to Delta children as the place they were taken to have their tonsils removed in the days when that procedure was so routine few of us escaped it.

The Delta was the sound of gins running late into the night and the smell of the cottonseed oil mill, which reminded those passing through the towns of ham frying. And there was another smell I always associated with the Delta—the smell of land, of earth, of things growing—honeysuckle and clover and freshly mown fields of wild onion.

Saturday was the big day of the week in the Delta of my childhood. Country folk, black and white, came in to buy their staples and to visit. Big pigeon-toed boys with bosomy girls in tow walked the streets to show off their prizes. Mothers sat in cars eating grapes they had bought at Mr. Lillo's fruit stand and nursing their babies. My father liked to drive downtown on a Saturday night and park in front of Mr. Cobb's Rexall Drugstore, which afforded a good view of the traffic up and down the sidewalk. On Saturday mornings the boys from town got their hair cut, and some of the planters could be seen getting their shaves at the barbershop. There they sat—two, sometimes three chairs filled with men reared back with hot towels over their faces while the ceiling fans overhead cooled them. Talk of the weather. Talk of Bilbo and the speech he'd made one time in Rosedale or Ruleville. That Bilbo! Talk of "high water," meaning the river was rising.

I never knew any Delta planters who resembled Big Daddy in Tennessee Williams's play *Cat on a Hot Tin Roof;* nearly all the planters I remember lived in the towns and drove out to their "places," sometimes with a pair of bird dogs on the backseat, or if they resided on their plantations lived in unpretentious houses whose yards were filled with tractors and steel drums and flocks of guineas.

I don't know why it was, but fine distinctions were made between farms and plantations, just as between farmers and planters. Yet some of the planters avoided the word *plantation,* which signaled wealth, or at least unlimited credit. If you had asked them what they did, they would probably have said "farm," no matter if they farmed a thousand acres. The planters I knew, most of them, were also doctors or lawyers or owned banks or businesses. Some ran for—and usually won—political office.

In the Delta there was always the memory of floods—people talking about something far removed from that subject would establish the time by whether it was before or after the flood of '27. I was not yet three—too young to remember it—when the levee broke and the river rushed through and spilled onto the fields and towns in its path, but I was told that I was in the car with my family when my father drove down somewhere near Shaw to see the closest edge of the floodwaters. I do remember a time in the early thirties when the river rose to the top of the innermost levee and my father talked of putting our furniture up on scaffolding and heading south to Louisiana. Sand boils could be seen in the fields just outside the levee as seeping river water bubbled to the surface. Some families did arrange to leave, but my father tarried and the water receded.

The Delta had a reputation as an unhealthy place to live, in large measure because of its swamps that bred mosquitoes and its periodic outbreaks of malaria and yellow fever. In the years just before and after the turn of the century, trains were not permitted to stop in many of the Delta towns when there was word of a yellow-fever epidemic somewhere up or down the line but were instead waved through by men armed with shotguns. The yellow-fever scare had long since passed by the 1930s, but doctors regularly prescribed quinine—a syrupy dose called Cocoa Quinine if you were a child—to ward off or cure malaria.

And there were other fears I remember from my childhood: of spinal meningitis, lockjaw, hydrophobia (the word then for rabies), infantile paralysis (polio). The sight of a strange dog foaming at the mouth could strike terror in the heart of a community. The sheriff's men were summoned to dispatch the animal, being sure to aim for the heart rather than the head, so that the head could be sent to the rabies lab in Jackson. In the early years settlers had to contend with wildcats, bears, panthers, and alligators. Still, the Delta's reputation was that of a place where fortunes could be made and where in any case things happened.

One thing that gave the Delta its vitality was its quite extraordinary mix of nationalities and cultures. Blacks composed something like 70 percent of the population, an even higher percentage in one or two of the Delta counties, yet from the white perspective they were a largely unacknowledged presence. In our county, Bolivar, whites accounted for only one-fourth of the population in 1930.

In both of the towns where I grew up there were a number of Jewish merchants, like the Lamensdorfs and Aarons in Shelby and the Kamiens and Kaplans in Cleveland, all of them highly regarded citizens. It was the same all over the Delta. There were also families of Italian, German, Syrian, Greek, and Chinese ancestry. One of the Shelby druggists, Mr. Domengeaux, was Cajun French, or possibly a descendant of emigrants who had come directly from France, and I believe Mr. Latiolais also. Both had come to the Delta from Louisiana. Those of German descent had settled a little to the east of Shelby, at what was sometimes called Germania. Many of the Italians—like the Sacco, Ferretti, Bramucci, and Belenchia families—owned farms around the town. A few followed family trades and were barbers or shoemakers.

The Chinese often lived in the back of the small grocery stores they operated. Most of their customers were blacks, though the Delta was full of exceptions: the Chinese-owned Modern Store in Cleveland was for years the best grocery store and meat market in the town, and it was the store overwhelmingly favored by the families who made up the establishment. But at the same time the Chinese were not allowed to attend the white public schools and as a result started a school of their own. They had earlier encountered the same restriction in Clarksdale and Greenville. Eventually the ban was lifted.

In these Delta towns there were always some of mysterious lineage or rumored to be of mixed blood or concealed parentage, babies found on doorsteps, alcoholic bachelor uncles said to be locked in padded rooms upstairs, ladies with TB who lived apart from their families on sunny sleeping porches, never seen on the streets or at the picture show. Hotheaded planters' sons who shot and killed their fathers. Suicides. Madness. A lot of stories. No wonder the Delta produced writers!

Most of all the Delta is for me now, in memory, people. The Rogers brothers, Walter and Jesse, veterans of the rubber-gun wars, kings of the cottonseed-hull mountain—the nearest thing I would ever have to brothers. My friend Milton Dixon and his brother Dum-Dum, whose father hunted coons with my father in the swamps along the river. J. W. Thomas, a romantic figure to me as a child because he could fly a plane and operated a short-wave radio station in his home across the street from us.

And H. L. Wilkinson, lawyer, planter, the patron saint of our town—who owned or ran nearly everything in it including the hardware store and lumber company my father managed and the gin my great-uncle operated. Mr. H. L.—brother of Mr. L. B., Mr. M. M., and Mr. J. W.—lived in a big two-story home at the end of our block and passed our house every day as he came home for dinner from his office at the commissary. He always tipped his hat to the children.

And there was Miss Laura Mae Keeler, who lived in that enormous turn-of-the-century house on the road to Perthshire and who was a legend among us because sometime in the recent past she had tried to save a black man from a lynch mob that took him from her. The black man was driven through my part of the country in a slow procession that ended in his death by burning. There was ever a dark side to the Delta.

The Delta was girls with double names—Fannie Chance Blanchard and Mattie Lorraine Riggin and Dora Lillian Doolittle—called Fannie Chance, Mattie Lorraine, and Dora Lillian; and boys or men known by their double names or nicknames or initials—Joe Rice Dockery, Hiram Lee Roberts, Kildee Weathers, C. T. Jacobs. Jimmy Dick Hill gave the town of Midnight its name after winning a pot and the land on which the town was built at straight-up twelve in a high-stakes poker game—one of those Delta legends.

The Delta was my wife's Uncle Bill, a lawyer of the old school, two-time mayor of our town and a former district attorney. *W. W. Simmons,* he always signed himself in the bold hand of those educated in penmanship. He was a man of the law but, above all, of principle: the Atticus Finch of my boyhood.

And the Delta was Ben Wasson, the Greenville literary light and early friend of Faulkner's who left the Delta to seek his fortune in New York but who returned to bring others the word of farther horizons. Every Delta town of any size had at least one gifted exile. Carrie Avent, born on her father's three-thousand-acre plantation near Minter City, went on to perform in Europe and the Near East before an accident brought an end to her career as an Oriental dancer. Some dreamed of a stage career or wrote stories that were almost taken by *Harper's* or published poetry in one of the magazines that no one had ever heard of.

In Greenville there was a sort of colony of writers emerging, one of them Shelby Foote, who eventually went north to live in Memphis. The poet George Marion O'Donnell, who taught a creative writing class I took in college, came out of the small town of Belzoni. Some made a name for themselves in other ways, but they always, or almost always, came home, as Ben Wasson did, to become objects of awe and wonder by virtue of having once flown the coop—and sometimes as lessons in failure.

And of course there was William Alexander Percy, a man I never met but one of the first Mississippi writers I read, even before I discovered the great pleasure of reading Eudora Welty. I first read *Lanterns on the Levee* during my senior year in high school at the urging of the teacher who sent her class to the synagogue to hear the Great Books lectures. I read Will Percy's book again when I was in the navy during the war—a copy checked out of the library at the Brooklyn Navy Yard but never returned because, I asked myself, who else in the navy would want to read a Greenville, Mississippi, writer?

One thing I early observed, or thought I did, about my part of the country was the Deltans' uncompromising sense of the place as God's country—something like that of the lady in Natchez who reminded her grandson entering Harvard one fall not to tell anyone he was from Natchez: "They'd only be jealous." There was an air of superiority about Deltans that some of those in the North Mississippi hill country resented: all that rich land and the attitude to go with it! It manifested itself in the determination of Deltans to do things in style, to give their daughters a fancy wedding when they didn't know where their next crop was coming from, sometimes even (so the story goes) charging china and silver and crystal and God only knows what else and then returning it after the wedding.

Credit was in fact the currency and coin of the Delta. To insist on cash was not only gauche but mostly unheard of. As for style, if it was not everything, it most assuredly mattered: I knew one lady who rode the evening train from Cleveland to Boyle—a distance of three miles—and paid the fifty cents extra for the privilege of avoiding the chair car and riding in the Pullman.

But what was it that made the Delta the Delta? For one thing, its history. The "mysterious Yazoo–Mississippi Delta," as Eudora Welty once called it, was a vast wilderness of canebrakes and virgin forests that was opened to settlement late and remained relatively isolated until the coming of the railroad. A huge labor force was required to clear and drain the land, which stretched some two hundred miles north to south in the northwest corner of Mississippi. West to east the Delta ran from the Mississippi River to the Yazoo, and before the construction of a dependable levee system it was subject to frequent flooding. The land was in fact a floodplain shared by the two rivers. In the years before the Civil War, the labor used to clear and cultivate this land was slave labor supplied by planters with large numbers of blacks or the means to purchase them.

The Delta was in many ways still isolated and undeveloped when the railroad came through in the 1880s. Lawyers boarded coal-burning trains headed north from Louisiana and the southwest Mississippi hill country to become planters and entrepreneurs and bankers. At the same time there was a migration down from the northern end of the line. Railroad men built the depots, which were strung out in new towns laid out roughly five miles apart, many of them flag stops. That is, you could stand along the tracks and wave the train to a stop; otherwise, it went on through. Many of the stops were named for the men who had granted the railroads right-of-way through their plantations. Bookkeepers headed north to keep records of the wealth to come or to become bankers or merchants. The Delta was a place for those with energy and ambition and a taste for adventure.

In the 1930s the black Delta, with which whites had a limited acquaintance, was a world of colored schools, colored churches, and colored waiting rooms, restrooms, and water fountains. The passenger trains that came through these towns had coaches for colored only. Blacks came to backdoors, took their seats in the back rows of buses, sat in the balcony at the picture show, if it had a balcony, and were not permitted to vote or to enroll in all-white colleges or universities until the civil rights struggle of the 1950s and 1960s settled the matter.

Few of the women—white women—of the Delta worked outside the home in the 1930s. Those who did were usually schoolteachers. Others clerked in millinery shops or dry-goods stores. The Oberst sisters, Rosa and Mollie, came to Rosedale from Memphis before 1900 and opened a millinery and dressmaking establishment that served the town for the next fifty years. In the town where I grew up, Miss Irene Hale ran the only dress shop and millinery and later married one of the town's doctors. A few women, but only a few, worked at jobs ordinarily taken by men. Sis Bland, the only woman in the town permitted to play poker with the men and join them for their chili suppers, was superintendent of the Shelby Oil Mill. She also wore sporty men's clothes, drove sporty cars, and subscribed to *Esquire*.

Almost every Delta town of any size had a Woman's Clubhouse. The era of small-town country clubs was just beginning, and the Woman's Clubs provided a setting for social events such as receptions and teas as well as local entertainment. According to the *Bolivar Commercial*, the county newspaper, my mother often performed "aesthetic dancing" there and might appear in the costume of a Mexican senorita or a Scottish lass or even a Japanese geisha. The clubs sponsored civic projects such as city beautification.

Bridge games were endemic to the town, and bridge parties often got underway in the morning and proceeded into the late afternoon, with a break for a lunch of tomato aspic and open-faced cucumber sandwiches and chicken salad. All written up in the paper with verve and imagination by the ladies who spent their weeks on the phone gathering items for the personals column. Mrs. O. P. Bland and her daughter Miss Sis Bland had motored to Memphis on Thursday. "The opening of a night-blooming cereus was the occasion for a delightful gathering of a few friends at the home of Mr. and Mrs. J. P. Shelby on Tuesday evening."

"The north-bound passenger train at noon Tuesday struck a Ford car at the crossing in front of Sharp-Lawson Hardware Co. and badly damaged the car." No mention of the driver—possibly L. B. Wilkinson, whose grandson tells the story of his grandfather losing three cars to the train.

A snouted Greyhound bus visited us twice daily, once headed north to Memphis, the second time going south, probably bound for Vicksburg. There were always suitcases—or grips, as they were called then—strapped to the top of the bus and passengers peering from the open windows. In our town the bus stopped on the street in front of the Shelby Hotel. But those who favored rail travel and could afford it left the Greyhound to others. In the 1930s, as the Depression deepened, the railroad dropped its rates to a cent a mile, so that a one-way ticket to Memphis, one hundred miles up the rails, cost a dollar.

The life of the town quite literally centered on the railroad. In those days there were four passenger trains a day, and some of the towns were served by a local known as the Peavine. Mail came and went by train, sorted in the mail car or baggage car; the trains brought Christmas bicycles from Sears Roebuck and caskets containing the bodies of those who had died away and were being returned home for burial. Freights carrying long strings of boxcars rolled slowly through the towns, occasionally stopping to pick up a boxcar on the siding at the cotton compress or the oil mill or to drop off a car loaded with lumber.

Racing the trains was one of the simple pleasures of my childhood. My father would head south on Highway 61 as "Number 15" pulled away from the depot and would race the train to the crossing—that is, the point where the road left the east side of the tracks and crossed over to the west, where it remained until it once more crossed to the east somewhere south of Mound Bayou. On winter nights the dark came early and the headlight of the train, the lights in the windows of the coaches, and the red glow of fire in the engine as the fireman stoked the firebox was for a boy an unimaginably exciting sight. Then my father slowed the car and the train was gone—engine, tender, baggage car, chair cars, diner, Pullman.

The Shelby depot where I waited all those evenings for the whistle of the southbound train is now a branch of the Bolivar County library. The COLORED WAITING ROOM signs that I remember from my childhood are gone but occasionally turn up at antique auctions—or did. Those still circulating are almost certainly reproductions—proof, if any were needed, that things have indeed changed.

No one climbs the water tank anymore, as I did once, in the belief that when I reached the top I could see Memphis. Still the imprint of the place is on me. In me. Ask me where I'm from and without a moment's thought I'll say, "The Delta."

One Writer's Sense of Place

Elizabeth Spencer

I learned about the importance of place in fiction the hard way, by trying to do without it. In my first novel I was hoping to bring to life a girl's many wanderings with her family—her father being a bridge contractor—and how, after her parents' deaths, she wound up in a job with a federal agency in a small county seat in Mississippi. How could I depict a life spent wandering throughout much of the USA without knowing anything particular about it, only that it was a bore to ride long distances in a car? What then does the beginning writer do? Imagination will carry you a part of the way, but unless you want to write about another planet where you could make up everything, it won't carry much authority. What I did was a common mistake: I tried to cover up my ignorance by writing "lyrically."

Reading over the day's output I thought it was great at the time, but then I got to that town where my heroine wound up, and lyricism flew out the window to visit more poetic spirits. Realism took up with masterful force, for I was now on native ground.

I knew how to ride in pickup trucks and how the Delta differed from the hills and what local people felt about it all. I knew how to cut through paths in the woods to reach remote houses and what the houses looked like. I knew what the weather might be at any season. I knew what people said to each other and where they were and what they were doing at the time. I knew (most important) what had happened in the past to affect the present.

This last of course wasn't there already; it had to be invented. But I learned that to invent from the known to the unknown is not such a feat—in fact, to work this way can many times become pure pleasure, even fun.

I encountered something else, rather strange: I believed what I made up! Yes, I knew it! I can say I "knew" it because what I made up was like what *might* have happened there, in that place, and therefore not open to question, at least not from me and, as it turned out, not from readers either.

I am speaking of *Fire in the Morning*, my first novel; and, truth to tell, I would just as soon people forgot it. It was an early effort, derivative as most early efforts are, and though it was greeted with more favorable criticism than it deserved, I view it now mainly as something I learned from. Pages of "lyricism" fell in the wastebasket. What emerged was a story of a man's struggle with the past. So where did that girl go? She was still important, for he married her, and in so doing gave her a place to come to, a home. But she was ignorant of all that the place implied and through ignorance stirred up quarrels from the past that like sleeping dogs were better left alone. She stumbled, in fact, on history.

Now that I had learned a way, I proceeded to apply that selfsame method to most of what I was to write in the future. My second book, *This Crooked Way*, was set in the Delta. I am from the hills, but near enough to the Delta to have seen and heard a lot about it. One evening at twilight my uncle was talking on the porch. Someone had asked how a man of our acquaintance had acquired so much Delta land and prosperity. My uncle said, "Like any other country boy, he came down from the hills dragging a cotton sack and came out owning the field." That was it in a nutshell, for the Delta, with all its rich land, was settled later than the hills, and the hill boys were quick to see what could be done there. I picked one of them out of nowhere (but I believed he existed) for my story. Now in this one I learned to build a narrative not out of a single terrain, a small town much like my own, but to manage with bits and pieces I could have heard about and put them when needed around my central characters. I knew what sawmills looked like and the people who ran them; I had seen local stock auctions, had attended country revivals, knew what planters' houses looked like, what people vividly told about tornados. It was all there through hearsay or actual sight and only had to be worked with and built into story, like a monkey climbing up a tree from branch to branch.

So it went in one effort after another until, after three novels set in my home turf of Mississippi, I ran into the high wall. By then I had lived for five years in Italy and had married and moved to Canada. How to continue in these unfamiliar settings? Someone had complimented me once by saying I didn't have to write about the Deep South; I could, in fact, write about anywhere I wished. I was therefore tempted. I had learned firsthand quite a lot about Italy, had been enchanted with an enchanting country, also had had a few spells of disillusionment.

Further, through the interest of the *New Yorker* in my work, I had begun to sell short stories. Three they bought had been set in Mississippi, but why not one set in Italy?

It would have to be Florence: once on a European trip I had encountered that city for the first time and felt I would never again be the same. It found its mark with one more wanderer, and I could only hope to return. This I was able to do when with the help of a Guggenheim I got to spend the first of those years in Italy.

When I began to write *The Light in the Piazza* I was in Montreal during a blizzard. All I remembered of Italy seemed to swirl in the radiant light I had found there. Uncertain of my ground in some ways (how did I know exactly what Italians thought about anything?), I rounded up some southern tourists and turned them loose on Florence, or was it Florence I turned loose on them? I could remember so much of the exact layout of the city: its monuments, palaces, museums, and towers, its interiors of frescos and paintings, its churches and fountains. Later, when about to see the story published, I checked on the exactness of my memories and found them, in just about every case, correct. This is almost alarming, because when *not* engaged in imagining the story, I could not have done it. Imagination feeds into the real, and vice versa.

One actual occurrence is for me, for some reason, needed in a story, be it long or short. For *The Light in the Piazza* this occurrence was one that happened when I was sitting in the stands put up in the Piazza della Signoria observing the annual soccer game—*calcio,* played in medieval costume. Odd to remember, I was with Allen Tate, who was then sojourning in Rome and had come to Florence to attend some Roman Catholic conference. A small antique cannon, brought to signal the game's opening, fired unexpectedly, and a man near it was burned with the powder. I used this at a pivotal moment in the story.

But my recent memories of the place itself were what saw this story through. Some places are ever ready to stir feelings and imprint their images. Eudora Welty has written eloquently of this quality of places; Walker Percy spoke of it as "the vibes." Although I had started out to write a short story, so many memories came flooding back, plus my interest in the characters continued to grow, until to my surprise I had a novella, still in print after forty-odd years, named for what started me on it during the dark of a Montreal blizzard—light.

Some odd questions arise in connection with place. Must it be a known place? "Write what you know!" choruses of creative-writing teachers cry. Like their response to all rules, creative students mutter to themselves, "Do I have to?" The imagination is a willful, unpredictable power. In writing a novel called *No Place for an Angel,* I found myself, without planning to, writing page after page laid in Texas, and furthermore doing it so convincingly that many people from Texas have asked me how I knew the state so well. I didn't. No excuse was possible except that once I drove my parents across that interminable state on a trip west. Further, much of east Texas resembles the South I knew—Louisiana, Mississippi—because the terrain is similar and the way the towns and houses are built comes certainly from the southern people pushing west to settle there.

We come to similar mysteries, such as Joseph Conrad inventing a whole country in Central America for his novel *Nostromo.* His reasoning might say he had known places like it; but that would be after the currents of his powerful imagination had finished running and the vision was complete.

I was recently a judge for the National Book Awards and learned that Andrea Barrett, our winner, had never seen the setting, she told me, of the story "Ship Fever," which took place in Quebec City in the last century. Yet the feel of the place was real. Much can be "worked up," out of reading or research, else the historical writer would be doomed to give up. Still, I think William Styron's *Confessions of Nat Turner* could only have been written by a Virginian. Ideally, the feelings the fiction writer finds in the characters arise out of a known place.

Problems: Places are changing fast. My hometown of Carrollton is much the same because it never grew. Some landmarks have burned down, been pulled down, decayed. A friend visiting her home there with a guest found herself describing houses actually gone. "Carrollton," she concluded, "is not a place, it's a state of mind." And this is what Eudora Welty meant in her fine essay on the river country when she spoke of the all but vanished towns there. "A place that ever was lived in is like a fire that never goes out."

Problems: Can one dote on a place too much? William Faulkner—a proof, if any was needed, of the power of place—asked too much of the reader when he wrote interminably about the lock on the jailhouse door in his imagined Jefferson, Mississippi. Now I will hear complaints from the devotees of Yoknapatawpha County—how dare I?

Problems: When place turns into landscape does something weaken? Yes, it does. To speak of a landscape means the speaker is no longer in it. A farm owner never speaks of his property as landscape. It may be one, but only to a visitor, or someone who used to live there.

Problems: Time marches on and change occurs naturally, or is caused by nature's wild and wayward upheavals. But in addition there is the added trouble of "development." While you are admiring your landscape, or cherishing it in memory, up springs a shopping mall, trees are cut down, superhighways march through, and motels and fast-food restaurants—all planned from afar (who knows where?)—not only disturb what once was there but destroy it. Yet the living also are marching through, creating their own sense of where they are, though the places seem to have no past, no memory, only a conclusive Now.

Imagine Hemingway or Faulkner walking through the local mall. Hemingway would get out as fast as possible; Faulkner would remember what used to be there and lament the present. Henry James wouldn't go at all. Eudora Welty would discover things. An exotic bird, for instance, would escape from the pet shop and go winging overhead, pursued by a boy with a net on a long pole. A little girl would be trying to blow up a red balloon.

I myself once was waiting impatiently for a connection in the Salt Lake City airport. It looked discouragingly like any other airport in the United States. I could be anywhere. Then at a distance down the huge hallway, thick with the usual signs of gates and counters, I saw two little girls approaching. They were stopping before the people waiting, one by one. I was next. Surely they were distributing Mormon literature. If not that, wanting answers to a questionnaire. No escape, for there they were. Did I have a pink lipstick? A treasure hunt! I might have, I said, and searched happily. (I had played that game back in junior high in Carrollton, Mississippi.) I found one! They checked the item off their list and scurried on, giggling.

This is still a beautiful country. We only need to find the blue highways and travel down them forever.

Place in My Fiction

Martha Lacy Hall

> The world of appearance in [fiction] has got to *seem* actuality.... Place
> being brought to life in the round before the reader's eye is the readiest
> and gentlest and most honest and natural way this can be brought about.
> —EUDORA WELTY, "PLACE IN FICTION"

I think of place in my writing as being laid in close and intimate spots. I cannot remember consciously setting out to present a geographic place. Instead, I tell my reader about a certain house or a particular room—the kitchen, a sunporch located across the back of a big white house, the rows of wretchedly poor shacks in the Negro section of a small, comfortable town during World War II. Of course, the larger place is the South, but I am assuming the reader does not need written notification about this locale. What I am eager to tell about is the blue-striped cushions on the porch furniture and the pecan pie coming out of the oven. Or I want to describe the landscape outside a certain house, as in my story "The Snakeshooter" (2002): "the Louisiana bog plants in one end of the pool, the tail spikes of pickerelweed that closed their blue flowers at five o'clock; soft green parrot's feather flowing like fern over one side of the pool; water hyacinths." Fears, pain, and chuckles. Haircuts. Corns removed from tender toes. The details and feelings associated with place, place as the setting for human experience and its complications, large and small.

It has taken me a good while to believe that thinking of my fiction in terms of place is an appropriate subject for me to contemplate. Of course, I am a southern writer. Being from the South informs all my stories. I spent the first eighteen years of my life in Magnolia, Mississippi; that period and nearly fifty years in Baton Rouge, Louisiana, provided the experience from which I build my fiction.

In coming to terms with this assignment, I proceeded in my diffident way to read through my work, passages here, passages there, looking for the most notable

examples of place. On what place or places did I rely for those tales that I have
seemed determined to tell? Where were they? Intending to help myself by doing
some sketchy reading of my stories, I found that I actually enjoyed rereading
them; and, as one might guess, I found myself reading longer and longer passages and then whole stories; eventually, I reread all the stories in *Music Lesson*
(1984); and then, inevitably, I did the same with the entirety of *The Apple-Green
Triumph* (1990), but I didn't reread my first collection, *Call It Living* (1980). For
any writer who must take an analytical turn of any kind about his own writing,
I recommend this sort of investigation. And, with a naïveté with which most
authors are probably not encumbered, I urge you to reread your own fiction.
That will almost certainly restore your sagging confidence and even entertain
you. In any case, that is what happened to me after I suffered a long and frustrating lapse in my writing of fiction.

As a part of my preparation to write this piece, I picked up Louisiana State
University Press's lovely paperback reprint of Walter Sullivan's second novel, *The
Long, Long Love* (1959), from its Voices of the South series. I read the whole
novel in one all-night sitting. Our honored guest himself provides fine examples
of how to write about place. We find illustrations in scenes that unfold as cars
drive through the streets of Nashville and in scenes set in rooms of the family's
city house and within their country house—Adams' Rest. Walter Sullivan has an
enviably smooth talent for acquainting his readers with the places he knows intimately—in Nashville and elsewhere in Middle Tennessee—as well as with the
people who live within this region. All springs from the comfortable places we
see along the way of the story's progress. The author provides fictive evidence of
Frederick J. Hoffman's axiom that "place is indispensable to scene. . . . It is only
when a scene is identified with place that the full powers of the literary imagination can be challenged and used." Knowing this area of Tennessee—Nashville,
Shelbyville, Chattanooga—from childhood visits to those towns, I can testify that
Walter Sullivan awakens and enforces my old and lasting love for the memorable
and softly beautiful parts of Tennessee I experienced as a child. Place.

Sullivan returns to Nashville in "Love's Mysteries," which was published by
Sewanee Review in the fall 2001 issue. Here he gradually but surely reveals the
solution to a family's long unanswered questions about its beloved member
Henry, who has died recently after having mysteriously separated himself from
his siblings for many years. His sister Dolores solves this mystery by going back
to Nashville to visit the old family home, where she and Henry and the others
grew up in comfortable and loving circumstances. Once Sullivan artfully takes
us into the intimate confines of the old house, the stunning revelations about

Henry (the answers begin at the front gate)—what he has been doing during the years of his silence—are revealed quickly. The old house proves to be the perfect place for Dolores to find at last the truth that she can report to the rest of the family. ("There it was, a Taco Bell on one side and . . . an office building on the other. The house itself, from the outside at least, was the same as ever.") At this house, with its "small yard . . . still green, and the iron fence surrounding it still [standing], its spikes casting a striped shadow on the sidewalk," the revelations of past and present are all bound together, on the point of being discovered by Dolores and enjoyed by the reader. I think that the action would not have been so perfectly joined had Dolores and Jewel (Henry's lover) been walking in some anonymous space when they met for the first time and realized their relation to each other. Definite place is better than indefinite space. We read "Love's Mysteries" glad to have been granted a warm and authoritative place for Dolores to solve the family's sense of mystery about her brother Henry. I might add, one writer, in this case myself, can relish another writer's good fortune in success-fully executing a mystery that turns upon a death, a child's death in an accident.

A small continuing mystery: what happened to Henry during all those years that he refused to have anything to do with his family? The viewpoint character and protagonist, Dolores, is as perplexed about her brother after she has learned the truth as she had been in starting out to return to the family home. Every writer would like to write a mystery with a surprise ending. Any writer would be proud to be the author of "Love's Mysteries."

I like houses, as I have said; and I like to think and write about them, setting the plots of stories in houses that live in my memory of places that have affected my thinking both recently and long ago. One such house, the details of which stick forever in my memory, is plain and unremarkable. There is just something about it, especially a six-foot rattlesnake skin hanging on the wall of the study. Nothing else otherwise distinguishes it. But you just don't forget that one strik-ing item, especially if you give it a shake to hear the long-dried rattles chatter when you pass by. That is all that made the house special for me. Everything else was unexceptional but an olive tree by the back porch. It was about six feet high. The foliage was little splays of leaves on tender stems. Every summer there were olives in abundance, green and hard and bitter. They never became edible, and the owner, who had a daughter my age, warned us not to put them in our mouths. Were they poison? They might have been.

The matter of place can be strange. The house to which I allude was in my mind as I wrote one of my favorite and most popular stories—"Privacy." I placed the

narrator, Jane, in the backyard, where she watched and listened to the goings-on
of three people, two of them next-door neighbors. During the unfolding action
Jane was not inside the house, and at the end of the story she goes no farther
than her kitchen. There is no talk of her house—not of the olive tree, certainly
not of the rattlesnake skin; only some yard furniture far back in the yard is mentioned. Nonetheless, as I wrote "Privacy," I was in that house. While I wrote
about Miss Coralie, Mr. Buddy, Mr. Henry George, and Ada Maude, all but Ada
Maude were placed in their houses on adjoining lots, where their stories are revealed. Here is an instance of what Eudora Welty means when she says that place
"has the most delicate control over character too: by confining character, it defines
it." She adds an essential point: "Every story would be another story, and unrecognizable as art, if it took up its characters and plot and happened somewhere
else. Imagine *Swann's Way* laid in London, or *The Magic Mountain* in Spain."

In an essay entitled "The Economy of Revelation" (1990), written for *The
Whole Story: Editors on Fiction,* George Core, who published "Privacy" in *Sewanee
Review* in the winter 1984 issue, writes that the story "could not have been written without the author's strong sense of place." He quotes a letter of mine: "The
most compelling force . . . was the setting, the narrator's house and yard, the geographic position in the rather small singular neighborhood." In that letter I
added, "I could not have invented 'Privacy' without the sturdy sense of where the
narrator was." The narrator's vantage point enables her to eavesdrop without
being detected. On the other hand, as my editor has said, "the form of the story
proceeds from the setting, just as its action unfolds from the temperaments of
its characters, especially Miss Coralie." She is the protagonist, of course, and my
favorite character in the story; I love her for being almost fearless, private and
reserved, cool and nice.

In that essay Core plumbs the personalities of "Privacy"—Miss Coralie, of
course, Mr. Buddy, Ada Maude, Mr. Henry George; and he does not neglect the
storyteller, Jane. I must say that my appreciation for and realization of these
figures took on new life after he published this study of my people in this favorite setting. As he notes, the arrangement of the houses on abutting lots is a
necessary factor in establishing Jane's post of observation and enabling her to
see the action and tell her story. The geography of my corner—with the adjacent lots and houses separated by thick shrubbery—is a unique stage. From her
vantage Jane can keep watch on everybody involved. And on the day of the action proper she simply takes her seat on a lawn chair in her backyard to watch
and listen. This process yields a great surprise when the love affair of Miss Coralie

and Mr. Henry George is revealed against the background of Handel's *Water Music* and his *Royal Fireworks.* "Lovers. Miss Coralie and Mr. Henry George."

I had many memorable experiences in what has become for me "Jane's house." I went to my first funeral there. The coffin sat in front of that rattlesnake skin. And there is a World War II story associated with this same house—a shocker that few people are now alive to remember. I and a few others have lived long enough to recall it all. But, if I placed another story in this ordinary house down on Railroad Avenue in Magnolia, it would probably be another tale with no real connection to the house. I would just roam through it while I wrote, forever supported in my imagination by the snakeskin and the olive tree.

I grew up in a turn-of-the-century house that was a few blocks from the rattlesnake house. In my "investigative" reading for this essay I realized that I had set a number of stories in that family home, moving about the old large rooms—for example, in "Lucky Lafe," where Lafe and his lifelong friend sit in the dining room reminiscing about the drama at home and overseas during World War II. Perhaps I should have provided more details of that house. I remember it so vividly—handsome woodwork, ornate doors, transoms made to open and close with hardware too stiff from lack of use to function properly; the mantelpieces that framed five fireplaces; a blue ceiling on the front porch—a wraparound with an unusually long swing. And I recall many other things. With a pencil I could draw all of it in large and small detail with no hesitation. It was built by a lumberman, who I have always assumed had easy and cheap access to fancy woodwork.

But I didn't appreciate that house fully because it lacked several features that I had idealized and thought necessary. It had no back stairs, for example, as did a house down the street that I often visited. And it had no window seat that bulged to the outdoors and was outfitted with a cushion and pillows. These—the backstairs and the window seat—were the only missing items of a serious nature, and they were simple enough to provide in the stories I set in that house.

This old clapboard house was cooled in the hot summers by an attic fan, ceiling fans, and strategically placed oscillating fans. On nice summer days we opened the big windows, and a breeze stretched the sheer curtains into the rooms. The house was heated by steam, which was then an oddity, with radiators in all the rooms; but it was heated even more by grates filled with coal flushed red, the ashes sifting into bricked pits that were cleaned out periodically. As a child I watched several middle-of-the-night fires in the neighborhood caused by such coal fires. I peered out from the porches of our house, shivering in terror. I wrote about one such fire in "The Painter," a story about a young man who becomes depressed and hangs himself in his garage. That house still stands, but mine is gone. It crumbled in upon itself from neglect, and one day not many years ago when I was visiting the town I made a nostalgic pass by the lot where it had been. Grass was growing smoothly over the site, and I couldn't help thinking I was viewing a lot in a well-cared-for cemetery. I've never been back except in my imagination and memory. I don't dare return for fear that something has arisen or been created that would cause me pain beyond the sadness of the house's loss.

Writers who have grown up in small southern towns may experience blocks that prevent or complicate their writing, but that does not occur because they have nothing to write about. As Flannery O'Connor long ago observed, anyone who has survived childhood has more than enough experience to write about. As I have said, I lived in Magnolia, Mississippi, for only eighteen years; but I was aware even then that I was being exposed to a remarkable assortment of personalities. And all events, such as a burning house or a womanless wedding at the courthouse, were important—and memorable—introductions to basic fear and even terror, also to sidesplitting laughter that resulted when one watched the city fathers prance down the center aisle in their wives' long dresses—in my father's case a yellow organdy gown in which he played the mother of the bride while loudly weeping throughout the ceremony. Look at Mr. Dickey Becker in "The Man Who Gave Brother Double Pneumonia." A barber, he continues to appear in my stories under one name or another, flapping hair clippings off his sheet and dusting the necks of his customers.

An entirely different place in the little town is the cemetery, the prettiest spot in Magnolia. The family plots were bound with masonry copings and furnished with graves marked by marble angels, lambs, still other animals, and architectural memorials. In that town there remain many stories yet to be written. The same stories might be duplicated in place from Canada to the Gulf of Mexico, but, were the setting changed, they would necessarily be vastly different. The same should he said of many another writer from Thomas Hardy to William Faulkner to living writers in and out of the South.

The great writer anchors his or her fiction in a specific place and shows us what is signified in Eudora Welty's observation that "location is the crossroads of circumstance, the proving ground of 'What happened? Who's here? Who's coming?'—and that is the heart's field." The human heart in conflict is the stuff of fiction, and place provides it with what Shakespeare calls "a local habitation and a name." What more can we ask?

Imagination in Place

Wendell Berry

I have been invited to write an essay about "the role of place in [my] work, especially in [my] fiction." It should be obvious to readers that the role of place in my work has been important, and yet the relationship between my place and my work seems dauntingly complex insofar as I have been conscious of it, and I believe I have been only partly conscious of it.

By an interworking of chance and choice, I have happened to live nearly all my life in a place I don't remember not knowing. Most of my forebears for the last two hundred years could have said the same thing. I was born to people who knew this place intimately, and I grew up knowing it intimately. For a long time the intimacy was not very conscious, but I certainly did not grow up here thinking of the place as "subject matter," and I have never thought of it in that way. I have not lived here, or worked with my neighbors and my family or listened to the storytellers and the rememberers, in order to be a writer. The place is precedent to my work, especially my fiction, and is, as I shall try to show, inevitably different from it.

By the same interworking of chance and choice, though somewhat expectably, I have lived here as a farmer. Except for one great-grandfather, all of my family that I know about have been farming people, and I grew up under instruction, principally from my father but also from others, to learn farming, to know the difference between good farming and bad, to regard the land as of ultimate value, and to admire and respect those who farmed well. I never heard a farmer spoken of as "just a farmer" or a farm woman as "just a housewife." To my father and his father especially, the knowledge of land and of farming was paramount. They thought the difference between a good farmer and a bad one was just as critical as the difference between a good politician and a bad one.

• • •

In 1964, after several years of wandering about, my wife, Tanya, and I returned to Kentucky with our two children and bought the property known as Lanes Landing, on the Kentucky River, about a mile from the house where my mother was born and raised and about five miles from my father's home place. The next summer we fixed up the house and moved in. We have been here ever since. Or Tanya and I have; our children are farming nearby.

Before we moved here, I had known this place for thirty-one years, and we have now lived here for thirty-nine. We raised our children here. We have taken from this place most of our food, much of our fuel, and always, despite the difficulties and frustrations of a farming life, a sustaining pleasure. Also, nearly everything I have written has been written here. When I am asked how all this fits together, I have to say, "Awkwardly." Even so, this has been the place of my work and of my life.

This essay is most immediately obstructed by the difficulty of separating my work from my life, and the place from either. The place included in some of my work is also the place that has included me as a farmer and as a writer.

In the course of my life and of my work as a farmer, I have come to know familiarly two small country towns and about a dozen farms. That is, I have come to know them well enough at one time or another that I can shut my eyes and see them as they were just as I can see them now as they are. The most intimate "world" of my life is thus a small one. The most intimate "world" of my fiction is even smaller: a town of about a hundred people, "Port William," and a few farms in its neighborhood. Between these two worlds, the experienced and the imagined, there is certainly a relationship. But it is a relationship obscure enough as it is, and easy to obscure further by oversimplification. Another difficulty of this essay is the temptation to oversimplify.

As a lot of writers must know, it is easy for one's family or neighbors to identify fictional characters with actual people. A lot of writers must know too that these identifications are sometimes astonishingly wrong, and are always at least a little wrong. The inevitability of this sort of error is explainable, and it is significant.

Some of my own fiction has seemed to me to be almost entirely imagined. Some of it has drawn maybe as close as possible to actual experience. The writing has sometimes grown out of a long effort to come to terms with an actual experience. But one must not be misled by the claims of "realism." There is, true enough, a kind of writing that has an obligation to tell the truth about actual experience, and therefore it is obliged to accept the limits of what is actually or provably known. But works of art, insofar as they are works of imagination, come of an impulse to transcend the limits of experience or provable knowledge in order to make a thing that is whole. Of course no human work can become whole by including everything, but it can become whole in another way: by accepting its formal limits and then answering within those limits all the questions it raises. Any reasonably literate reader can understand Homer without the benefit of archaeology, or Shakespeare without resort to his literary sources.

It seems to me that my effort to come to terms in writing with an actual experience has been, every time, an effort to imagine the experience, to see it clear and whole in the mind's eye. One might suppose, reasonably enough, that this could be accomplished by describing accurately what one actually knows from records of some sort or from memory. But this, I believe, is wrong. What one actually or provably knows about an actual experience is never complete; it cannot, within the limits of memory or factual records, be made whole. Imagination "completes the picture" by transcending the actual memories and provable facts. For this reason, I have often begun with an actual experience and in the end produced what I have had to call a fiction. In the effort to tell a whole story, to see it whole and clear, I have had to imagine more than I have known. "There's no use in telling a pretty good story when you can tell a really good one," my mother's father told me once. In saying so, he acknowledged both a human limit and a human power, as well as his considerable amusement at both.

I believe I can say properly that my fiction originates in part in actual experience of an actual place: its topography, weather, plants, and animals; its language, voices, and stories. The fiction I have written here, I suppose, must somehow belong here and must be different from any fiction I might have written in any other place. I am pleased to suppose so, but the issue of influence is complex and obscure, and the influence of this place alone cannot account for the fiction and the other work I have written here.

Both my writing and my involvement with this place have been in every way affected by my reading. My work would not exist as it is if the influence of this place were somehow subtracted from it. Just as certainly it would not exist as it is, if at all, without my literary mentors, exemplars, teachers, and guides. Lists are dangerous, but as a placed writer I have depended on the examples of Andrew Marvell at Appleton House, Jane Austen in Hampshire, Thomas Hardy in Dorset, Mark Twain in Hannibal, Thoreau in Concord, Sarah Orne Jewett on the Maine coast, Yeats in the west of Ireland, Frost in New England, William Carlos Williams in Rutherford, William Faulkner and Eudora Welty in Mississippi, Wallace Stegner in the American West, and in Kentucky, James Still, Harlan

Hubbard, and Harry Caudill—to name only some of the dead and no contemporaries. Over the years I have kept fairly constantly in my mind the Bible,
Homer, Dante, Shakespeare, Herbert, Milton, and Blake. I have taken much consolation and encouragement from Paul Cézanne's devotion to his home landscapes in Provence and Samuel Palmer's work at Shoreham. I have remembered
often the man of Psalm 128 who shall eat the labor of his hands, and Virgil's
(and Ronsard's) old Cilician of *Georgics* IV. Over the last twenty years or so, I
have contracted a large debt to certain writers about religious and cultural tradition, principally Ananda Coomaraswamy, Titus Burckhardt, Kathleen Raine,
and Philip Sherrard—again, to name only the dead. Now that I have listed these
names, I am more aware than before how incomplete any such list necessarily
must be, and how necessarily confusing must be the issue of influence.

I will allow the list to stand, not as an adequate explanation, but as a hint at
the difficulty of locating the origins of a work of fiction by me (or, I assume, by
anybody else). And I must add further to the difficulty by saying that I don't believe I am conscious of all the sources of my work. I dislike learned talk about
"the unconscious," which always seems to imply that the very intelligent are able
somehow to know what they don't know, but I mean only to acknowledge that
much of what I have written has taken me by surprise. What I know does not yield
a full or adequate accounting for what I have imagined. It seems to have been
"given." My experience has taught me to believe in inspiration, about which I
think nobody can speak with much authority.

My fiction, anyhow, has come into being within the contexts of local geography and of local culture, of the personal culture of reading, listening, and
looking, and also within the contexts of what is not known and of the originat-
ing power we call inspiration. But there is another context, that of agriculture,
which I will need to deal with at more length.

I was brought up, as I have said, by agrarians and was conscientiously instructed in a set of assumptions and values that could be described only as agrarian. But I never saw that word in print or heard it pronounced until I was a
sophomore at the University of Kentucky. At that time I was in a composition
class whose instructor, Robert D. Jacobs, asked us to write an argument. I wrote,
as I recall, a dialogue between two farmers on the condemnation of land for the
construction of a highway or an airport. The gist of my argument was that the
land was worth more than anything for which it might be destroyed. Dr. Jacobs
didn't think much of my argument, but he did me a valuable service by identifying
it as "agrarian" and referring me to a group of writers, "the southern Agrarians,"

who had written a book called *I'll Take My Stand*. I bought the book and read at least part of it about three years later, in 1956. It is a valuable book, in some ways a wonder, and I have returned to it many times since. My debt to it has increased.

I must have become a good deal interested in the southern Agrarians during my last years at the university, for with my friend and fellow student Mac Coffman (Edward M. Coffman, the historian) I drove up to Kenyon College to talk with John Crowe Ransom on that subject. But it is hard now for me to tell how much I may have been influenced by the southern Agrarians and their book at that time. Ransom by then was disaffected from *I'll Take My Stand* (though his elegant introduction, "A Statement of Principles," is still the best summary of agrarian principles versus the principles of industrialism). And I think I encountered not much at the University of Kentucky that would have confirmed my native agrarianism. It seems to me now that my agrarian upbringing and my deepest loyalties were obscured by my formal education. Only after I returned to Kentucky in 1964 did I begin to reclaim what I had been taught at home as a growing boy. Once I was home again, the purpose and point of that teaching became clear to me as it had not before, and I became purposefully and eagerly an agrarian. Moreover, because I had settled here as a farmer, I knew that I was not a literary agrarian merely but also a practical one.

In 1970 I published in the *Southern Review* a small essay, "The Regional Motive," that I suppose was descended from, or at least a cousin to, the essays of *I'll Take My Stand*. But in my essay I said that "the withdrawal of the most gifted of [the southern Agrarians] into . . . Northern colleges and universities invalidated their thinking, and reduced their effort to the level of an academic exercise." Whatever the amount of truth in that statement, and there is some, it is also a piece of smartassery.

I received in response a letter from Allen Tate. As I knew, Tate could be a combative man, and so I was moved, as I still am, by the kindness of his letter. He simply pointed out to me that I did not know the pressing reasons he and his friends had moved to the North. And so when I reprinted my essay I added a footnote apologizing for my callowness and ignorance, but saying even so, and as I remember with Tate's approval, that I might appropriately "warn that their departure should not be taken either as disproof of the validity of their [agrarian] principles, or as justification of absentee regionalism (agrarianism without agriculture)."

The parentheses around that concluding phrase suggest to me now that I was making a point that I had not quite got. The phrase, which appears to have been only an afterthought thirty-two years ago, points to what now seems to me the major fault of *I'll Take My Stand:* the agrarianism of most of the essays, like the regionalism of most of them, is abstract, too purely mental. The book is not impractical—none of its principles, I believe, is in conflict with practicality—but it is too often remote from the issues of practice. The legitimate aim (because it is the professed aim) of agrarianism is not some version of culture but good farming, though a culture complete enough may be implied in that aim. By 1970 I had begun to see the flaws and dangers of absentee regionalism, and especially of southern absentee regionalism. Identifying with "The South," as if it were somehow all one and the same place, would not help you to write any more than it would help you to farm. As a regional book, *I'll Take My Stand* mostly ignores the difficulty and the discipline of locality. As an agrarian book, it mostly ignores also the difficulty and the discipline of farming, but this problem is more complicated, and dealing with it took me longer.

Of the twelve essayists, only Andrew Lytle and John Donald Wade appear to speak directly from actual knowledge of actual farming in an actual place. And a passage in Andrew Lytle's essay, "The Hind Tit," points the direction I now must take with this essay of mine. He has begun to write about "a type" of farmer who has two hundred acres of land, but he does so with a necessary precaution:

> This example is taken, of course, with the knowledge that the problem on any two hundred acres is never the same: the richness of the soil, its qualities, the neighborhood, the distance from market, the climate, water, and a thousand such things make the life on every farm distinctly individual.

Thus he sets forth the fundamental challenge, not only to all forms of industrial land use, but to all other approaches to land use, including agrarianism, that are abstract.

The most insistent and formidable concern of agriculture, wherever it is taken seriously, is the distinct individuality of every farm, every field on every farm, every farm family, and every creature on every farm. Farming becomes a high art when farmers know and respect in their work the distinct individuality of their place and the neighborhood of creatures that live there. This has nothing to do with the set of personal excuses we call "individualism" but is akin to the holy charity of the Gospels and the political courtesy of the Declaration of Independence and the Bill of Rights. Such practical respect is the true discipline of farming, and the farmer must maintain it through the muddles, mistakes, disappointments, and frustrations, as well as the satisfactions and exultations, of every actual year on an actual farm.

. . .

And so it has mattered, undoubtedly it has mattered to my fiction, that I have lived in this place both as a farmer and as a writer. I am not going to pretend here to a judgment or criticism of the writing I have done. I mean only to say something about the pressures and conditions that have been imposed on my writing by my life here as a farmer. Rather than attempt to say what I have done, I will attempt to speak of farming as an influence.

Having settled even in so marginal a place as this, undertaking to live in it even by such marginal farming as I have done, one is abruptly and forcibly removed from easy access to the abstractions of regionalism, politics, economics, and the academic life. To farm is to be placed absolutely. To do the actual work of an actual farm one must shed the clichés that constitute "The South" or "My Old Kentucky Home" and come to the ground.

One may begin as an agrarian, as some of us to our good fortune have done, but for a farmer agrarianism is not enough. Southern agrarianism is not enough, and neither is Kentucky agrarianism or Henry County agrarianism. None of those can be local enough or particular enough. To live as a farmer, one has to come into the local watershed and the local ecosystem, and deal well or poorly with them. One must encounter directly and feelingly the topography and the soils of one's particular farm, and treat them well or poorly.

If one wishes to farm well, and agrarianism inclines to that wish above all, then one must submit to the unending effort to change one's mind and ways to fit one's farm. This is a hard education, which lasts all one's life, never to be completed, and it almost certainly will involve mistakes. But one does not have to do this alone, or only with one's own small intelligence. Help is available, as one had better hope.

In my farming I have relied most directly on my family and my neighbors, who have helped me much and taught me much. And my thoughts about farming have been founded on a few wonderful books: *Farmers of Forty Centuries* by F. H. King, *An Agricultural Testament* and *The Soil and Health* by Sir Albert Howard, *Tree Crops* by J. Russell Smith, and *A Sand County Almanac* by Aldo Leopold. These writers bring the human economy face-to-face with ecology, the local landscape, and the farm itself. They teach us to think of the ecological problems and obligations of agriculture, and they do this by seeing in nature the inescapable standard and in natural processes the necessary pattern for any human use of the land. Their thinking has had its finest scientific result thus far in the "Natural Systems Agriculture" of the Land Institute in Salina, Kansas. Natural Systems Agriculture returns to the classical conception of art as an imitation of nature. But, whereas Hamlet saw art as holding a mirror up to nature, and thus in a sense taking its measure, these agricultural thinkers have developed as well the balancing concept of nature as the inevitable mirror and measure of art.

In addition to books specifically about agriculture and ecology, I have been steadily mindful, as a farmer, of the writers mentioned earlier as literary influences. And I have depended for many years on the writing and the conversation of my friends Gene Logsdon, Maurice Telleen, Wes Jackson, and David Kline. I have been helped immeasurably also by the examples of Amish agriculture, of the traditional farming of Tuscany as I saw it more than forty years ago, of the ancient agricultures of the Peruvian Andes and the deserts of the American Southwest, of the also ancient pastoral landscapes of Devonshire, and of the best farming here at home as I knew it in the 1940s and early '50s before industrialization broke up the old pattern.

What I have learned as a farmer I have learned also as a writer, and vice versa. I have farmed as a writer and written as a farmer. For the sake of clarity, I wish that this were more divisible or analyzable or subject to generalization than it is. But I am talking about an experience that is resistant to any kind of simplification. It is an experience of what I will go ahead and call complexification. When I am called, as to my astonishment I sometimes am, a devotee of "simplicity" (since I live supposedly as a "simple farmer"), I am obliged to reply that I gave up the simple life when I left New York City in 1964 and came here. In New York, I lived as a passive consumer, supplying nearly all my needs by purchase, whereas here I supply many of my needs from this place by my work (and pleasure) and am responsible besides for the care of the place.

My point is that when one passes from any abstract order, whether that of the consumer economy or Ransom's "Statement of Principles" or a brochure from the Extension Service, to the daily life and work of one's own farm, one passes from a relative simplicity into a complexity that is irreducible except by disaster and ultimately is incomprehensible. It is the complexity of the life of a place uncompromisingly itself, which is at the same time the life of the world, of all Creation. One meets not only the weather and the wildness of the world, but also the limitations of one's knowledge, intelligence, character, and bodily strength. To do this, of course, is to accept the place as an influence.

My further point is that to do this, if one is a writer, is to accept the place and the farming of it as a literary influence. One accepts the place, that is, not just as a circumstance, but as a part of the informing ambience of one's mind and imagination. I don't dare to claim that I know how this "works," but I have no doubt at all that it is true. And I don't mind attempting some speculations on what might be the results.

To begin with, the work of a farmer, or of the sort of farmer I have been, is particularizing work. As farmers themselves never tire of repeating, you can't learn to farm by reading a book. You can't lay out a fence line or shape a plow-land or fell a tree or break a colt merely by observing general principles. You can't deal with things merely according to category; you are continually required to consider the distinct individuality of an animal or a tree, or the uniqueness of a place or a situation, and to do so you draw upon a long accumulation of experience, your own and other people's. Moreover, you are always under pressure to explain to somebody (often yourself) exactly what needs to be done. All this calls for an exactly particularizing language. This is the right kind of language for a writer, a language developing, so to speak, from the ground up. It is the right kind of language for anybody, but a lot of our public language now seems to develop downward from a purpose. Usually, the purpose is to mislead, the particulars being selected or invented to suit the purpose; or the particulars dangle loosely and unregarded from the dislocated intellectuality of the universities. This is contrary to honesty and also to practicality.

The ability to speak exactly is intimately related to the ability to know exactly. In any practical work such as farming the penalties for error are sometimes promptly paid, and this is valuable instruction for a writer. A farmer who is a writer will at least call farming tools and creatures by their right names, will be right about the details of work, and may extend the same courtesy to other subjects.

A writer who is a farmer will in addition be apt actually to know some actual country people, and this is a significant advantage. Reading some fiction, and this applies especially to some southern fiction, one cannot avoid the impression that the writers don't know any country people and are afraid of them. They fill the blank, not with anybody they have imagined, but with the rhetorically conjured stereotype of the hick or hillbilly or redneck who is the utter opposite of the young woman with six arms in the picture by the late ("Alas") Emmeline Grangerford, and perhaps is her son. He comes slouching into the universe with his pistol in one hand, his prong in another, his Bible in another, his bottle in another, his grandpappy's cavalry sword in another, his plug of chewing tobacco in another. This does harm. If you wish to steal farm products or coal or timber from a rural region, you will find it much less troubling to do so if you can believe that the people are too stupid and violent to deserve the things you wish to steal from them. And so purveyors of rural stereotypes have served a predatory economy. Two of the southern Agrarians, I should add, countered this sort of thing with knowledge. I am thinking of John Donald Wade's essay "The Life and Death of Cousin Lucius" in *I'll Take My Stand* and *A Wake for the Living* by Andrew Lytle.

If you understand that what you do as a farmer will be measured inescapably by its effect on the place, and of course on the place's neighborhood of humans and other creatures, then if you are also a writer, you will have to wonder too what will be the effect of your writing on that place. Obviously this is going to be hard for anybody to know, and you yourself may not live long enough to know it, but in your own mind you are going to be using the health of the place as one of the indispensable standards of what you write, thus dissolving the university and "the literary world" as adequate contexts for literature. It also is going to skew your work away from the standard of realism. "How things really are" is one of your concerns, but by no means the only one. You have begun to ask also how things will be, how you want things to be, how things ought to be. You want to know what are the meanings, both temporal and eternal, of the condition of things in this world. "Realism," as Kathleen Raine said, "cannot show us what we are, but only our failure to become that to which the common man and the common woman inadequately, but continually, aspire and strive." If, in other words, you want to write a whole story about whole people—living souls, not "higher animals"—you must reach for a reality which is inaccessible merely to observation or perception but which also requires imagination, for imagination knows more than the eye sees, and also inspiration, which you can only hope and pray for. You will find, I think, that this effort involves even a sort of advocacy. Advocacy, as a lot of people will affirm, is dangerous to art, and you must beware the danger, but if you accept the health of the place as a standard, I think the advocacy is going to be present in your work. Hovering over nearly everything I have written is the question of how a human economy might be conducted with reverence, and therefore with due respect and kindness toward everything involved. This, if it ever happens, will be the maturation of American culture.

I have tried (clumsily, I see) to define the places, real and imagined, where I have taken my stand and done my work. I have made the imagined place of Port William, its neighborhood and membership, in an attempt to honor the actual place where I have lived. By means of the imagined place, over the last fifty years,

I have learned to see my native landscape and neighborhood as a place unique in the world, a work of God, possessed of an inherent sanctity that mocks any human valuation that can be put upon it. If anything I have written in this place can be taken to countenance the misuse of it, or to excuse anybody for rating the land as "capital" or its human members as "labor," my writing would have been better unwritten. And then to hell with any value anybody may find in it "as literature."

Part

III

EXPLORATIONS 1

PLACE IN MODERN
SOUTHERN FICTION

Faulkner's Wilderness

H. L. Weatherby

I

Faulkner is, of course, the triumphant example in America today of the mastery of place in fiction. . . . I am not sure, as a Mississippian myself, how widely it is realized and appreciated that these works of such marvelous imaginative power can also stand as works of the carefulest and purest representation." That is, of course, Eudora Welty in "Place in Fiction," and she proceeds to demonstrate an "imaginative power" little short of Faulkner's in re-creating place in "Spotted Horses"—"It could happen today or tomorrow at any little crossroads hamlet in Mississippi. . . . We have the Snopeses ready, the Mrs. Little-johns ready, nice Ratliff and the Judge ready and sighing, the clowns, sober and merry, settled for the evening retrospection of it in the cool dusk of the porch; and the Henry Armstids armed with their obsessions, the little periwinkle-eyed boys armed with their indestructibility; the beautiful, overweening spring, too, the moonlight on the pear trees from which the mockingbird's song keeps returning."[1] The passage continues; I pause for the pear tree because it lets something into the story, puts it in touch with something beyond "the carefulest and purest representation."

She says "pear trees," but there seems to be only one, and that a presence in the story qualifying all the rest: "The pear tree across the road opposite was now in full and frosty bloom, the twigs and branches springing not outward from the limbs but standing motionless and perpendicular above the horizontal boughs like the separate and upstreaming hair of a drowned woman sleeping upon the uttermost floor of the windless and tideless sea." There is no accounting fully for the effect of this passage; it is a good example of what Welty calls Faulkner's

---

1. Welty, *Stories, Essays, and Memoir,* ed. Richard Ford and Michael Kreyling (New York: Library of America, 1998), 790–91.

"shoot[ing] the moon."[2] The whole is epiphanic; the combination of language
and cadence carries the reader beyond anything that analysis can quite account
for. But the details are nonetheless important. In a story of mad (comically mad)
activity we encounter transcendent stillness. The branches do not *spring* but
stand. They are *motionless,* and the figurative sea is *windless* and *tideless.* The
woman is also motionless—*drowned* (dead) or, as on second view, *sleeping,* and
her location, the very adjective, takes her and us out of motion; when one reaches
the *uttermost,* there is nowhere further to move. Hers, the pear tree's, is another
dimension, transcending time and death. Yet this visionary moment is very much
in the story's place—"across the road opposite"—and fully consonant with "the
carefulest and purest representation."

Such moments are not uncommon in Faulkner—when place, without ceas-
ing to be believably local, touches on ineffable possibilities. "Barn Burning" affords another instance. Throughout that story, too, Mississippi's "beautiful, overweening spring" is a presence, and when Sarty Snopes repudiates "the old blood,
which he had not been permitted to choose for himself" and thus "betrays" his
criminal father for righteousness sake, the springtime earth receives him. The
torn sleeve of his rotten shirt when Major de Spain's Negro servant tries to hold
him defines the virtue of his deed; like ancient Christians coming to baptism, he
leaves old garments, the clothing of "the old blood," behind him. However, were
it not for the vernal night into which he runs, the issue of his sacrifice would remain unclear; there we find what he sacrificed himself for. He awaits daylight
(that in itself is symbolically important), which he knows is near, both because
"the slow constellations wheeled on" and because the call of the whippoorwills,
"as the instant for giving over to the day birds drew nearer and nearer," became
"constant and inflectioned and ceaseless, so that . . . there was no interval at all
between them." Their music embraces him: "He went on down the hill, toward
the dark woods within which the liquid silver voices of the birds called unceas-
ing—the rapid and urgent beating of the urgent and quiring heart of the late
spring night. He did not look back."[3] He is now the pariah—also the archetypal
child lost in the woods. But he is also the child in Goldengrove, where birdcalls
are liquid silver, where the night has a beating heart, and where, in the culminating chiasmus, the beating becomes a quiring (perhaps of Shakespeare's "young
eyed cherubims" who so engage Faulkner elsewhere). Place takes the child beyond

2. Faulkner, *The Hamlet* (New York: Random House, 1940), 281; Welty, *Stories, Essays, and
Memoir,* 790.
3. Faulkner, *Collected Stories* (New York: Random House, 1950), 25.

place and affords a momentary apprehension of something beyond apprehension, for which the world—family, blood, past—is well lost. Of course he did not look back.

II

Neither did Ike McCaslin. If we may speak, as such passages seem to warrant our doing, of "spiritualized" or "sacramental" place in Faulkner, of place opening to something beyond itself, surely the finest instance, the most fully developed such place, is the wilderness in *Go Down, Moses*—in "The Old People," "The Bear," and "Delta Autumn."

That is not to suggest—and one must insist again on the accuracy of representation—that the "Big Bottom" is allegorical and thus reducible to its metaphysical significance. Like the settings of "Spotted Horses" and "Barn Burning," it is a physically believable part of the Yoknapatawpha world. We know, in fact, precisely where it is—in the old days, when Ike first hunted and until Major de Spain sold the timber rights, only thirty miles from Jefferson; by 1940, in "Delta Autumn," with the retreat of the wilderness before the logging crews, a long day's journey, across and down the Delta, by automobile and motorboat. Within it, we know exactly what happens, where, for how long, and the state of the weather. When Sam Fathers takes Ike to see, for the first time, Old Ben's twisted paw print, every facet of the scene is realized. The ride, when Ike has "finished his dinner" (midday, of course, when southerners always ate dinner), takes "more than three hours through the rapid shortening sunless afternoon, following no path, no trail even that he could discern." Sam places Ike on "the one-eyed mule which would not spook at the smell of blood, of wild animals" (foreshadowing Ike's riding her again—when we learn that her name is Katie—on the climactic day when Old Ben is killed). "The other one" (Sam's mount) *will* spook, and does—"jerking and wrenching at the rein while Sam held it, coaxing it forward with his voice"—signal that they have reached the print. "Then, standing beside Sam in the thick great gloom of ancient woods and the winter's dying afternoon, [Ike] looked quietly down at the rotted log scored and gutted with claw-marks and, in the wet earth beside it, the print of the enormous warped two-toed foot."[4] Here again is "the carefulest and purest representation."

---

4. Faulkner, *Go Down, Moses* (New York: Random House, 1942), 200. Subsequent parenthetical references are to this edition.

But like the pear tree and the whippoorwills, such details, without losing any of their specificity, point beyond themselves. Well before this winter afternoon's ride (indeed, at the beginning of the story), the reader has learned that these "ancient woods" constitute a dimension of experience—something one "enters." Ike "entered it"; the phrase occurs twice—when he arrives for his first hunt and later when he goes alone to track Old Ben (195, 208) and sees again "the print of the enormous warped two-toed foot." The first time, "it seemed to him at the age of ten he was witnessing his own birth." And Faulkner adds, "He entered his novitiate to the true wilderness" (195). Such language, with its obvious religious resonance—baptism (being born again) and ascetic renunciation—immediately sets the wilderness apart; this place makes spiritual demands. "Sam and Old Ben and the mongrel Lion were taintless and incorruptible" (191); the adjectives imply ascetic self-denial, even chastity. Sam is wifeless and childless (as Ike will come to be), and "the old bear," who embodies the wilderness, is "solitary, indomitable, and alone; widowered childless and absolved of mortality" (193–94). These figures are pure like the wilderness they represent and serve. Ike must become like them to "enter it."

Why, "one morning . . . in the second week" (197), does Ben come close (but unseen) to Ike's stand? Sam Fathers's answer: "He come to see . . . who's new in camp this year, whether he can shoot or not, can stay or not" (198). "'You mean he already knows me, that I aint never been to the big bottom before, aint had time to find out yet whether I . . .' He ceased again, staring at Sam; he said humbly, not even amazed: 'It was me he was watching.'" Sam answers only, "You watch tomorrow" (201). And tomorrow, when the bear comes again (still unseen), Ike "only heard the drumming of the woodpecker stop short off, and knew that the bear was looking at him. . . . Then it was gone. As abruptly as it had stopped, the woodpecker's dry hammering set up again. . . . 'I didn't see him,' he said." "'I know it,' Sam said. 'He done the looking'" (203). There is an inner life in this place, to which both the bear and the woodpecker belong, of which only the "taintless" can become a part, and which only Sam, who has long ago completed his novitiate, can understand and interpret.

Faulkner hints, moreover, that this inner life, to borrow Eliot's phrase, is both in and out of time. Ike "could see them, the two of them, shadowy in the limbo from which time emerged and became time: the old bear absolved of mortality and himself who shared a little of it" (204). That "little of it" he must lose. *Relinquishment* (207), the controlling word in the story, is his means of doing so. That happens when "he entered it" the second time, going alone the next June to track the bear, first with gun, watch, and compass, then without the gun (Sam tells him to leave it behind—"'It's the gun.' Sam said. . . . 'You will have to choose'" [206])—and finally with nothing, complete relinquishment. "The leaving of the gun was not enough. . . . It was the watch and the compass. He was still tainted." Leaving these, and even the stick for snakes, he is like Sarty Snopes, "a child, alien and lost in the green and soaring gloom of the markless wilderness" (208). It is surely of no slight importance that the "watch . . . had been his father's" (207) and thus represents the "old blood," the tainted McCaslin past, which a decade later, in order to be true to the wilderness, he will also be bound to "relinquish." But the watch is of course also time, and Ike meets the bear in that "shadowy . . . limbo" before time. Lost in the woods, having placed himself in serious danger by his relinquishments, Ike sees and follows the unmistakable and rapidly dissolving "crooked print," each indentation filling with water as he watches and leading him back to the watch and compass "glinting where a ray of sunlight touched them. Then he saw the bear." Again an epiphanic scene—the ray of sunlight, for instance, in the "soaring gloom." And an intersection of the timeless with time—Ike is back to the watch, but the bear does not "emerge, appear," as it would in time. Rather "it was just there, *immobile, fixed* in the green and windless noon's hot dappling." Nor does it walk away; "it faded, sank back into the wilderness *without motion*" (209, emphases mine). Now Ike has truly "entered it," that mystery of the place; he has met "the old bear . . . absolved of mortality." As for "himself who shared a little of it"—without gun, watch, and compass, less of it.

This episode anticipates the culminating moment of vision in part 5 of "The Bear," when Ike returns two years after the death of Old Ben to the graves of Sam Fathers and Lion, where "Old Ben's dried mutilated paw" rests in a tin for axle grease (again Faulkner's precision of detail) nailed to a tree "above Lion's bones" (328). Once more Ike sees in and through place to a mystery both inherent in and transcending place, "the myriad life which printed the dark mold of these secret and sunless places [the shadowy and pretemporal limbo?] with delicate fairy tracks [Old Ben's rapidly dissolving print?]." This life is temporal, "breathing and biding," but also, like the revelation of the bear, "immobile." Ike quits "the knoll which was no abode of the dead because there was no death, not Lion and not Sam." The ensuing lyrical passage could be read as mere naturalistic pantheism or Romantic nature mysticism—Lion and Sam are "not held fast in earth but free in earth and not in earth but of earth," a part of "air and sun and rain and dew and night, acorn oak and leaf and acorn again, dark and dawn and dark and dawn again." But if the reader has attended carefully to Faulkner's presentation of the wilderness as a mystical place that makes genuinely religious demands on those who "enter it," he is likely to be skeptical of a reading that cancels the mystical and religious by reducing life beyond death to a merely physical continuation of existence in the seasonal cycle—"Rolled round in earth's diurnal course / With rocks and stones and trees." Nor does the passage itself allow for such reduction. Although Lion and Sam are now "of earth" and "myriad," they are nevertheless "*undiffused* of every myriad part" (emphasis mine). If we take that statement at face value, we must conclude that to become a part of "leaf and twig and particle" does not destroy human (or canine) identity. ("*[Sam] probably knew I was in the woods this morning long before I got here,* he thought.") It is rather to be "translated" (Faulkner's specifically Christian term) into that transcendent dimension of experience to which this sacramental place gives access— to be of it, myriad, but also beyond it, undiffused. What follows supports such a reading: Old Ben is not diffused. Rather, "they would give him his paw back even, certainly they would give him his paw back: then the long challenge and the long chase"—but now beyond time and death—"no heart to be driven and outraged, no flesh to be mauled and bled" (328–29).

This scene and this language recall the earlier hunting story in *Go Down, Moses,* "The Old People," and may depend in part for their interpretation upon it. There Ike kills his first deer, and Sam Fathers marks him with the buck's blood. At the end of that day, which is also the end of that season's hunt, as Ike and the rest are leaving the wilderness, Ike now "forever one with the wilderness which had accepted him," they "all heard the unmistakable and unforgettable sound of a deer breaking cover" (178). Boon, who has glimpsed him, swears he is enormous with fourteen points, a claim that meets with skepticism. While the dogs run him, Sam directs Boon and Walter Ewell, whose rifle "never missed," to stands and leads Ike down a ridge to "a tremendous pin oak in a little thicket." There they wait in a silence so complete that Ike even believes his breathing has stopped, while "the wilderness ceased to breathe also, leaning, stooping overhead with its breath held, tremendous and impartial and waiting" (181–82). Into this suspension of natural life comes a manifestation of that other, more than natural life which the wilderness harbors and a sight of which, as when Ike first sees Ben, it sometimes vouchsafes to its initiates. First there is "the flat single clap of Walter Ewell's rifle" and "the mellow sound of [his] horn"; then, "coming down the ridge, as if it were walking out of the very sound of the horn which related its death," an immense buck, "tilting its head to pass the antlers through the undergrowth," then leaping with "winged and effortless ease," "passing within twenty feet of them, its head high and the eye . . . full and wild," "while up the ridge Walter

Ewell's horn was still blowing them in to a dead buck"—but only "a little spike buck which had still been a fawn last spring" (183–84).

That what Boon, Ike, and Sam saw was an apparition—perhaps the very buck Ike had shot that morning—is not certain but hinted strongly at the end of the story. In bed with McCaslin that night at Major de Spain's house in Jefferson, Ike tells his cousin what he saw. Mistaking McCaslin's ensuing silence for disbelief, Ike protests: "You dont believe it . . . I know you dont." "Why not?" answers McCaslin. And then to Ike's "But I saw it! . . . I saw him!" (the indecision between *it* and *him* sustaining the ambiguity of the vision), McCaslin makes an astonishing response: "I know you did. So did I. Sam took me in there once after I killed my first deer" (186–87).

Thus the story ends; but just prior to this McCaslin has offered what might be considered a rationale for the mystery of the wilderness. Since physical life wears out "long before you have exhausted the possibilities of living . . . all that must be somewhere." Where? Not in "the scoured and icy stars" of the freezing night, to which McCaslin points through the window, but in the burgeoning earth. "Suppose they dont have substance, cant cast a shadow" (186–87)—they may nevertheless be present, as Ike later believes that Sam and Ben and Lion are still present in the woods. Faulkner seems to be hinting that like them the great buck, while dead—"in earth" and "of earth"—is still also alive, retaining identity, "undiffused," like Ben still participating in "the long challenge and the long chase" but now free from time and death, with "no heart to be driven and outraged, no flesh to be mauled and bled." Perhaps place—at least a mystical place like the wilderness—contains within its present time its entire, now timeless, past. Sam, and now the fully initiated Ike, can mediate between the two dimensions, for, like his mentor, Ike can now speak the language of "the old people." He addresses "the old one," the huge rattlesnake who punctuates the moment of vision above Sam's and Lion's graves, with the same salutation with which Sam had saluted the mysterious buck: "Chief . . . Grandfather" (330, 184).

Faulkner returns to the theme in "Delta Autumn." Ike, now himself old, recalls "the names, the faces of the old men he had known and loved and for a little while outlived, moving again among the shades of tall unaxed trees and sightless brakes where the wild strong immortal game ran forever before the tireless belling immortal hounds, falling and rising phoenix-like to the soundless guns" (354). "Immortal game" run by "immortal hounds" among "unaxed trees and sightless brakes"—that is the hunt, the game, the hunters, and the place (Ben, Sam, Boon, General Compson, Major de Spain, and the rest, and the wilderness as it had been)—translated into the timeless dimension that the great buck inhabits and that Ike, at nearly eighty, is soon to enter. "Unaxed" is poignant, for the wilderness, which is under attack in part 5 of "The Bear," has now, in "Delta Autumn," been all but destroyed, the land it occupied reduced to "ruthless mile-wide parallelograms wrought by ditching [and] dyking machinery" (342) operated by men who have not learned relinquishment. This place, the medium of the mystery, will soon be gone. Conversely, "Phoenix-like" carries, as the Phoenix always does, the hint of resurrection, and Ike's reverie, if nostalgic, is not despairing. In fact, he here comes to understand more fully than before what the wilderness means and what relinquishment means. He "suddenly...knew why he had never wanted to own any of it, arrest at least that much of what people called progress." Why? "It was because there was just exactly enough of it. He seemed to see the two of them—himself and the wilderness—as coevals... the two spans running out together." Then comes an important distinction: "not toward oblivion, nothingness, but into a dimension free of both time and space" (354). That would be the dimension in which immortal hounds run immortal game, in which Ben will get his paw back, in which there is no death. It is as though the very fragility of the wilderness, its mutability, implies the immutable life beyond it, of which it has been for Ike the vehicle. The final relinquishment is of the wilderness itself; it will have done its work.

Earlier Ike had tried to hold on to it. He was "directly under the bear" (211)—so close that, as he tells McCaslin later, he could see "*a big wood tick just inside his off hind leg*" (296). Sam Fathers does not need to ask why Ike didn't shoot; he only remarks the fact: "You've done seed him twice now, with a gun in your hands.... This time you couldn't have missed him." All Ike needs to answer is "Neither could you.... You had the gun" (212). Both recognize tacitly what the death of Ben will mean. Five years later, in the McCaslin plantation office, McCaslin asks again: "*But you didn't shoot when you had the gun.... Why?*" McCaslin answers his own question with his much discussed reading of "Ode on a Grecian Urn": "*She cannot fade, though thou hast not thy bliss... Forever wilt thou love, and she be fair*" (296–97). McCaslin's point is clear: overtaking the girl and the subsequent sexual consummation would, like killing the bear, end the chase. Better to stop short and perpetuate desire in the ritual of the love chase and the hunt. That, McCaslin correctly understands, was Ike's motive, conscious or not, for not shooting. What Ike comes to understand in "Delta Autumn" transcends Keats's paradox. The "Urn" is a profoundly secular poem; that is its power. Art offers the only permanence to be had, the only means of immortalizing the chase and preserving *both* beauty and desire; and the cost is high—

death. The lover and the girl, the hunter and the game, can only be preserved by being frozen in paint or sculpture; not shooting and thus holding on to the wilderness and the chase is, in effect, to attempt that. But where the "Urn" offers no alternative, Ike's subsequent understanding does—that "dimension free of both time and space" into which the hunt is translated. There "she cannot fade," yet the lover *may* have his bliss. Keats's perception is aesthetic; Faulkner's is religious.

III

Failure fully to recognize the sacramental character of the wilderness and the religious demands it makes has in my judgment distorted interpretation. There is a long-standing debate as to whether Ike was right to relinquish his inheritance: did Faulkner mean us to approve or not? Those who think he did are largely concerned with race and regard Ike's action as a noble repudiation of his family's allegedly wicked, southern, slaveholding past. Conservative critics such as Cleanth Brooks—whose reading of these stories is the best we have—argue convincingly against such a simplistic and ideologically motivated reading (in the long conversation with McCaslin, Ike seems rather to be a patriotic southerner) and distrust Ike's refusal of land and patrimony. What neither group has taken sufficiently into account is that the primary motive for Ike's refusal may not be social or political but spiritual, not primarily his tainted family (though that is, of course, an important factor) but the wilderness itself, not what he is giving up but what he is giving it up for. Brooks comes very close. To characterize the wilderness he uses, as I have, the term *sacramental:* Ike "had learned from Sam Fathers a conception of nature that amounts to the sacramental."[5] Brooks is also at pains to argue that Faulkner is no primitivist or pantheist (and Sam Fathers no noble savage and Ike no American Adam), but that his understanding of nature is informed by Christianity and takes both the Fall and Redemption into account. Since redemption requires relinquishment, why does Brooks not approve of Ike's? One reason, I suggest, is too heavy a reliance on Wordsworthian analogies. Like Faulkner, Brooks argues, Wordsworth "came out of the Christian tradition," and in his nature poetry "a great deal of Christianity" remained.[6] The argument is persuasive to a point. Certainly Wordsworth's natural scenes open upon spiritual dimensions. But there are elements in "The Bear" and "Delta

5. Brooks, *William Faulkner: The Yoknapatawpha Country* (New Haven: Yale University Press, 1963), 262.
6. Ibid., 41.

Autumn" that distinguish the Mississippi wilderness from Wordsworth's places, and it is these differences that most fully justify Ike's action.

One of these elements is the concreteness and precision of detail—the sheer circumstantiality of Faulkner's places—with which we began. Place in Wordsworth is always at the vanishing point, less a concrete circumstance than an occasion for the meditation that ensues upon it. After the initial scene painting—admittedly detailed—the location "a few miles above Tintern Abbey" ceases to matter. Now the poet's concern is with "something far more deeply interfused," which is as much a function of his perception as of the scene perceived—what eye and ear "half create, / And what perceive." In Faulkner, location never ceases to matter. By analogy with Wordsworth, Brooks calls Faulkner a "nature poet";[7] it would be more accurate to say that whereas Wordsworth is a nature poet, Faulkner is a poet of place. Perceiving "something far more deeply interfused" in "The Bear" and "Delta Autumn" is never at the expense of the physical scene, nor is there the faintest suggestion that men like Ike or Sam Fathers "half create" the spiritual reality they discover in the wilderness. Rather, they are the humble recipients and servants of a mystery. And that mystery is itself circumstantial and precise. Wordsworth's "something far more deeply interfused" remains only "something." Not only is it half created by the imagination of the perceiver; its nature is unspecified, and indeed unspecifiable. To use Wordsworth's own language, it is merely an *intimation* of immortality. By contrast, what Ike receives from the wilderness is very specific—that "dimension free of both time and space" hitherto communicated to him in time and space—in the wilderness—and to which in "Delta Autumn" he looks forward beyond his death and that of the wilderness. What Faulkner appears to be talking about is something as simply religious as eternal life, anticipated as it were sacramentally in this transient life. For whatever reason, Brooks seems to miss this. When he comments on the visionary passage in part 5 of "The Bear," he stresses a mysticism confined to nature: "The life which flourished in the great dog and in the old man has simply merged itself with the fountain of life; the drop has been swallowed up in the great heaving ocean of being."[8] That sounds considerably more Wordsworthian than Faulknerian—no mention of Old Ben's getting his paw back.

I presume to quarrel with Brooks on these matters because he comes so much closer than Faulkner's other interpreters to "getting it right"—to recognizing the spiritual implications of these stories and of the wilderness. What is lacking,

7. Ibid., phrase used as title of chapter 3.
8. Ibid., 32.

in my judgment, is that he does not take his own claim of sacramentality seriously enough and thus does not see clearly what the wilderness means to Ike. It is for that reason, I believe, that he remains uneasy about Ike's repudiation. Roth Edmonds's mistress in "Delta Autumn" accuses "Uncle Isaac" of irresponsibility in repudiating his inheritance; Roth, she claims, has been "spoiled" by wealth that was not rightfully his—that Ike should have kept. And when Ike admonishes her to forget Roth, go north, and marry someone of her own race, she taunts him, asking him whether he has forgotten "anything [he] ever knew or felt or even heard about love" (363). As to her first charge, that Ike erred in relinquishing the plantation to McCaslin, Brooks reminds us that other and more respectable figures, including General Compson, have also criticized Ike's move, and Brooks adds, "If Ike's renunciation was a kind of vicarious atonement, an act of sacrifice and expiation . . . the act can also be viewed as a dodging of responsibility." And the girl's question about love, says Brooks, "goes sharply home. For there [in love], whether or not through his own fault, Isaac is a failure." Brooks therefore warns against regarding Ike's "motivation as obviously saintlike"; "the reader must weigh these other interpretations of his motives and criticisms of his actions."[9]

Roth's mistress certainly has her point (although the fact that she is herself an illegitimate descendent of Lucius Quintus McCaslin and is continuing, with Roth, the long pattern of incest and miscegenation—that she is part of the old tainted blood—strengthens Ike's position); and part 4 of "The Bear" illustrates how complex the issue of relinquishment is. But in focusing only on Ike's forebears and their despicable conduct toward their slaves, we overlook the wilderness and its demand that Ike become like "Sam and Old Ben and the mongrel Lion . . . taintless and incorruptible"; like Sam Fathers, childless; like the bear, "widowered childless and absolved of mortality" (191, 194). We misread these stories unless we take with full seriousness Ike's statement to McCaslin that "Sam Fathers set me free" (300) or if we fail to appreciate Ike's recognition, just before the epiphany in part 5, that "the woods would be his mistress and his wife" (326). Brooks almost condescends to a "streak of asceticism" in Ike—acknowledging it "is not at all to rob Isaac of his dignity and pathos." (Is it not, possibly, to identify the source of his dignity and pathos?) He is "one of Faulkner's most interesting and touching characters. But Faulkner has not set him up as a model."[10]

Asceticism makes sense only in reference to its object. If one is not convinced that the end for which one sacrifices is worth the sacrifice, that the spiritual

9. Ibid., 273–74.
10. Ibid., 274.

blessing for which the desert father denies the flesh and leaves the world is indeed spiritual and a blessing, something far more beautiful than the flesh and the world, the self-denial seems ridiculous, perverse. If Ike's seems so to Brooks and others, that is perhaps because they have not taken the wilderness with full seriousness—as a convincing vehicle of a convincing spiritual reality, of something more beautiful, and indeed more substantial, than the McCaslin plantation—or, indeed, marriage and progeny—can offer. Just before his martyrdom, Eliot's Becket says to the uncomprehending priests who are trying to save him from what they see as self-destruction, "I have had a tremor of bliss, a wink of heaven, a whisper, / And I would no longer be denied." Allowing, of course, for the vast difference in idiom, I suggest that Ike is saying something equivalent to the uncomprehending McCaslin, to his equally uncomprehending wife, and ever since to uncomprehending critics, to all of whom his relinquishment makes as little sense as Becket's willing death makes to the fourth knight—a "verdict of Suicide while of Unsound Mind." Unless one has had "a tremor of bliss, a wink of heaven"—has "entered it," has seen Old Ben "just there, immobile, fixed in the green and windless noon's hot dappling," has discovered that "there was no death, not Lion and not Sam," has glimpsed the hunt translated into a "a dimension free of both time and space"—he can scarcely understand that what such moments anticipate and promise is well worth whatever cost. In a traditional Christian context, it is God's revelation of himself through dogmas, church, and sacraments (or perhaps directly, in visions) that gives saints and martyrs their winks of heaven. In the nondogmatic context of Faulkner's fiction—at least in these stories—it is place that serves that purpose by becoming a medium for the sacred and numinous and thus affording those who take the sacramental nature of the wilderness seriously an understanding of Ike's motives.

Place in Katherine Anne Porter's Miranda Stories

Portrait of the Artist as a Rebellious Texas Belle

William Pratt

There have not been many full-fledged literary studies of Katherine Anne Porter's work, because it has always presented a challenge to the critic.[1] At her best there was no one better, but she had her limitations, which are not easy to define. She wrote one story, "Flowering Judas," that placed her among the most gifted fictional innovators of the twentieth century, fit to be compared with James Joyce and Virginia Woolf. But it was an exception, unlike anything else she did—unless it would be "The Jilting of Granny Weatherall," another superbly written stream-of-consciousness narrative. A more notorious exception was her only novel, *Ship of Fools*, which became a sensational bestseller as a book and gained even greater popularity as a movie, a showcase for Hollywood stars and a box-office hit, winning her fame and wealth in her old age. It took her twenty years to produce the novel, which drove reviewers wild, their appraisals ranging from extravagant praise that she had finally crowned her fictional career with a full-length work to bitter condemnation that she had produced a botched narrative unworthy of a writer of merit. In retrospect, her long-awaited novel may have earned the sort of critical assessment Henry James gave to the Russian novelists, whose works he says in the preface to *The Tragic Muse* are "large loose baggy monsters."

Henry James was one of her acknowledged masters, with whom she invites comparison, not for depth and range of characters or richness and variety of scene so much as for her impeccable style. And indeed she was a stylist, though

---

1. One critic who clearly met the challenge was Robert Penn Warren, in his essay "Katherine Anne Porter: Irony with a Center," published in *Selected Essays* (New York: Random House Vintage, 1966), 136–56.

she herself said otherwise, staunchly maintaining, "I don't believe in style. The style is you." She went on to say, in the same *Paris Review* interview, "You do not create a style. You work, and develop yourself; your style is an emanation from your own being."[2] Maybe she was right in declaring that the best stylists—and she is certainly one of them—do not consciously work at producing a style, since it is inherent in their way of using words. It was her belief that "there is a basic pure human speech that exists in every language. And that is the language of the poet and writer." There is no doubt she knew what she was talking about, since true style is bound to be praised wherever it appears and for whatever reason, and her distinctive style is one of the marks of her superiority as a writer. To be compared as a stylist with Henry James is enough in itself.

She could even be called an international novelist, as James preeminently was, but not most of the time. She was not one of the "lost generation" of Scott Fitzgerald (whom she loathed) or Ernest Hemingway. Normally, and most characteristically, she was a southern writer, whose paragon was William Faulkner, the comparison that suited her best work, and in her, as in him, place becomes an important consideration. She wrote about her region, the east Texas farm country, with the same authority Faulkner showed about his Mississippi plantations, and, being older than he was, she was never under his influence. But like him, she had a strong affinity for place; once, in a letter to Eudora Welty, she extolled the virtue of "Place as a brimming frame: place as sense of form; as equilibrium."[3] She had been born in Indian Creek, Texas, a Southwest frontier town, not in a Deep South plantation town like New Albany, Mississippi, where Faulkner was born. Nor, contrary to her claims, did she derive from a landed southern family, accustomed to luxury but robbed of it by the war. Rather, she grew up in reduced circumstances quite unlike those of her surrogate heroine, Miranda. Her biographer learned with some difficulty that, through Miranda, Katherine Anne Porter (christened Callie Russell Porter) greatly improved "her family's social and material status."[4] Her grandmother, unlike Miranda's, had no family farm but lived in a small house in Kyle, Texas. They had no Negro servants emancipated from slavery, and she was educated in a Methodist school in San Antonio rather than in a convent school in New Orleans like Miranda. One is tempted to

2. Barbara Thompson, "An Interview with Katherine Anne Porter," in *Katherine Anne Porter: A Critical Symposium,* ed. Lodwick Hartley and George Core (Athens: University of Georgia Press, 1969), 18.

3. *Letters of Katherine Anne Porter,* ed. Isabel Bayley (Boston: Atlantic Monthly Press, 1990), 498.

4. Joan Givner, *Katherine Anne Porter: A Life* (New York: Simon and Schuster, 1982), 72.

say that Miranda is to Porter what Stephen Dedalus is to James Joyce; she herself said that "Miranda and no other represents me: my surrogate, my witness, my shadow."[5] But it is now clear that, unlike Joyce, Katherine Anne Porter created her "shadow" as much from imagination as from life. Making a myth of one's own and one's family's past—just think of Faulkner—is a trademark of southern writers, and Katherine Anne Porter was better at it than most.

Nevertheless, she claimed she was a native southerner, and her fiction if not her biography earns her the right to that claim. She was definite about it: "I'm a Southerner by tradition and inheritance, and I have a very profound feeling for the South."[6] She is quite naturally one of the writers we think of when we speak of the Southern Literary Renascence of the twentieth century, which in one generation made the South a literary landscape worthy of comparison with the New England landscape of the nineteenth century, the New England of Hawthorne and Thoreau. She is even, in a sense, more southern than Faulkner, for her regional accent was never as idiosyncratic as his, whether he was writing complex stream-of-consciousness monologues or hard-hitting naturalistic descriptions. Her accent is not markedly regional at all, yet she had an ear for southern speech and captured it memorably, as in the indirect dialogue of "The Source" or the direct dialogue of "The Journey," or any of the other stories in "The Old Order," which as a series of short stories is comparable with Faulkner at his best. "The Old Order" delineates the antebellum South as a culture in a way that is brief but precise, defining it as well as any southern writer ever has.

The six stories in "The Old Order" are dramas of both character and place, which together make up southern culture. Initially, the stories concern the Grandmother, who after the Civil War has become the head of the family following the death of her husband, a late casualty of the war, and it was she who "built a house large enough to shelter them all, of hand-sawed lumber dragged by oxcart for forty miles," as it was she who "got the fields fenced in and the crops planted." Thus she made the farm what it was, and then taught the younger generation, both black and white, how to live: "The Grandmother's role was authority, she knew that; it was her duty to portion out activities, to urge or restrain where necessary, to teach morals, manners and religion, to punish and reward her own household according to a fixed code."[7] What was the source of

5. Quoted in the obituary for Katherine Anne Porter in the *New York Times,* Friday, September 19, 1980.

6. Thompson, "Interview," 8.

7. *The Collected Stories of Katherine Anne Porter* (New York: Harcourt, Brace and World, 1965), 328. Subsequent parenthetical references are to this edition.

this code? It came from the tradition of families living on the land, inheriting the doctrines of Christianity, among them "the dogma that children were conceived in sin and brought forth in iniquity," a tradition she imparted to the younger generations, to Miranda's father, Harry, and to Miranda herself. She claimed, and justly, "I have planted five orchards in three states"—in Kentucky, Louisiana, and Texas. The farm she built in east Texas after the Civil War, to which she returns every summer from the town where she lives, supplies her deep need for a "homecoming," which to her meant living in harmony with nature—that is, place—specifically, "the black, rich soft land and the human beings living on it." The stories in "The Old Order" were Katherine Anne Porter's tribute to the culture that nurtured her imagination and that is at the center of her best fiction.

Southern literature was her milieu, and the entire region of the South was her place, though she wrote mostly about the part of it she knew best, which was east Texas and southwest Louisiana, of which New Orleans was the regional capital. She appreciated "the spirit of place" praised by D. H. Lawrence in his *Studies in Classic American Literature* and responded warmly to the Mexican setting of Lawrence's *The Plumed Serpent*: "There is no laborious building up of local color, but an immense prodigal feeling for the background, for every minute detail seen with the eyes of a poet. He makes you a radiant gift of the place."[8] Like Lawrence, Katherine Anne Porter did not write of a single place but of many places, each briefly but memorably described, as in her short novel "Old Mortality," whose action occurs in her part of the South but which has three clearly marked sections and several different settings. It moves from the east Texas farm country, where Miranda grew up, to the city of New Orleans, where her revered Aunt Amy had once lived and died, first to a convent school, then to a racetrack where she meets her Uncle Gabriel, then to his house in a shabby section of the city, and finally to a train taking her back to her part of Texas, where she travels with Cousin Eva to the funeral of Uncle Gabriel, who is to be buried next to Amy, and where her father meets them on a small-town railway platform. Of these varied settings, Miranda especially likes the vacations from school spent on her grandmother's farm, but she elopes before she finishes school, and when she returns to her birthplace, the little town in Texas where Uncle Gabriel's funeral is to be held, it is with a sense that it is no longer her home, for, as we learn in the last episode of her life, in "Pale Horse, Pale Rider," Miranda has left the South and gone west to a city in the Rocky Mountains to live and work as a reporter on a newspaper.

8. Katherine Anne Porter, "Quetzalcoatl," in *The Days Before* (New York: Harcourt Brace, 1952), 264.

Miranda is a model of good manners, brought up to respect the Old Order, personified by her grandmother. But Miranda is conscious that she is not going to be part of it, for though at the beginning of her longest story, "Old Mortality," she shows how much she admires Aunt Amy, hallowed by her family as the ideal beauty of the previous generation, she knows she cannot emulate her. Her destiny is to be a child of the Old Order, an extension of the antebellum South, who must grow up in the New Disorder. As a result, she is a troubled young woman seeking her identity, a member of "the lost generation" to which Katherine Anne Porter swore she never belonged. She is a woman struggling to find herself and her true calling, from the moment she first goes to the circus with her family as a very young girl and is terrified by what the adults think amusing and has to be taken home bawling. The world appears to her a frightening place, where she is unsure of how to react to others and in doubt about who she is. It remains terrifying at the edge of death in the influenza epidemic of 1918 in "Pale Horse, Pale Rider," and at the childhood memory of the death of a mother rabbit, prompted by the sights and smells of a foreign sweets market, in a Proustian recollection of the past at the end of "The Grave," where she is briefly glimpsed twenty years later, ten years beyond "Pale Horse, Pale Rider," at about twenty-nine, the oldest the reader ever sees her, and yet she is just as uncertain as ever about who she is and what she should be doing. There is none of Stephen Dedalus's cool confidence about the future in her, and if she is an artist, she doesn't seem to know it.

The Miranda stories amount to a scant nine works of fiction, or about 150 pages in all, varying greatly in length, from the brief episode of "The Witness" to the extended tale of "Old Mortality," in other words from vignette to nouvelle, or as she preferred to name the fictional categories, from short story to short novel. In chronological (but not publishing) order, they are "The Source," "The Journey," "The Witness," "The Circus," "The Last Leaf," "The Fig Tree," "The Grave," "Old Mortality," and "Pale Horse, Pale Rider." If she had thought of presenting these as nine consecutive chapters, instead of nine widely scattered stories, they might form a bildungsroman depicting the education of a southern girl from childhood to maturity at the turn of the twentieth century. But apparently Porter never conceived of the stories as a sequence, and in fact she published them separately and nonconsecutively, over a period of almost thirty years, from "The Grave" and "The Circus" in 1935 (appearing at different times and in different magazines) to "The Fig Tree" in 1960, a story that belongs in the middle of the Miranda stories, but which the author thought she had lost. So they appeared in haphazard fashion and did not seem to have a unified intention until all were in print. Then, and only then, was it possible to see Katherine Anne Porter's full achievement in its true light. Although some critics regretted that she never emerged as the major writer she promised to become, it was clear at last that she had done what only major writers do: she had created a coherent group of stories set in a definite place, gathered around a central character, and unified by theme, a body of work the sum of which was greater than the parts.

It is highly instructive to follow the Miranda story consecutively, through its nine separate episodes, not all of which involve her as a character but all of which point to her as the heroine of Katherine Anne Porter's imaginary South. She is not even mentioned in the first story, "The Source," but the main character is called the Grandmother, implying that there are already grandchildren like Miranda. The Grandmother goes to the farm from the town in the summer, taking her family along with her, and quickly restores order to a place that has grown disordered without her. Her place is a farm deep in the country, large enough to be a southern plantation, with a house flanked by an orchard and a barnyard, and an extended family of blacks and whites. Choosing "The Source" as the title of this first story in the Old Order sequence implies that the Grandmother's character derives from the Agrarian setting in east Texas, that character and place are inseparable. Indeed the Grandmother, whose given name is Sophia Jane, and who is known to both black and white members of her family as *Miss* Sophia Jane, incarnates the Old Order of the South. She had moved from the eastern frontier of Kentucky to the western frontier of Texas, and then had survived the South's defeat in the Civil War as well as the loss of her husband. She lives as the matriarch of a family, most of whose men have been killed in the war, and she imposes on her family the proper manners and the racial hierarchy that she has always known. Although Miranda is not named in "The Source," it is clear that she will grow up with the Grandmother as her symbol of authority.

Miranda's name is briefly mentioned in the second story, which is entitled "The Journey," as a recalcitrant young girl who pulled up the entire mint bed and offered it to a stranger who had simply asked for a sprig of mint. Clearly, she is already a young rebel, though most of the time she listens to the Grandmother and accepts her commands. The story is about the Grandmother and Nannie, her black servant, who was bought in a slave auction before the Civil War, and who after emancipation continues to serve the woman to whom she once belonged. There is no hint of embarrassment in the story about the dominance of one race over the other, but the Grandmother assures Nannie that she will join her in Heaven after death, since she is a good Christian who believes that "God does not know whether a skin is black or white. He sees only souls" (336). Miranda tacitly receives her education in social manners at her Grandmother's knee, absorbing the lesson that black and white will one day be reconciled in Heaven, though accepting on earth, as most native southerners of Porter's generation did, the natural superiority of one race over the other. Katherine Anne Porter gives a detailed historical account of a slave auction in this story, one that seems quite objective and realistic, horrifying though it might seem to later generations. Miranda of course is not present for any of these past events, but as the grand-daughter she inherits an instinctive knowledge of family history, and as a young girl she knows the black Nannie as well as she knows her own white Grandmother.

She also knows Uncle Jimbilly, the husband of Aunt Nannie, who has "got over his slavery very well," she thinks, but who enjoys telling the children hair-raising stories about the whippings that used to be inflicted on the black slaves by their white masters. He is a kindhearted old man in Miranda's eyes, whose job is to carve little wooden tombstones for the family pets who die and have to be decently buried. His wife has been the mammy to Miranda's father's genera-tion, but in "The Witness" she chooses a measure of personal freedom, electing at the end of her life to live in her own cabin, separate but still firmly located on the family farm. Miranda quite naturally grows up thinking that blacks and whites are members of the same family, and she likes it that way.

And she grows up with a strong sense of family solidarity, which protects her when she goes out into the world in "The Circus," where she is seated in a long row with white cousins and black servants in the grandstand of the big tent. But their protectiveness allows her to leave the family and be taken home by one of the black servants, crying all the way because she has been frightened by the daredevil tricks of the circus performers, with their cruel painted smiles, giving them in her eyes "a look of haughty, remote displeasure, a true grown-up look." She is still a child and retreats into the arms of Dicey, the colored maid who looks after her, and cries herself to sleep. "The Circus," more than any of the Miranda stories, shows that from her first encounter with the big world outside the fam-ily, symbolized by the circus, it seems a forbidding and hostile place, even when it tries to be friendly and amusing—unlike the family farm in "The Fig Tree," where she spends her summers as a contented little girl who enjoys life in the country.

Most of all, she grows up knowing about death, first from the baby chicken that dies in "The Fig Tree," which she thinks is still saying "Weep, weep" after she buries it, until she learns from Great Aunt Eliza that the sound is only the sum-mer noise of tree frogs. And in "The Grave" she confronts both birth and death in the family burial ground, where she and her brother dig in the earth of a grave and discover treasures: a silver dove and a golden ring. The dove is identified as the screwhead of a coffin by her brother, Paul, who wants to keep it, while the ring is a wedding ring that Miranda puts on her thumb, suddenly feeling like a young woman, though she is only nine. It is in this story that she witnesses the death of a mother rabbit, which her brother shoots and skins with a knife as she watches in fascination, especially amazed when he exposes the womb with the tiny unborn baby rabbits inside. It is this sight that she buries in her memory for twenty years, until suddenly it emerges in a foreign market at the sight of candied sweets in the shape of animals. She is transported in her mind back to the childhood incident when she witnessed death and birth at once, "mingled sweetness and corruption," in the mother rabbit her brother killed, and she re-lives the past as a memory of "the time when she and her brother had discovered treasure in the opened graves." In neither "The Fig Tree" nor "The Grave" is death portrayed as a morbid fact of life; instead it is a symbolic resurrection, in the pleasant sound of the tree frogs that she had wrongly identified with the dead chicken, and the sight of the precious ornaments fortuitously found in the an-cestral grave, the silver dove and the golden ring.

It is in "Old Mortality" that Miranda learns about death as a physical fact that brings human existence to an end, in the person of Aunt Amy, who is re-membered by her brother Harry, Miranda's father, as a spirited beauty who sadly died young, before Miranda was born, but who continues to live in her mind in the oval portrait on the wall. Miranda looks admiringly at the portrait as the story begins, an eight-year-old girl fascinated with the family legend of Amy's reckless behavior that led to her early death, which made her a romantic heroine in the family's eyes, one who could never be equaled by anyone of a younger generation. It is in this story that Katherine Anne Porter describes the ideal south-ern belle, just as she exists in the minds of those like Miranda's father who idealize Amy, and in the minds of the little girls—Miranda and her older sister, Maria— who look at her portrait with envy and wish they could be like her but know they will never reach her degree of perfection:

> There were points of beauty by which one was judged severely. First, a beauty must be tall; whatever color the eyes, the hair must be dark, the darker the bet-ter; the skin must be pale and smooth. Lightness and swiftness of movement were important points. A beauty must be a good dancer, superb on horseback, with a serene manner, an amiable gaiety tempered with dignity at all hours. Beautiful teeth and hands, of course, and over and above all this, some mysteri-ous crown of enchantment that attracted and held the heart. It was all very exciting and discouraging. (176)

Miranda looks at the portrait of Amy and then thinks about herself, a small, thin, snubby-nosed, freckle-faced girl, and knows it is no use trying to live up to this ideal, much as she would like to. Nevertheless, her family sets greater store by memories than by facts, and she becomes more interested in Aunt Amy's past than in her own present, and so "She believed for quite a while that she would one day be like Aunt Amy, not as she appeared in the photograph, but as she was remembered by those who had seen her" (177). She fails in that attempt, but succeeds in becoming a far more responsible young woman than Amy, after learning the awful truth about Amy's sudden death, which may have been the suicide of a very unhappy bride on her honeymoon, not the fated death of a beautiful young woman. Such a romantic death, she knew, was the subject of poems and stories by Edgar Allan Poe, whom their father speaks of as "our greatest poet," meaning that he was southern. Miranda is as southern as her father, so much so that she admires John Wilkes Booth, the assassin of Abraham Lincoln, who shouted "Sic semper tyrannis" as he leapt from Lincoln's booth to the stage of Ford's Theatre, and to her the moral of the story of Lincoln's death is that "one should always have Latin, or at least a good classical poetry quotation, to depend upon in great or desperate moments" (180). She even thinks it would be good to have Lincoln's assassin in the family, so loyal is she to the antebellum South she inherits.

But even more, she admires Uncle Gabriel, who had married Aunt Amy after a long, frustrating courtship, and who, after Amy's sudden death on their honeymoon in New Orleans, wrote an epitaph for her, the four lines of which are Katherine Anne Porter's own poetry at its best:

> She lives again who suffered life,
> Then suffered death, and now set free
> A singing angel, she forgets
> The griefs of old mortality. (181)

It is an epitaph worthy of Poe, and it gives the story its name, for mortality is the theme, starting with the remembered death of Aunt Amy as a haunting young woman, and finishing with the death of Uncle Gabriel as a wasted old man shackled to a bitter, cynical second wife ironically named Miss Honey. Miranda had heard much in her younger years of Gabriel Breaux and thought of him as a dashing beau, who was desperately in love with Amy but unable to win her, until he suddenly found himself destitute, disinherited by his rich grandfather, and just as suddenly attractive to the woman he had unsuccessfully courted until then. In a headstrong change of mind, Amy eloped with him to New Orleans, where she seemed at first to enjoy the festivities of the Mardi Gras but then took a fatal dose of the medicine prescribed for her tuberculosis, dying in rather mysterious circumstances as described in a letter from her nurse to the Grandmother. But Gabriel was still in love with her when he buried her, the verses he had written for her inscribed on her tombstone.

Miranda sees him for the first time in the flesh in New Orleans, where, in the second episode of the story, he appears as the haggard, drunken owner of a racehorse, named Miss Lucy after Amy's horse, which wins a race at 100 to 1 odds and makes them all temporarily rich. Miranda and her sister, Maria, are glad to escape from the confines of their convent school to be taken by their father to the racetrack, but they are appalled by the appearance of Uncle Gabriel, who has become such a sodden hulk that Miranda can't believe he was once the handsome husband of the irresistible Aunt Amy. She is thoroughly disillusioned to see him as he is, a man who has wasted his life after Amy's death, and in the final episode she is returning home for his funeral, having eloped herself (like Aunt Amy) and distanced herself from the family she now reproaches for smothering her with protective affection. We see into her mind as she watches her estranged father talk convivially with Cousin Eva, the black sheep of the whole family, the chinless wonder who has never married but has campaigned tirelessly for women's rights, and we find that Miranda sees herself as totally alone in the world, with a husband she knows she is going to leave, and a family she has already abandoned. It is hardly the life she dreamed of as a young girl, yet it is the life she has chosen, and she is determined to make whatever she can of it on her own. She thinks to herself, as the family gathers for Uncle Gabriel's funeral, that she will never again be theirs to command; she will live her own life, make her own mistakes, try to be completely honest with herself, not be influenced by legendary memories and impossible ideals. She has now become a familiar fictional figure—the modern exile. She has left her place (and past) behind, and she is at least dimly aware of the consequences. "Oh, what is life, she asked herself in desperate seriousness, in those childish unanswerable words, and what shall I do with it?" (220). She realizes that being perfectly candid with oneself is as perilous as being full of vain dreams about the future, and all she can do is face courageously whatever comes, without the assistance of those who love her most. "Old Mortality" ends with a chilling but unforgettable sentence, which is the final thought in Miranda's mind as she dutifully attends the family funeral: "At least I can know the truth about what happens to me, she assured herself silently, making a promise to herself, in her hopefulness, her ignorance"

(221). The paradox of this final sentence resonates, throwing a harsh light on the unconscious self-deception of Miranda, which is made plain with the last word, *ignorance,* the author's subtle criticism of her moral blindness. This moral blindness is not hers alone: it is the inevitably limited vision of every human being. The story of Miranda has become universal, now that her rebellion against the family has placed her in unfamiliar territory, outside the circle of protection in which she grew up, a prey to an impersonal fate, and a lonely hostage to a friendless world.

Given such a bleak outlook, Miranda's full story can only end in her death, so it would seem. But actually the final episode is worse, because the death that nearly takes her out of the world in "Pale Horse, Pale Rider," during the influenza epidemic of 1918 at the end of World War I, spares her miraculously but takes her lover away, leaving her more desolate than ever. She was only eighteen at the end of "Old Mortality," when she joined her family for the last time at Uncle Gabriel's funeral, but she is already married, unhappily it appears, since she will soon be divorced. The final story takes place six years later, when she is twenty-four, and has been for three years a reporter on a newspaper far from her home in Texas. The paper is called the *Blue Mountain News,* almost the same as the *Rocky Mountain News* on which Katherine Anne Porter herself worked in Denver, when she too nearly died of influenza in 1918. In the story, the city on "a plateau a mile high" is portrayed as a place of alienation, in which Miranda's life derives meaning solely (no family here, no farm to belong to, no past) from a young soldier (also a displaced Texan) named Adam, who might have become her second husband but who dies in the same flu epidemic that nearly carries her off. She has become displaced herself, with few spiritual resources, and the few that are left are fragile.

The story is mostly about death, with the title borrowed from a Negro spiritual she remembers from her childhood in Texas, and in her delirium Miranda imagines death as a rider on horseback: the Pale Horse, Pale Rider is the figure of death on a white horse, drawn from the last book of the Bible, the Apocalypse or Revelation. She and Adam sing the spiritual together, intoning, in advance of what happens in the story, its prophetic line: "Pale horse, pale rider... done taken my lover away" (394). But in spite of the dominant imagery of death, the story is not morbid, for like "The Grave" and "Old Mortality" it is redeemed by realism and humor and by the purity of the style, since it is beautifully narrated in a poetic prose that makes death seem almost welcome, a soothing presence rather than a menacing force. Certainly Katherine Anne Porter might have created further episodes in the story of Miranda, but for reasons of her own she chose to end it with a journey into death, one that ends with a return to life at the end. Miranda is miraculously released from the delirium of imagining she is dead but recovers only to find that she has lost the one person who made her life worth living. When she awakens from her long dream of death, she finds herself alone in "the dead cold light of tomorrow." Her story ends while she is still a young woman, yet more alone than ever, in what may be a final loneliness, for the ominous last sentence is "Now there would be time for everything" (317). The irony this time is not that of being trapped in self-deception; it is an endless, cosmic irony, for whatever remains of her life seems futile without Adam. At the end of "Old Mortality," she was hopeful but ignorant; now it seems she is merely hopeless, with nothing to look forward to except her own death at some indefinite time in the future.

It is a somber ending for Miranda, yet it seems a logical consequence of the choice she has made: to leave her native place, to rebel against her family and her upbringing, breaking the code of unfailing courtesy and family affection in which she has been raised, a clearly selfish decision for which she must pay the price. The death of Adam is devastating to her because she still wants to love and be loved, though she had told herself she wanted a solitary fate. She has the solitary fate, but it is all she has. As the last story begins, she is telling herself half-consciously, "Nothing is mine, I have only nothing but it is enough, it is beautiful and it is all mine" (270). However, as the story ends, she believes that the lover she has lost is "more alive than she was, the last intolerable cheat of her heart; for knowing it was false she still clung to the lie, the unpardonable lie of her bitter desire" (317). She rises from the sleep of death still thinking of her loss, in a silent and empty room. It is not what she wanted, but it is what she must endure, and endure it she will, since her resolve is still strong, and her will has survived the illness, just as the Grandmother had survived the war and the loss of her husband. Miranda seems as indomitable in her desolate loneliness as the Grandmother was in ruling her family. The continuity of strong feminine will lives on, a stubborn remnant of the Old Order that she still possesses and a steadying force in the midst of the New Disorder that surrounds her. That is heroism, but it is of the tragic variety, for it is bought at the high price of alienation.

Katherine Anne Porter never arranged her Miranda stories into the novel she might have written; but, taken together, they coalesce, forming the fictive continuity of such a novel. More than anything else she wrote, they are the heart of her achievement, her personal myth of the South, based on her own family memories, enriched by her imagination and graced with her style. Miranda is her original creation, developed out of her own experience of growing up in a close family and then deciding to strike out for herself. But universal truths are contained in each episode, from the child's first encounter with the forbidding outside world in "The Circus," to the little girl's discovery of treasures in the family cemetery in "The Grave," to the young woman's attraction to the legends of the past from which she must separate herself in "Old Mortality," to the mature woman's struggle with death and the loss of love in "Pale Horse, Pale Rider." What is most remarkable about Miranda's growing up is her constant sense of self-possession through all her adventures and misadventures, for she seems to be sure that her search for identity has a direction, that, despite her uncertainty about what she wants to become, she will remain true to herself, consistent in her character, holding fast to what is essential in her. If Miranda differs in many ways from the author who created her, she embodies a truth about human nature that Katherine Anne Porter voiced in her most candid interview: "We change, of course, every day; we are not the same people who sat down at this table, yet there is a basic and innate being that is unchanged."[9] Watching her pass from childhood to maturity in a few brief but decisive episodes, the reader knows that since Miranda has persevered up to now, she is likely to accept the death of her lover as she accepted the death of the baby chicken, and Aunt Amy, and Uncle Gabriel, and the Grandmother, at different stages of her life, for she has proved convincingly that she has the fortitude to face whatever misfortunes await her, until the ultimate moment when she must accept her own death; and, in her final story, she has shown she is prepared even for that. Readers of Katherine Anne Porter, having followed Miranda from childhood in her native Texas to the brink of death in distant Colorado, know all we need to know about her.

9. Thompson, "Interview," 21.

Place in Robert Penn Warren's Life and Work

Joseph Blotner

I had regularly taught Robert Penn Warren's *All the King's Men* in my courses, and becoming a friend of the author and an occasional guest in his Connecticut home while I was writing William Faulkner's biography had deepened our relationship. And I already knew many of Red Warren's friends in addition to the scholars who had written on his extensive body of work and the writers who had collaborated with him. When I started meditating another biography, his life was the logical choice for me. Closest of all to him was his former student Albert Erskine, for many years his editor at Random House. He had been my editor too for a dozen years, and when I broached the idea of writing Red's biography, Albert intimated that it would be demanding for many reasons. He may well have known something I didn't: that Warren had already declined requests from two excellent writers to do the job. And he had said that his poems already constituted a kind of "shadowy biography." I waited, and then on my next visit to New York I decided I would ask Albert more specifically. Again he responded simply. "Go ahead and ask him," he said.

Remembering D. H. Lawrence's famous warning, "Don't trust the teller, trust the tale," I determined that I would begin with the story that Warren had provided, directly and indirectly, in his writing. The two modes would prove to be inextricably mixed. Basic to his work was the sense of place, especially that place where he had lived his life, most particularly in his growing years. He had made use of it in some of his earliest published work. While still a Rhodes scholar at Oxford he had undertaken the novelette to be called "Prime Leaf" (1931). Set in Kentucky and Tennessee, it was infused with his memories of the land, such as the tobacco farms his beloved Grandpa Penn had owned, and with tales of the "Black Patch War" between farmers and the growers' associations. Even as he became a published novelist, the home region provided the physical background for his few short stories, particularly the best of them, "Blackberrry Winter." The locale was middle Tennessee, extending from a Bardsville farm to the city in Charlestown and Nashville.

He built on similar material for his novel *Night Rider* (1939), with the generating action and violent climax deriving again from history, including wide-ranging state politics as well as the Black Patch War. Steadily increasing his scope and command of native materials, he set the principal action of *At Heaven's Gate* (1943) in a southern city, reinforcing it with segments set variously in Nashville, Memphis, and New York, with labor troubles at a mill providing contrast. His great leap forward came with the range he demonstrated in *All the King's Men* (1946), where the narrator, Jack Burden, leads the reader from the contrasting settings of protagonist Willie Stark's rural home to the affluent comfort of Burden's Landing and the estate of Jack's true father. For the vivid and complex political milieu of the state capital, Warren drew on his years as a Louisiana State English professor in Baton Rouge. His exploration of wider landscapes provided a contrast using a theme he would employ elsewhere, the flight to the West, one of the results of his California sojourns.

Deliberately extending his temporal and spatial range as well as his style, he reached back more than a century in *World Enough and Time* (1950) into Kentucky political history. Again, he employed the theme of flight to the West with Grand Guignol violence in a bizarre swamp kingdom. *Band of Angels* (1955) began in Kentucky and then moved from Ohio to New Orleans against a background of Civil War violence. Warren expanded these concerns with *Wilderness* (1961), ranging from battlefields to the New York draft riots. Except for this last, his remaining novels over the next two decades were set for the most part in what James H. Justus calls "Warren's *Terra*."[1] For *The Cave* (1959), *Flood* (1964), *Meet Me in the Green Glen* (1971), and *A Place to Come To* (1977), this was primarily Tennessee. Although there were brief excursions to Alabama, Florida, Chicago, Hollywood, and even Paris, the focus most often fell on the town of Fiddlersburg, with dramatic events provided by accidental entombment, by the deliberate reshaping of the land, by homicide, and by penitentiary melodramatics. Warren's last novel ranged over many years and great distances, in America and beyond it, and the title of this narrative of Jediah Tewksbury's long odyssey, *A Place to Come To*, carried its meaning succinctly.

Warren's use of place is attuned to the needs of his novels, but his deepest aspirations are represented best in his poems. They are inhabited by the family

1. Justus, "Warren's *Terra*," *Mississippi Quarterly* 48 (Winter 1994–1995): 133–45.

constellation that provided material throughout his career—the Penn grand-parents, his father and mother, his son and daughter and their mother, Eleanor, his second wife and his great love. A shadowy presence in a few poems is his first wife, Cinina, whose marriage became a purgatory to which he was faithful for twenty years. These characters are supported by scores of others. Some bring place with them into the poems so that it grows more precise and recognizable as time goes on. One of his earliest, "Kentucky Mountain Farm," looks back at "History among the Rocks," at early settlers and subsequent bloody conflict. With a wide lens he ranges far and high, following to altitude one of his most enduring images, the sunset hawk who scans all beneath him. But this was not, he insisted, a vision drawn from early memories. He had never seen this part of his native state, he declared, and the poem was pure invention. Appearing almost as near the end of his oeuvre as the earlier one is to its beginning, "Old Time Childhood in Kentucky" focused on "the world I was in" and then extended the view with intimations of the way it would change. Tobacco rows and the cane-brakes gave way to memories of retold battles, and further to cave mouths and skeletons that summon up reflections on geological time. This was becoming a familiar progression, from the present and immediate to the recent historical, then the far distant, and finally to the unfathomable past, as "In eons back I grew there in that submarine depth and lightlessness."[2]

Stops along the way from early residence in Kentucky to mature years in Connecticut provided material for his best work. In midcareer his unhappily ended time at Louisiana State University in Baton Rouge melded the particular and the general. "Bearded Oaks," which would become his most anthologized poem, began with a view of bayou country and proceeded geologically with this meditation: "We live in time so little time / And we learn all so painfully, / That we may spare this hour's term / To practice for eternity" (65). Decades later, with love focused on his four-year-old daughter, he shifted to another continent to provide the scene for joy snatched from the world's uncertainty. "To a place of ruined stone we brought you, and sea reaches. / *Rocca:* fortress, hawk-heel, lion-paw, clamped on a hill" ("To a Little Girl . . . in a Ruined Fortress," 103). Coincid-ing with his newfound joy as husband and father, these Italian scenes enriched his use of landscape as metaphor.

Other poems such as "Rattlesnake Country" offered precise commentary on remembered places and still further mixed this mode with the metaphorical.

2. *The Collected Poems of Robert Penn Warren,* ed. John Burt (Baton Rouge: Louisiana State University Press, 1998), 561. Subsequent parenthetical references are to this edition.

"Dragon Country: To Jacob Boehme" began graphically: "This is the dragon's country, and these his own streams. / The slime on the railroad rails where he had crossed the track" (133). For some readers the poems concerned primarily the awareness of evil and the need for fighting it. It also showed his propensity for increasingly expanded vistas and metaphysical leaps.

But his most searching poems consistently employed basic images drawn from light and darkness, from sun and moon. Central to these was the human figure, usually a man's, reaching upward and seeking for meaning or some kind of affirmation. Poems such as "Cthonian Revelation: A Myth" often evoke the darkness of a cave and nameless depths. In contrast, an upward striving informed "Why You Climbed Up" and "Why Boy Came to Lonely Place." Warren often referred to himself as a seeker, and this is the posture of "Man in Moonlight," as it had been for "Youth Stares at Minoan Sunset" when he "spreads his arms to the sky as though he loves it—and us." A compelling image of great power for Warren was that in "Watershed" as the "sunset hawk now rides / The tall light up the climbing deep of air" (38), an image that reappears as "king of the air" in "Red-Tail Hawk and Pyre of Youth."

Warren's broadest canvases, *Audubon: A Vision* (1969) and *Chief Joseph of the Nez Perce* (1983), demonstrated again how he could range over time, space, and history, but the title of the book that appeared between them was more true to the way he continued to explore other dimensions. *Can I See Arcturus from Where I Stand?* (1975) began by pursuing truth with "A Way to Love God" and "Old Nigger on One-Mule Cart Encountered Late at Night When Driving Home from Party in the Back Country." It concluded with the poet in "Another Land" with another love, fresh from the near-death experience, looking into the starlight, and seeking truth as he looks for the constellation.

When I had first asked him for help, Warren had replied that he could not undertake anything then, but a year later I heard from him again. There were files in his study in Fairfield, Connecticut, that might be of use to me, he wrote, and there were some stories that had circulated in his hometown of Guthrie, Kentucky, that he wanted to correct. He would prove a ready respondent to a wide range of questions, and he would readily give access to books and papers I needed. His accounts of the diversions of adolescence were filled with memories of fields and forests, strenuous upward climbs and chilling descents into caves and woody labyrinths. This would be true of recollections of western desert scenes as well as southern lowlands. Guthrie was still clear and present in his mind with memories of earliest childhood, of classroom endeavors as well as the friendships and injuries of adolescence.

As I made preparations for my first visit, one friend asked if I knew Eleanor Clark Warren. I did not, and it was only later that I read her son's characterization. "She was like a vast force of nature," Gabriel Warren said, "tides, glaciers, climate change, continental drift, and yes, sometimes earthquakes and vulcanism."[3] These images were appropriately drawn from nature. As vigorous as her husband, she spent time outdoors as avidly as he did despite her impaired vision. So she brought with her a zest for the ski slopes that provided a counterpart to the many poems in which he cleaved the waves, striking out toward the horizon, his long strokes providing a rhythmic counterpoint to verses he composed. And in poems she was a figure out of nature, a nude swimmer emerging from the water, a nurturing mother nursing her baby.

In different places and times the Warren family contributed varied lore. His sister, Mary Cecilia Warren Barber, supplied memories of the childhood and adolescence that made him call Guthrie "a place to be *from*." In several sessions Rosanna Warren patiently offered sensitive responses to my questions with revealing comments about the father-daughter relationship between these two poets. A talented sculptor and sailor, Gabriel Warren sought the sea as enthusiastically as his father did and became a model for figures sailing into storms or standing alone in night scenes, stretching upward, the figure of a seeker, the same stance his father used to characterize himself.

From his early years, *The Divine Comedy* provided a place to which he returned often, but integral to all was his use of the land, and the piedmont of Kentucky and Tennessee provided the background for most of his fiction and poetry. He drew on it for his first story, first poems, and first novel. Writing my study took me farther afield than I could have imagined. To understand the background of "Prime Leaf" and *Night Rider,* I had to locate the "Black Patch," an area that is oval-shaped on the map and comprises thirty-five counties in Kentucky and eighteen in Tennessee stretching over two hundred miles from the Mississippi River on the west to the Cumberland on the east. Tobacco was the farmer's money crop, not the bright leaf air-cured burley of the North Carolina piedmont but the "dark-fired" tobacco cured by smoldering fires in tightly chinked barns. Warren knew the region early, especially the counties of Todd and Christian, Trigg and Calloway. As a child he swam in their streams and climbed down to explore their caves. As a man he returned to ride with his father through the southern Kentucky countryside over roads where the old man would point

3. Gabriel Warren in an unpublished tribute to his mother, Eleanor Clark Warren, written for her memorial service.

out distant houses and fields where Warrens had lived and now lay. He did extensive research for his writing when he needed to, but he preferred recourse to memory, indignantly denying that *Night Rider* was a historical novel. "The events belonged to my early childhood," he said. "I remember the troops coming in when martial law was declared." In another conversation he said of *Night Rider, At Heaven's Gate,* and *All the King's Men* that they were not history: "I never did a day's research in my life on these novels. They were coming out of the world I lived in, but not a historical one."[4]

After immersion in Kentucky and Tennessee history, I shifted to Louisiana. Warren saw and heard Huey Pierce Long once during the time he taught at Louisiana State University. Years after the novel's 1946 publication he would write, "When I am asked how much *All the King's Men* owes to the actual politics of Louisiana in the 30's, I can only be sure that if I had never gone to Louisiana and if Huey Long had not existed, the novel never would have been written." But "for better or worse, Willie Stark was not Huey Long. Willie was only himself, whatever that self turned out to be, a shadowy wraith or a blundering human being."[5] Living in Louisiana between 1934 and 1942, Warren quickly assimilated the culture and history of that part of the South. And he brought the sense of place into its depiction as he had done with the midsouth of Kentucky. He learned its seasons and their changeability. In their first spring there, he and Albert Erskine put in an early garden, losing it to frost even before their sunburn had stopped smarting.

The narrator, Jack Burden, conveys more than plain sight and sound.

> On up Number 58, and the country breaks. The flat country and the big cotton fields are gone, now, and the grove of live oaks way off yonder where the big house is, and the white-washed shacks, all just alike, set in a row by the cotton fields with cotton growing up to the doorstep.... That's all left behind now. It is red hills now, not high, with blackberry bushes along the fence rows, and blackjack clumps in the bottoms and now and then a place where the second-growth pine stands close together if they haven't burned over for sheep-grass, and if they burned over, there are the black stubs. The cotton patches cling to the hillsides, and the gullies cut across the cotton patches. The corn blades hang stiff and are streaked with yellow.... There were pine forests here a long time ago but they are gone.[6]

4. *Talking with Robert Penn Warren,* ed. Floyd C. Watkins, John T. Hiers, and Mary Louise Weaks (Athens: University of Georgia Press, 1990), 27, 260.

5. Warren, "*All the King's Men:* The Matrix of Experience," *Yale Review* 53 (Winter 1964): 161, and *All the King's Men* (New York: Modern Library, 1953), v.

6. Ibid., 4.

Much observation and many memories came together in the creation of this panorama. "I was living in a melodrama ... and the biggest part of the 'happening' was probably that I lived in Louisiana—that 'banana republic'. . . when Huey P. Long held it as his fief."[7] Remembering Long and his fief from the distance of Italy in the later 1930s and seeing it through Dante, Shakespeare, Spenser, and Machiavelli and in terms of fascist politics, Warren was able to seize the possibilities of the action, an action rooted in place.

Both early and late he returned to Kentucky for the sense of place in his fictions. One summer morning in 1945 while he was consultant in poetry at the Library of Congress, his close friend Katherine Anne Porter crossed the hall from her office and flung a document down on his desk. It was called *Confession of Jereboam Beauchamp.* "This is for you," she told him. "I'm giving you a novel." He had done library research for *At Heaven's Gate,* but now he meant to write "a straight historical novel." To compose *World Enough and Time* he steeped himself not only in the tragic story of a "young idealist who can't find an object for his idealism" but also in the larger account of the disastrous panic of 1819. There were some scenes grisly enough for a Grand Guignol performance, along with others recalling the events in the Capulet tomb. Yet at the same time they were grounded in an achieved visual reality. In *The Cave,* set more than a century later and focusing on a deep place of the earth in Tennessee, Warren drew on youthful experiences that had provided both event and metaphor for poems as well as novels.

It was as if he was striving for an effect his friend Eudora Welty described: "the world of appearance in the novel," she wrote, "has got to *seem* actuality. . . . Place being brought to life in the round before the reader's eye is the readiest and gentlest and most honest and natural way this can be brought about." For this effect Warren drew on a wide range of phenomena: plantation life, abolitionism, the war, and reconstruction. And the results would be commensurate. "The moment the place in which the novel happens is accepted as true," Welty continues, "through it will begin to glow, in a kind of recognizable glory, the feeling and thought that inhabited the novel in the author's head and animated the whole of his work."[8]

Just as former students and young friends responded whenever I asked for help, so did Red's old friends and colleagues. This research drew me back often

7. *Talking with Warren,* ed. Watkins, Hiers, and Weaks, 272.

8. Welty, "Place in Fiction," in *The Eye of the Story: Selected Essays and Reviews* (New York: Random House, 1978), 121.

to Tennessee and Kentucky. At Vanderbilt, a few writers and teachers were able to describe the ambience of the university from Red's student days to his bitter departure as a faculty member years later. Early in my work I had turned to Walter and Jane Sullivan, who took me to see places that were crucial in Red Warren's experience. One was the place he recalled as "the place where I wanted to live": "The place I thought was heaven to me, after my years of wandering, was middle Tennessee."[9] A young horseback-riding friend had told him of a cabin on his father's estate. To the Warrens it was "a lovely spot . . . down the hill in a grove with lots of old wisteria and honeysuckle." Fifty years after they "had worked like dogs putting the place in order," we drove in the Sullivans' car over the whole area, by now built up in suburban styles, until Walter and Jane found the landmarks that identified the Warrens' lovingly named Pennfolly (adapted from Benfolly, the old house bought for Allen Tate and his wife by Allen's brother Ben). We walked the overgrown paths while memories came flooding back to Jane and Walter.

Since his first stay in Montana in 1935, Warren had been fascinated with the history of Chief Joseph of the Nez Perce. At last he began to tell the tragic story in verse. Finally, 104 years after the chief's surrender to overpowering numbers, Warren had eight of the poem's nine sections written and rewritten. But there was one problem. He had carefully followed both the U.S. Cavalry and the Indian accounts of the climactic battle, but still he could not see how, in that terrain, fifteen hundred cavalrymen could go undetected until their sudden attack ended the Battle of the Little South Bear Paw Mountains. So he decided to do what he had done for *Brother to Dragons,* to see for himself the land where the crucial events happened. Two young friends, Stuart Wright and David Quammen, met him at Great Falls, Montana. They told me in detail what they found after their long car ride. "The battlefield itself is a long sloping meadow that leads down to a hidden swale, where Joseph's people had their camp." Soon Warren was deep in thought, making notes from time to time. "There was a clear depression," Stuart remembered, "sort of a declivity. And we completely lost sight of the camp itself, which meant that looking in the other direction you couldn't see anything. And that was the answer. That's how the cavalry did it. They were able to slip into that point and actually wait for the attack to begin, because they could not be seen."[10] So Warren did his homework and his fieldwork, and thanks

9. *Talking with Warren,* ed. Watkins, Hiers, and Weaks, 272.
10. Quoted in Joseph Blotner, *Robert Penn Warren: A Biography* (New York: Random House, 1997), 464.

to his friends who confided in me I knew how he had found his answers for the action that led to the climax of his poem.

During the remainder of his life, Warren's verse would show his readiness to shift from the timeless past to the historical present, and by implication to the largely unforeseeable future. *Chief Joseph of the Nez Perce* encompassed both that western battle grounded in the nineteenth century and a "New Dawn" in the twentieth with the cataclysm marking the beginning of the atomic age and its world-changing power. The locales could scarcely have been more different, the Montana hills and the Bikini atoll. Warren tried to explore the resonance of this latter eponymous place name. And, as with earlier images of place, in this poem he explored the dimensions of one place—literal and suggestive, physical and metaphysical.

The Outside of the Inside
The Vision of Time and Place in Eudora Welty

Lewis P. Simpson

The place is the comfortable, old-fashioned living room of the Tudor style house across from Belhaven College on Pinehurst Street in Jackson, Mississippi. The time is an evening in the later 1970s or, perhaps, the early '80s. We are a small group: my wife and I, another couple, and our hostess, Eudora Welty, who has lived in this house since the early 1920s. This was when her father, on the rise in the insurance business, had built it and moved his family from the house on Jackson's North Congress Street where Eudora had been born in 1909. She lived most of her ninety-two years in the house on Pinehurst and did nearly all her writing there—in an upstairs room before a window that opened on the street, "her post of observation," as Walter Sullivan has termed it.[1]

On the evening I refer to, for some reason I can't now remember, I am recalling the time two or three years earlier when my wife and I were in San Francisco and saw what we took to be relics of the age of the "flower children" wandering here and there in the streets and parks. Eudora says that she has wondered what has happened to the flower children. We drift on in our conversation to other subjects. It is some time before I notice Eudora is no longer taking part in the talk. Later, when it is time for us to be taking our leave, she rouses and says in her soft, inimitable voice (Mississippian in tone and inflection, yet never, like Faulkner's, quite so distinctly so): "I wonder what has happened to them? I wonder what has happened to *all* of them?"

It takes me a moment to realize why Eudora had fallen silent some time back in the evening. She had become completely preoccupied with wondering about the fate of the youthful dissidents of the sixties. I wanted to find out what had

---

1. Sullivan, "Eudora Welty 1909–2001," *Sewanee Review* 109 (Summer 2001): 482.

gone on in her reverie about the flower children. But it was late and not a time to linger.

The fate of those who become lost in the world: what salvation is there for them? Is this not one way to sum up the subject of Eudora Welty's fiction? And if we do so, are we not in a larger sense summing up the subject of all her contemporaries—of all those who came into the world in the time before, during, or immediately after the First World War? And, for that matter, of all the European and American novelists who have come into the Euro-American world since it fell to pieces in August 1914 and everybody became lost in the ruins?

In his later years Robert Penn Warren increasingly felt that his writings were a personal response to this question. When I reread Eudora Welty's short stories and novels following her death in July 2001, I sensed more than I had before the subtle lyric quality not only of her fiction but of her small body of carefully crafted essays and reviews as well. That is to say, I felt more distinctly than before the autobiographical cast of her writings. I refer to the way in which she suggests a subtle struggle to define a sense of personal identity in the face of being lost in the world. I have come to feel indeed that her stories and essays often turn on a paradoxical desire both to reveal and to conceal this struggle. "I'm just a private person," she told an interviewer in 1986. Then she added enigmatically: "But I tell my innermost secrets through my fiction. It's all there."[2]

Welty usually wrote about American southerners, the people she says she knew best, but she occasionally wrote a few memorable stories about people from elsewhere. I am thinking of "Music from Spain" but more particularly of "The Bride of the Innisfallen" and, more particularly still, of the haunting story she first published in the *New Yorker* in 1952 called "No Place for You, My Love."

In "The Bride of the Innisfallen" the chief character is identified only as an "American girl." She has come to England with her husband, but when the reader encounters her at the beginning of the story she is seated in a compartment of a train at Paddington Station waiting to leave for Fishguard, where the passengers will transfer to the *Innisfallen,* an overnight ferry to Cork, Ireland. After arriving in Cork, she walks about in the city for almost the whole of a rainy day in a strange state of joy. As evening comes on she shelters herself from the rain in the "warm doorway" of a pub and, hearing the voices coming from within, drops a

---

2. Quoted in Ann Waldron, *Eudora: A Writer's Life* (New York: Doubleday, 1998), 332. Compare "A writer's whole feeling, the force of his whole life, can go into a story.... But your private life should be kept private" (*Writers at Work: The "Paris Review" Interviews,* 4th series, ed. George Plimpton [New York: Viking Press, 1976], 281).

telegram she has composed to send to her husband into a gushing street drain and walks "without protection into the lovely room full of strangers." She has no idea what may happen to her in that room; nor, on the basis of the evidence presented in the story, does the reader. And, on the same basis, one can say, neither does the author of the story, human relationships in Welty's stories being at times comically, at times pathetically, at times tragically, but always mysteriously irresolute.[3]

In "No Place for You, My Love" there are two characters, a man and a woman, each, like the chief character in "The Bride of the Innisfallen," nameless; though unlike the American girl who goes to Cork, they are pointedly described as non-southern Americans. The man is a "businessman" from Syracuse, New York; the "girl" (as the author refers to her), whom the man judges to be younger than he is, perhaps thirty-two, is from Toledo, Ohio. Strangers to each other, they meet in New Orleans on a hot Sunday afternoon in July. Each has come to Galatoire's with a group of southern friends. Mutual friends in the two parties see each other across the restaurant, and the groups combine into one luncheon party. When the man from Syracuse meets the woman from Toledo, he thinks — himself "long married" — that here is a woman who is having an affair, "with a married man most likely." The girl from Toledo thinks, "It must stick out all over me.... People in love like me, I suppose, give away the short cuts to everybody's secrets." As the luncheon progresses the man and the girl — two outsiders, "two Northerners keeping each other company," though they say nothing about it to each other — experience the sense of having discovered a bond. Thus it is that after the luncheon they find themselves, at the suggestion of the man, driving out of the city in his rented red Ford convertible to see what the world is like "South of New Orleans." In the "*degrading* heat," as the girl calls it, they drive down a concrete strip flanked by raging insects and cluttered with crayfish and terrapins; eventually they cross to the other side of the Mississippi River on a ferry crowded with people enjoying a Sunday outing (*Stories*, 561–63 passim).

Among the several passengers who get out of their cars to walk about the deck is a boy with an alligator on a chain. "Both respectable and merciful, their hides," the woman thinks. "Deliver us all from the naked in heart" (*Stories*, 568).

---

3. Welty, *Stories, Essay, and Memoir*, ed. Richard Ford and Michael Kreyling (New York: Library of America, 1998), 561. Subsequent parenthetical references to Welty's stories are to this edition.

After they get off the ferry and resume their southward trek on the west side of the great meandering river, the man asks himself:

> Had she felt a wish for someone else to be riding with them? He thought it was more likely that she would wish for her husband if she had one (his wife's voice) than for the lover in whom he believed. Whatever people liked to think, situations (if not scenes) were usually three-way—there was somebody else always. The one who didn't—couldn't—understand the two made the formidable third. (*Stories,* 568)

As the man from Syracuse and the girl from Toledo drive into an even more intense heat than they have felt before, the pavement ceases and the road, flanked by fishermen's shacks, becomes one made of the shells of mollusks. They continue until they come to the little town named Venice at the end of land, where, as darkness descends around them, they turn around and shortly afterward find a bar and restaurant, a "homey place," housed in a barnlike structure and run by the owner, bartender, and cook. Here at Baba's Place they order sandwiches and beer. Later, when they no longer sense the brief initial curiosity their presence has aroused in the local patrons, they join them on the dance floor and move to "a slow piece" emanating from the jukebox.

> Surely even those immune from the world, for the time being, need the touch of one another, or all is lost. Their arms encircling each other, their bodies circling the odorous, just-nailed-down floor, they were, at last, imperviousness in motion. They had found it, and had almost missed it: they had had to dance. They were what their separate hearts desired that day, for themselves and each other. (*Stories,* 576)

Later, "in the thickening heat," they dance to a lively song, while Baba joins "the mosquito-voiced singer" on the record in singing the chorus of "*Moi pas l'aimez ca.*" Finally, "bathed in sweat," they depart for the return to New Orleans. Once the man stops the car to clean the windshield of bugs; a little later he stops, puts his arm around his companion, and kisses her, "not knowing ever whether gently or harshly." His loss of the capacity to make this "distinction" brings him back to an awareness of the world they have come out of. "They had ridden down into a strange land together and were getting safely back—by a slight margin, perhaps, but margin enough." But even as he mutters, "We're all right now," and lights a cigarette, "something that must have been with them all along suddenly, then, was not," rises, "tall as panic," and cries out, "like a human," and then drops back (*Stories,* 579–80).

The girl from Toledo and the man from Syracuse go back across the river to the east side, this time by "the bridge" (the Huey P. Long Bridge, completed in December 1935, three months after Long's assassination; this and other details, as well as the general atmospheric aura of the story, indicate its setting may be the later 1930s or the early 1940s). Back in the city, the man finds the hotel where his companion is staying, and, apparently without having ever exchanged names, the two part, with a restrained handshake, on the sidewalk at the hotel entrance. Looking back the man from Syracuse thinks he sees a man strolling across the lobby to meet the girl from Toledo.

Two or three years after writing her story about the strange journey two strangers take into a strange place, Welty wrote an essay that, although it bears an impersonal title, "Writing and Analyzing a Story," is largely a reflection on her personal—one is tempted to say deeply personal—experience in writing "No Place for You, My Love." The only essay in *The Eye of the Story*, the compilation of selected essays and reviews Welty published in 1978, in which she examines one of her own stories, it is prefaced by the remark that it is in actuality not so much a critical analysis as "a piece of hindsight from a working point of view." The author explains that shortly after she had completed a story called "No Place for You, My Love"—"a story, told in subjective terms, of a girl" who is "caught fast in the over-familiar, monotonous life of her small town, and immobilized further by a prolonged and hopeless love affair"[4]—she made a summertime visit to New Orleans.

One day during her visit "an acquaintance" had invited her to take a drive through the country south of the city. When she returned home to Jackson she discovered that during her journey into "that once-submerged, strange land of 'south from South,'" the story she had just written had come into her "head in an altogether new form." As a result she discarded the first version and, though retaining the title, wrote "a new version from scratch" to accord with her realization that the image of the strange world she had just journeyed through had "stamped itself" on her imagination as the "very image of the story's predicament" she was seeking to portray in "No Place for You, My Love." Conceiving that the point of view she had employed in the first version of this story—the subjective view of the southern girl "sealed in her world, by nature and circumstance"—had worked to the story's "detriment," the author "escaped" the mind of this girl altogether by divesting her of the "half-dozen familiars" she had around her and

4. Welty, *The Eye of the Story: Selected Essays and Reviews* (New York: Random House, 1978), 111. Subsequent parenthetical references are to this edition.

transforming her into a midwesterner. Then she "invented a single new character, a man whom I brought into the story *to be* a stranger." "I was to keep out of
his mind too," Welty adds; and thereby "had double-locked the doors behind
me" (*Eye*, 110–11).

Escaping from the minds of her characters, Welty discovered, as she "wrote
further into the story," that "something more real, more essential, than the characters were on their own was revealing itself." She had found the true point of
view: "outside" the characters—"suspended, hung in the air between two people,
fished alive from the surrounding scene":

> In effect, though the characters numbered only two, there had come to be a sort
> of third character along on the ride—the presence of a relationship between
> the two. It was what grew up between them meeting as strangers, went on the
> excursion with them, nodded back and forth from one to the other—listening,
> watching, persuading or denying them, enlarging or diminishing them, forgetful
> sometimes of who they were or what they were doing here—in its domain—
> and helping or betraying them along. (*Eye*, 111–12)

In the course of their journey through the place that is the lower reaches of
Louisiana, Welty observes, her characters come into touch with "something wilder
than ordinary communication between well-disposed strangers," with something
that responded to "the speed of the ride pitted against the danger of an easy or
conventionally tempting sympathy." The "heat that in itself drives on the driver
in the face of an inimical world" is "demoniac"—being at once "more ruthless and
more tender, more pressing and acute than their automatic saving ironies and
graces" (*Eye*, 113).

The defeat of the saving ironies is, to be sure, implicit in what Welty says is
the subtle "plot" of the "little story," which is the "vain courting of imperviousness in the face of exposure."

> Deliver us all from the naked in heart, the girl thinks (this is what I kept of
> her). . . . Riding down together into strange country is danger, a play at danger,
> secretly poetic, and the characters, in attempting it as a mutual feat, admit noth-
> ing to each other except the wicked heat and its comical inconvenience. The
> only time they will yield or touch is while they are dancing in the crowd that to
> them is comically unlikely (hence insulating, nonconducting) or taking a kiss
> outside time. Nevertheless it happens that they go along aware, from moment
> to moment, as one: as my third character, the straining, hallucinatory eyes and
> ears, the roused-up sentient being of that place. Exposure begins in intuition;

and the intuition comes to its end in showing the heart that has expected, while it dreads, that exposure. (*Eye*, 113)

Welty sums up her intention in "No Place for You, My Love" as her desire "to make the story's inside outside, and then leave the shell behind" (*Eye*, 112–13). She had "no wish to sound mystical," she says, but, she admits, if she could, she "did expect to sound mysterious now and then"; for she regarded her story as paradoxically "a circumstantial, realistic story in which the reality *was* mystery."

> The cry that rose up at the story's end was, I hope, unmistakably, the cry of that doomed relationship—personal, mortal, psychic—admitted in order to be denied, a cry that the characters were first able (and prone) to listen to, and then able in part to ignore. The cry was authentic to my story: the end of a journey *can* set up a cry, the shallowest provocation to sympathy and love does hate to give up the ghost. A relationship of the most fleeting kind has the power inherent to loom like a genie—to become vocative at last, as it has already become present and taken up room; as it has spread out as a destination however unlikely; as it has glimmered and rushed by in the dark and dust outside, showing occasional points of fire. Relationship *is* a pervading and changing mystery; it is not words that make it so in life, but words have to make it so in a story. Brutal or lovely, the mystery waits for people wherever they go, whatever extreme they run to. (*Eye*, 114)

In the original version of "No Place for You, My Love," Welty says, she had aspired to tell "a story of concealment, in terms of the hermetic and familiar," but she had somehow ended up with a story that concealed "what I had meant to show." Transformed into a story about a journey a girl from Toledo and a man from Syracuse take on Sunday afternoon into the coastal extremities of Louisiana, the new version embodied what she wanted it to: the revelation of the mystery of the relationship between two human beings revealed through the power of the "sentient being of that place" (*Eye*, 113).

It is curious that in "Place in Fiction," published a year after the essay on the writing of "No Place for You, My Love," Welty seems bent on modifying the emphasis on the mystique of place in her self-interpretation of this story:

> I think the sense of place is as essential to good and honest writing as a logical mind; surely they are somewhere related. It is by knowing where you stand that you grow able to judge where you are. Place absorbs our earliest notice and attention, it bestows on us our original awareness; and our critical powers spring up from the study of it and the growth of experience inside it. It perseveres in

bringing us back to earth when we fly too high. It never really stops informing us, for it is forever astir, alive, changing, reflecting, like the mind of man itself. . . . Sense of place gives equilibrium; extended, it is sense of direction too. Carried off we might be in spirit, and should be, when we are reading or writing something good; but it is the sense of place going with us still that is the ball of golden thread to carry us there and back and in every sense of the word to bring us home. (*Eye*, 128–29)

Yet the sense of place in "No Place for You, My Love" is distinctly otherwise. "Feeling" in her "story's grip," Welty says it became "literally apparent—that secret and shadow are taken away in this country by the merciless light." She continues: "I was writing of a real place, but doing so in order to write about my subject. I was writing of exposure, and the shock of the world." (Or, she might have said, exposure to the shock of the discovery that in "merciless reality" the world is a "place" in which the girl from Toledo and the man from Syracuse are forever lost [*Eye*, 112–13]). Is not the austere, ultimate implication of the journey they take through the coastal parishes of Louisiana on a Sunday summer afternoon their momentary glimpse of the veiled truth that there was no place for them in the world they have come out of, or the world they have come to, or the world to which they must return?

Reviewing *The Bride of the Innisfallen and Other Stories* in *Sewanee Review*, Louis D. Rubin was moved to comment that this work assures us that "a sensitive, discerning artist is steadily extending her range." As in all her work "a great deal goes on, much of it humorous, piquant, graceful, and beneath the surface there is another dimension entirely."[5] This other dimension, it occurs to me, is marked by the underlying conflict—the animating "tension"—in Welty's stories between her sense of place and her sense of time.

Although present from the beginning of her career as a storyteller, this tension revealed itself to Welty herself, one judges, only slowly, and she did not attempt to come to grips with it, at least in formal critical comment, until 1973, when she published "Some Thoughts on Time in Fiction" in the Eudora Welty issue of *Mississippi Quarterly*. Since, at the request of the publication's editor, the late Peyton W. Williams, I was serving as the special editor of this issue, I was privileged to read this essay as soon as it arrived from the hands of the author; with a certain sense of shock, I realized that in effect it constituted an important revision of Welty's essay "Place in Fiction," which since its publication in 1955 had

5. Rubin, *Sewanee Review* 63 (Autumn 1955): 671.

acquired something like classic status among her readers as the key to the inter-pretation of her fiction.

"Some Notes on Time in Fiction" begins with the statement that time and place—"the two bases of reference upon which the novel, in seeking to come to grips with human experience, must depend for its validity"—may seem to the novelist to operate together, that is, until the novelist "comes to scrutinize them apart" (*Eye*, 163). This self-conscious act reveals that place, "the accessible one, the inhabited one," the one possessing a "blessed identity," has not a friend but an implacable enemy in time—"anonymous," bearing "the same face the world over," telling "us nothing about itself except by the signals that it is passing," never giving "anything away" (*Eye*, 165). The essay on time in fiction also implies, it seems to me, another, and more subtle, revisionary emphasis in Welty's concep-tion not only of the basis of fiction but also of its form or forms. She had effec-tively begun her career with six notable short stories (including the classic tale "Petrified Man") that Cleanth Brooks and Robert Penn Warren published in the first series of *Southern Review*, and by the time the complete collection of her short stories came out in 1980, she had long since achieved the status of a master of this genre.

But in her essay on time in fiction Welty suggests that the form she most revered was not the short story but the novel, the literary form most deeply as-sociated with the modern preoccupation with time. Indeed, she says that "the novel is Time's child" (*Eye*, 165). Welty's meditation on time—which, it may be said, resembles a prose poem even more than her meditation on place—depicts the modern novel as having its fundamental meaning in its metaphorical rela-tion to the prime symbol of modernity, the mechanical clock. In making this observation, she refers to Mann and Proust: "Mann attacking the subjectivity of man's knowledge of time, and Proust, discovering a way to make time give back all it has taken, through turning life by way of the memory into art, left master-pieces that are clocks themselves, giant clocks stationed for always out in the world, sounding for us the high hours of our literature." But Welty makes it clear that she also regards Faulkner—whose work "is magnetized to a core of time"—as being among the makers of the "giant clocks stationed for always out in the world, sounding for us the high hours of our literature" (*Eye*, 172). Per-haps, for her, to be sure, Faulkner is the most significant clock maker. In the all-important distinction she makes in "Time in Fiction" between fictional time and the "arbitrary, bullying power" clock time exerts on the life of daily reality, her ap-peal is primarily to Faulkner—who, asserting in *Light in August* that "Memory believes before knowing remembers," has "crowded chronology out of the way many times to make way for memory and the life of the past."

> Remembering is so basic and vital a part of staying alive that it takes on the strength of an instinct of survival and acquires the power of an art. Remembering is done through the blood, it is a bequeathment, it takes account of what happens before a man is born as if he were there taking part. It is a physical absorption through the living body, it is a spiritual heritage. It is also a life's work. (*Eye*, 71)

As with Faulkner, the exploration of the spiritual heritage of the southern culture of memory—of the comedy and the tragedy of the perpetuation of this culture—became Eudora Welty's life's work as an eminently self-conscious, completely dedicated artist.

But there is a distinct difference between her vision of memory and Faulkner's. In creating the Yoknapatawpha stories, Faulkner was always deeply conscious of the intimate presence in his vision of southern history—and its relation to modern history—of the American Civil War, and of the South as the place where much of this war had been fought. He was in particular eminently aware of the transfiguring effect of the war on his native place, and especially of its consequences as these were embodied in the lives of the people of the state of Mississippi, including the members of his own family and, not least, his own life.

In my experience of reading Faulkner, however, I did not realize for a rather long time the significance of the fact that, as a member of the southern literary generation that came into its own in the 1920s and early 1930s, he belonged to the last generation of southern writers who experienced a vital personal connection with the Civil War through the daily presence in their lives of people who had not only survived its battles but were living embodiments of the drama of surviving the long and bitter aftermath of "the defeat" and the Reconstruction. This realization did not fully come to me until—thinking about the meaning of Welty's long career in American letters—it occurred to me how little, in contrast to Faulkner's stories, the memory of the Civil War counts for in her stories, how essentially different from Faulkner's is her sense of her relation to the southern culture of memory.

She had been born into this culture in Jackson, Mississippi, in 1909, not far from the Old State Capitol. Here Mississippians had taken the fateful step of withdrawing from the Union; here, a hundred years later, in 1973, they had held an official celebration of Eudora Welty's career (a "Eudorafication," her friend

Malcolm Cowley called it) and symbolically crowned her with the laurel wreath. Yet in Welty's case memory of the Civil War was not, as in Faulkner's case, a bequeathment of the blood. Welty understood perfectly what Quentin Compson means when he tells his Canadian friend Shreve on that frigid night in their Harvard dormitory room that to understand Quentin's attachment to the South he would have had to be born there: born like Quentin into the world of the flesh-and-blood survivors of "the defeat" and, as their flesh-and-blood heirs, have had the experience of living the long death of the southern nation after the Civil War. Welty's family history cut her off from this experience. She was the daughter of Christian Welty, a Yankee born in Ohio who, in 1904, opportunistically came to the capital city of Mississippi, entered the insurance business, and left as his highly visible legacy the Lamar Life Insurance Building, still a dominant feature of the Jackson skyline. He was accompanied on his venture into the Deep South by his bride, Chestina, who came from West Virginia—a state formed in the midst of the Civil War by Unionists, some of them, like her mother's family, the Andrews, originally Virginians who had exiled themselves from the slave South when they moved into the wild mountainous world of western Virginia.[6]

But while she did not share directly in the Faulknerian experience, at once vexing and stimulating, of blood memory—of believing before knowing remembers—Welty had the advantage of being free of the Faulknerian burden of the invariable association of memory with the memory of the Civil War. Free, it seems to me—with a less agonizing effort than is evident in Faulkner's struggle to do the same thing in, say, *The Sound and the Fury*—not only to conceive of fiction as time's child but also, in that "dark and painful novel," as Hermione Lee has called *The Optimist's Daughter*, to symbolize, in the story of Laurel Hand's return to Mt. Salus for her father's funeral, the reconciliation of place and its enemy, time.[7]

In *The Optimist's Daughter* time becomes a dimension of place and place a dimension of time. As, to be sure, it is not only in all her stories but also in the marvelously moving photographs collected in *One Time, One Place*, which may be taken to symbolize Welty's greatest achievement as a writer. This is, to paraphrase a haunting retrospective statement in the introductory essay to *One Time, One Place*, coming "to terms" with her own "lifelong exposure to the world"—

6. Welty, *One Writer's Beginnings* (Cambridge: Harvard University Press, 1984), 52–58.
7. Lee, "On Eudora Welty," *New York Review of Books* 67 (September 29, 2001): 32.

coming to terms, in other words, with an artist's lifelong exposure to time and place.[8]

Ironically, unless one saw them on exhibit in the Mississippi Department of Archives and History or, on occasion, in New York City and elsewhere, one had to wait nearly twenty years after the initial publication of Welty's photographs, until 1989, to see a published representation worthy of her images—this in the 1989 University Press of Mississippi collection, with a fine introductory essay by Reynolds Price and a provocative interview with the photographer herself.[9]

In the Mississippi edition one could finally appreciate the story Welty tells in the introductory essay to *One Time, One Place* about how early in her career as a writer she had discovered and confirmed the connection of place, time, and human relationships when she had taken a seminal journey—traveling by automobile to all eighty-two counties in her native state. This had been in fulfillment of her official duties as a "junior grade" public-relations agent of the Mississippi office of Roosevelt's Works Progress Administration during the years of the Great Depression. At night, in lonely country-town hotel rooms (cooled in summer by "loud electric fans"), she had written reports (for "county weeklies to publish if they found the space") about "newly opened farm-to-market roads" and new airfields "hacked out of cow pastures"; she had set down interviews with judges of juvenile courts, described putting up exhibits at county fairs, and written news stories about riding along on bookmobile routes, "distributing books into open hands like the treasures they were" (*One Time*, 7).

But Welty had had something else to think about at night in those country-town hotel rooms: the images of people and places she was capturing on film as she drove about in Mississippi; for, while she fulfilled the task of making a written record of what she did for the WPA with due diligence, the task that meant the most to her was the unofficial, self-assigned, largely private one of making a photographic record of life in 1930s Mississippi. Her work as an amateur photographer did not become generally known until 1971, when Random House published *One Time, One Place*. In the introduction to this volume, which one southern reviewer called "Miss Eudora's Picture Book," she explains that she took her pictures with a Kodak "one step more advanced than the Brownie" (*One Time*, 8). and developed them in the kitchen when she was back home in Jackson on weekends. To make enlargements she used a secondhand enlarger

8. Welty, *One Time, One Place: Mississippi in the Depression: A Snapshot Album* (1971; reprint, Jackson: University Press of Mississippi, 1996). Subsequent parenthetical references are to this edition.

9. Welty, *Photographs* (Jackson: University Press of Mississippi, 1989).

she got from the State Highway Department. "A better and less ignorant photographer would certainly have come up with better pictures, but not these pictures," she says; "for he could hardly have been as well positioned as I was, moving through the scene openly, and yet invisibly, because I was part of it, born into it, taken for granted" (*One Time*, 9).

Unfortunately, the meaning of Eudora Welty's photographs as a revelation of a story writer's search for the truth that is hidden in the outside of the inside is represented more clearly in her introduction to *One Time, One Place* than in their reproduction on rough paper in the Random House edition. Even so, one responds to the power Welty herself found in them.

> When a heroic face like that of the woman in the buttoned sweater—who I think must come first in this book—looks back at me from the picture, what I respond to now, just as I did the first time, is not the Depression, not the Black, not the South, not even the perennially sorry state of the whole world, but the story of her life in her face. And though I did not take these pictures to prove anything, I do think they most assuredly do show something—which is to make a far better claim for them. Her face to me is full of meaning more truthful and more terrible, and, I think, more noble than any generalization about people could have prepared me for or could describe to me now. I learned from my own pictures, one by one, . . . [that] we are the breakers of our own hearts. (*One Time*, 11)

Whether the relationship is that of the photographer taking a picture of the woman in the sweater, or the storyteller writing about the girl from Toledo and the man from Syracuse, it involves an undying presence of mystery. But the shock of experiencing a vision of place and time that reveals the mystery of "the living relationship between what is going on and our selves" suggests a measure of salvation. "I learned quickly enough when to click the shutter, and what I was becoming aware of more slowly was a story-writer's truth: the thing to wait on, to reach there in time for, is the moment in which people reveal themselves. You have to be ready, in yourself; you have to know the moment when you see it" (*One Time*, 12). We break our own hearts in the pathos, and not less the comedy, of our indifference to this moment.

> We come to terms as well as we can with our lifelong exposure to the world, and we use whatever devices we may need to survive. But eventually, of course, our knowledge depends upon the living relationship between what we see going on and ourselves. If exposure is essential, still more is the reflection. Insight doesn't happen often on the click of the moment, like a lucky snapshot, but

comes in its own time and more slowly and from nowhere but within. The sharpest recognition is surely that charged with sympathy as well as with shock—it is a form of human vision. And that is of course a gift. We struggle through any pain or darkness in nothing but the hope that we may receive it, and through any term of work in the prayer to keep it. (*One Time,* 12)

From the moment she first clicked the shutter of a camera, Welty knew that, though her vocation was to make stories, not pictures, her wish, indeed her "continuing passion," as is so poignantly illustrated by her picture—no, her vision—of the woman in a sweater, "would be, not to point the finger in judgment but to part a curtain, that invisible shadow that falls between people, the veil of indifference to each other's presence, each other's wonder, to each other's plight" (*One Time,* 12). Or, we might say, employing the kind of abstraction Welty despised, to point the finger to each person's isolation under the conditions of modern history.

The subtle drama of seeing into the outside of the inside, or the inside of the outside—and depicting the terrifying yet exalting truth of the story of human relationships under the historical circumstances in which we live our lives—this in abstract terms is the sum and substance of the story of our relationships with each other as told by Eudora Welty. While we may seldom transcend the conditions of our existence—may almost never penetrate the veil of our imperviousness to others; indeed do all we can to keep the veil intact; and consequently are doomed to be the breakers of our own hearts—one may in some special moment glimpse in a Welty story what lies beyond the veil and, whether the momentary vision is owing to the grace of God or the grace of art, or both, become in that cruel, but precious, moment healers of our own hearts.

I remember another evening in Eudora's living room. It is crowded with guests attending a reception she is giving during the "Eudorafication" in 1973. I am talking to Walker Percy about the Pulitzer that has just been awarded to Eudora for *The Optimist's Daughter,* and Walker is remarking in a confidential voice, "You know, it is about Eudora herself." In that moment, I think, I glimpsed the complex irony implicit in Eudora Welty's creation of the fictional Laurel Hand, the optimist's daughter.

Eudora Welty's Sense of Place

Denis Donoghue

I

In "A Worn Path"—the final story in *A Curtain of Green and Other Stories* (1941)—Eudora Welty tells of an old black woman, Phoenix Jackson, who lives "away back off the Old Natchez Trace." On "a bright frozen day in the early morning" one December she sets out to walk the long and only partly worn path to Natchez.[1] If you count small things and don't insist on catastrophes, much happens to her. Her skirt gets caught in a thorny bush, she negotiates a log thrown across a creek, and she imagines that a boy gives her a slice of marble cake. She gets through a barbed wire fence, comes on a scarecrow, meets a wagon track, finds a well and drinks from it, fends off a black dog only to fall into a ditch, gets a lifting hand from a hunter, pockets a nickel the hunter has dropped, and arrives at Natchez. There she asks a woman to lace up her shoes, finds the doctor's office, gets the bottle of medicine her grandson needs, accepts a nickel in Christmas charity from the nurse's attendant, decides to spend it on a paper windmill for her grandson, and sets off back the way she came. On the path to Natchez she had talked to herself and to the world: "Out of my way, all you foxes, owls, beetles, jack rabbits, coons and wild animals! . . . Keep out from under these feet, little bob-whites" (*Stories,* 171). She observed that a hill was pine going up, oak going down. A field of old cotton led to one of dead corn and then to a maze where the path lost itself. Phoenix Jackson walked on, talking "in the voice of argument old people keep to use with themselves" (*Stories,* 172). She doesn't expect the world to reply. Trees, hills, dogs, the sun, the creek have their places, but none of Phoenix Jackson's feelings assumes that the world should respond to her

1. Welty, *Stories, Essays, and Memoir,* ed. Richard Ford and Michael Kreyling (New York: Library of America, 1998), 171. All quotations from Welty's fiction are taken from this volume and from *Complete Novels,* ed. Richard Ford and Michael Kreyling (New York: Library of America, 1998). Subsequent parenthetical references are to these editions.

in kind. She does not stop to turn the things that surround her into a landscape or to think of them in that capacity. Everything she meets is just whatever it happens to be. The worn path becomes a presence, even a force to us, but not to Phoenix Jackson. If she had anything as improbable as a philosophy, it would be untroubled Realism. Her consciousness is barely distinguishable from her will. Getting to Natchez engages every form of her energy. She is incurious about anything else the world contains.

Eudora Welty is like Phoenix Jackson in only one respect. Place is immensely a value to her, but she does not assume that when she looks at the natural world it will look fondly back at her. She knows trees, flowers, and birds with remarkable familiarity and has the sensibility of an adept, which she attributes to Audubon in "A Still Moment," but she does not look for a neo-Wordsworthian relation between the world and the mind that contemplates it. Her fiction, like her photographs, is devoted to the people she sees and their relation to the places where they live and work, but she does not separate the places from the people or hold the landscapes up for separate attention. It is as if she read T. S. Eliot's *After Strange Gods* and took heed of his animadversions on the subject of landscape. Eliot had Hardy in view, a writer he disliked for "self-absorption," and it is possible that his dislike sent him into harsh generalization:

> In consequence of his self-absorption, [Hardy] makes a great deal of landscape; for landscape is a passive creature which lends itself to an author's mood. Landscape is fitted too for the purposes of an author who is interested not at all in men's minds, but only in their emotions; and perhaps only in men as vehicles for emotions.[2]

Welty does not think that a landscape should be susceptible to a character's mood or that a character is justified in seeking among trees, flowers, swamps, and rivers an intuition of a shared life. Pantheism does not seem to attract her. Relations occupy her mind, but she does not presume on their hospitality or go beyond reasonable limits of affiliation.

Otherwise put: Welty is not a symbolist, according to our standard definition of symbolism. But I am impelled by Guy Davenport's "That Faire Field of Enna" to think that we must distinguish, especially in reading Welty, two versions of Symbolism. The first is sufficiently indicated by reference to Thomas Carlyle, Gerard de Nerval, Stéphane Mallarmé, Arthur Symons, and the early William Butler Yeats. We find it in Mallarmé's program, "pour ne garder de rien que la

2. Eliot, *After Strange Gods: A Primer of Modern Heresy* (London: Faber and Faber, 1934), 55.

suggestion" (to retain only the suggestion). It is also well apprehended in *The Symbolist Movement in Literature,* where Symons writes of "a literature in which the visible world is no longer a reality, and the unseen world no longer a dream." And in "The Symbolism of Poetry," where Yeats writes: "The purpose of rhythm, it has always seemed to me, is to prolong the moment of contemplation, the moment when we are both asleep and awake, which is the one moment of creation, by hushing us with an alluring monotony, while it holds us waking by variety, to keep us in that state of perhaps real trance, in which the mind liberated from the pressure of the will is unfolded in symbols."[3]

It is not surprising that Davenport gives a severe account of these symbols and the literature in which they are favored. He is an Objectivist on principle and thinks that "the artist shows the world as if meaning were inherent in its particulars." He has no interest in exchanging particulars for essences:

> Psychology in the study of dreams defined the symbol as essentially opaque, a confusion rather than an epiphany of meaning. The darker the symbol, the richer it was thought to be, and ambiguity became a virtue in literature. James may be partly responsible, but then James posited for our pleasure in such things an ambiguity that is true of experience (we do not know each other's inner dark of soul, nor what is written in letters locked in a cupboard, nor what people see when they say they've seen a ghost). The symbols of the French *symbolistes* and their school from Oslo to Salerno, from Dublin to Budapest, were not properly symbols at all, but enigmas derived from the German doctrine of elective affinities among things and from Fourier and Swedenborg. These symbols so-called in the sensibilities of Baudelaire and Mallarmé became an abstract art, paralleling the disappearance of intelligible images in the painting of Malevich and Kandinsky a generation later. You cannot interpret a *symboliste* symbol, you can only contemplate it, like a transcendentalist brooding on the word *nature*.[4]

Not that Davenport is willing to give up symbols, but he proposes to change their character and to redeem them for a better tradition—Objectivism—by making them intelligible. He wants a symbol to be such that he can come to the end of it and know what he has come to the end of. He finds authority and

---

3. Mallarmé, *Oeuvres Completes* (Paris: Pleiade, 1945), 365; Symons, *The Symbolist Movement in Literature,* ed. Richard Ellmann (London: Constable, 1911), 4; W. B. Yeats, *Essays and Introductions* (London: Macmillan, 1961), 159.

4. Davenport, "That Faire Field of Enna," in *The Geography of the Imagination* (San Francisco: North Point Press, 1981), 269, 262.

precedent in Ezra Pound, James Joyce, Louis Zukofsky, sundry Objectivists, and (though he doesn't quite say so) Eudora Welty. But mainly Joyce:

> For the first time since Dante, symbols became transparent on Joyce's pages... Joyce, who rethought everything, rethought symbolism. It must first of all be organic, not arbitrary or fanciful. It must be logical, resonant, transparent, bright. From Flaubert he had learned that a true symbol must be found in an image that belongs to the narrative. The parrot Loulou in *Un Coeur simple* acts symbolically to make us feel the devotion, loneliness, ecstasy, and inviolable simplicity of Felicité.... In Joyce a rolled-up newspaper with the words *Gold Cup* and *Sceptre* among its racing news becomes a symbolic blossom around which two men, symbolic bees, forage. This is a deeper symbolism than more apparent ones in operation at the same time: Odysseus among the Lotus Eaters, a spiritually lost Jew longing to return to Israel ("and the desert shall blossom like the rose"), a man psychologically a drone to his queen-bee wife, a man named Flower enacting the suffering of a saint named Flower (Anthony) and his temptations; and on and on. Joyce's symbols are labyrinths of meaning, but they are logical, and they expand meaning. They are, as mediaeval grammarians said, *involucra*—seed husks asking to be peeled.[5]

The distinction between the two Symbolisms, whatever we call them—soft and hard, opaque and translucent, occult and intelligible, Romantic and Classic, Yeats and Joyce—bears on one's reading of Welty. She is classical in her affections. Her symbols are not dissociated, they are images that "belong to the narrative." It follows, as a quality and not as a defect, that they are not endless in purport. In the last pages of *The Optimist's Daughter* a bird, a swift, gets out of the chimney in the McKelva home at Mount Salus and flies from room to room. Laurel tries to catch it and set it free. An itinerant handyman, Mr. Cheek—"Bird in the house?... Sign o' bad luck, ain't it?" (*Novels,* 982)—tries to help, but he's no good. In the end, using two baskets, Laurel gets hold of the bird and releases it: "The bird was away. In the air it was nothing but a pair of wings—she saw no body any more, no tail, just a tilting crescent being drawn back into the sky" (*Novels,* 985). Readers are not invited to be as superstitious as Mr. Cheek. It is enough if we reflect that Laurel, too, is trying to get out of the house intact, now that it belongs to the dreadful Fay, her deceased father's second wife. Laurel quarrels with Fay, insisting on saying what she has to say. Then she leaves the house, consigning to memory every experience she cares for: "The memory can be hurt,

5. Ibid., 262–63.

time and again—but in that may lie its final mercy. As long as it's vulnerable to the living moment, it lives for us, and while it lives, and while we are able, we can give it up its due" (*Novels,* 992).

The relation between Laurel and the bird is local and bounded. Because it is an intelligible relation, it is limited as if on principle, and we do it sufficient justice by going through to the end of it. Interpretation is enough; unlimited divination is not required. Nor was it required, a few pages earlier, when Laurel recalled taking the train with her husband, Phil, from Chicago to Mount Salus and seeing "the long, ragged, pencil-faint line of birds within the crystal of the zenith, flying in a V of their own, following the same course down." There is no need to go into a swoon of reverie. The propriety of the image can be intuited without fuss: "All they could see was sky, water, birds, light, and confluence. It was the whole morning world" (*Novels,* 979). Interpretation starts a flight of analogy, and when the intelligibility of the analogy has been apprehended, the flight is brought to an end. We are still in the morning world. To say that the symbol is transparent is to say that it begins and, when its interpretation has been rationally fulfilled, ends.

Yeats, at least in his *symbolist* phase, would have regarded Welty's birds as merely allegorical and her method as a device for saying things that "could be said as well, or better, in another way." He despised the allegorical form of meaning, as in Tintoretto's *Origin of the Milky Way,* which impels us to say: "That woman there is Juno, and the milk out of her breast is making the Milky Way." When you have said that, you have given the meaning of the picture, and "the fine painting, which has added so much irrelevant beauty, has not told it better." But in neo-French Symbolism, according to Yeats, there are no such iconographies, no occasions to gratify one's hermeneutic zeal by saying that *that* stands for *this:*

> If you liberate a person or a landscape from the bonds of motives and their actions, causes and their effects, and from all bonds but the bonds of your love, it will change under your eyes, and become a symbol of an infinite emotion, a perfected emotion, a part of the Divine Essence; for we love nothing but the perfect, and our dreams make all things perfect, that we may love them.[6]

Welty might retort: "I love nothing but the imperfect, and my imagination shows all things imperfect, so I love them because they are not infinite." If there is a penumbra around her images—to call them that for the moment—no vagueness attends them but a sense of their participation in a recalled mythology. Davenport calls it mirage:

6. Yeats, *Essays and Introductions,* 147, 148, 148–49.

> She arranges images so that we see them in sharpest focus and simultaneously
> as a ghost of reality. When, for instance, a child is rescued from an on-coming
> train in *Delta Wedding*, we are made to see (if our imagination has its eyes
> open) the black, fuming chariot of Dis swooping down on Persephone picking
> flowers. The scene is not exactly a symbolic enactment; it is a mirage of it.[7]

Welty's procedure differs in that respect from the more elaborate correspondences of Joyce's *Ulysses* because Joyce's procedure keeps the Homeric mirage
going for the whole book, at least intermittently, while Welty's is occasional and
optional. When Maureen, in *Delta Wedding*, gets her foot caught on the trestle
and Uncle George tries to set it loose and fails, the Yellow Dog bears down on
them and the engineer only barely stops the train in time. It is optional whether
or not you think of Persephone and Dis. An occasional mirage gives you warrant
for thinking that the local image is not unique; there have been such imperfec-
tions before. One's sense of life is amplified without losing the immediate force
of the image.

Yeats called such correspondences "emblems" rather than "symbols," without
being consistent in maintaining the distinction. Emblems get their meaning "by
a traditional and not by a natural right."[8] We get our symbols from the natural
world—the sun, the moon, rivers, caves, swans—but our emblems from tradition, the history of cultures, literature, philosophy—as Yeats's poems and essays
feature Junzo Sato's sword, Milton's lonely tower, Plato's cave. But there is no
need to cultivate one at the expense of the other, though Paul de Man argues in
The Rhetoric of Romanticism that each entails its own philosophical disposition.
It seems to me that Yeats resorted to nature and to culture betimes, opportunistically; at a given moment he may have felt that one of these values was more reli-
able than the other. Sometimes he used a symbol as if it were primarily an em-
blem. The first stanza of "Coole Park and Ballylee, 1931" ends: "What's water but
the generated soul?"—not because nature and mind have collaborated to effect
that kinship but because Porphyry did it in *On the Cave of the Nymphs*.

II

If we think of Welty's commitment to images, emblems, and the art of mirage,
we see that it also governs her sense of place. She asks of a place only that it be itself and know itself in that being. Her places are not mere contexts of human

7. Davenport, "That Faire Field," 262.
8. Yeats, *Essays and Introductions*, 147.

and natural actions but, to begin with, they are places, not states of soul given an external form. All the better if a place acquires a certain force of presence corresponding to presence of mind and a quiet determination not to yield up its secrets to the first interrogation. The hill country of northeast Mississippi, where *Losing Battles* is set, has social but not sensitive bearing. What has happened to it is geological, but not teleological: mostly what has happened to it has been done by the people who have lived there, stretching back further than the historians can see. Welty comes to her sense of place not primordially but, as Davenport has shown, mythologically. These myths were local and immediate to the people who first heard them, but to us they are timeless, indicating patterns of experience we regard as nearly universal rather than regional. In Welty's hands they have the effect of making it appear not to matter much that her stories are set in one century rather than another. Time is important to them, but only so far as it has taken geographical and social lineaments.

It follows that it is not necessary to make a strict distinction, while reading Welty's fiction, between the values of space and time. Alexander von Humboldt pointed out that "in classical antiquity the earliest historians made little attempt to separate the description of lands from the narration of events the scene of which was in the areas described: for a long time physical geography and history appear attractively intermingled." The geographer Carl Ortwin Sauer has noted that "the literature of geography in the sense of chorology ["the study of the areal or habitat differentiation of the earth"] begins with parts of the earliest sagas and myths, vivid as they are with the sense of place and of man's contest with nature."[9] Herodotus is at once historian and geographer. There is no need to be strict in these designations unless we are willing to see the structures become sinister.

Modern preoccupation with time, as in Henri Bergson and Marcel Proust, has made us think that time and space are ideological rivals, and that each enforces a corresponding politics. Philosophers of space are thought to have a totalitarian impulse, concealed or not, while philosophers of time are deemed to be democrats. The dispute between Joseph Frank and Frank Kermode some years ago about "spatial form" seemed at any moment ready to turn rough with allegations of political bad faith. You could still start a row by proclaiming the merits of Wilhelm Wörringer's *Abstraction and Empathy,* Wyndham Lewis's *Time and*

9. Von Humboldt, *Kosmos* (Stuttgart and Tubingen, 1845), 1:64–65; Sauer, *Land and Life,* ed. John Leighly (Berkeley: University of California Press, 1965), 316–17 (von Humboldt quoted on 318, n. 5).

Western Man, and Pound's *Cantos* against choice philosophers of Time. But the disputants ought to acknowledge that one can denounce, as Samuel Beckett does in his book on Proust, "the poisonous ingenuity of Time in the science of affliction" without thinking that such ingenuity can be deflected by spatial analogies. Beckett thought that Proust wrote as he lived—in time. In that respect he was a Romantic, an Impressionist: "By his impressionism I mean his non-logical statement of phenomena in the order and exactitude of their perception, before they have been distorted into intelligibility in order to be forced into a chain of cause and effect." An artist who might be called classical, on the other hand, assumes "omniscience and omnipotence" and "raises himself artificially out of Time in order to give relief to his chronology and causality to his development."[10]

But to claim that Welty equably acknowledges space and place is not as innocent as it sounds, though she has not been drawn into a dispute on the lines of Frank versus Kermode. If she had to choose between Time and Space as values, I think she would choose Space, and if pushed further into the choice she might invoke places as devices against time. But generally she avoids the choice. Without claiming the authority of Herodotus, Humboldt, and Sauer, she makes space and place subsume the historical time in which her people, houses, and habitats have become what they are. She is acutely aware of the time it takes to become anything worthwhile. It follows that she writes with notable tenderness of families, traditions, old wisdoms, houses that have survived; and writes severely of things that have had not taken enough time to be remembered or worth remembering. We are expected to be alert to these intimations. When Laurel looks at Dr. Courtland—"Laurel looked for a moment into the experienced face, so entirely guileless. The Mississippi country that lay behind him was all in it" (*Novels,* 887)— we are expected to take the force and momentum of that Mississippi country and to know or guess whatever Laurel and Eudora Welty know of that country and its measure of experience and guilelessness. Fay's coming from Madrid, Texas, is to begin with no rebuke to Texas—not till it emerges that every word she speaks to Laurel about her family is a lie and that she is white trash, wherever she comes from. But any second wife would need to be an angel to survive comparison with Judge McKelva's Becky and, in Laurel's memory of it, the West Virginia that Becky came from:

> The first time Laurel could remember arriving in West Virginia instead of just finding herself there, her mother and she had got down from the train in early morning and stood, after it had gone, by themselves on a steep rock, all of the

10. Beckett, *Proust* (London: John Calder, 1965), 15, 86, 81.

world that they could see in the mist being their rock and its own iron bell on a post with its rope hanging down. Her mother gave the rope a pull and at its sound, almost at the moment of it, large and close to them appeared a gray boat with two of the boys at the oars. At their very feet had been the river. The boat came breasting out of the mist, and in they stepped. (*Novels,* 968)

No wonder the narrator comments, making Laurel's sense of life explicit: "All new things in life were meant to come like that."

Perhaps it is too much. Davenport, who will not hear an evil word about Eudora Welty, utters a sharp one—"wail"—when his mind turns to her silent politics. He permits himself some misgiving about her social discriminations, which are mostly discriminations of place and tone. With Fay McKelva in mind, along with Bonnie Dee Peacock from *The Ponder Heart,* he maintains:

Miss Welty has been fascinated before by these rapacious, weak-witted, pathologically selfish daughters of the dispossessed, and likes to bring them in sharp contrast with the decrepit chivalry and good manners of Mississippi gentry. The result, however complex and sensitive Miss Welty's handling of the misalliance, comes close to being a wail that an older order is being replaced by one that is by contrast barbarous and without transition.[11]

Some of these social distinctions are effected by standard means—exhibited vulgarity, lies, crassness, dreadful conversations, misbehavior at weddings, wakes, and funerals where good manners are expected—but often the rapacious, weak-witted, selfish people are shown living in places as obnoxious as their morals.

III

Eudora Welty has written of the sense of place in three essays, "Place in Fiction," "Some Notes on River Country," and "Writing and Analyzing a Story." The sentiment common to the three involves a feeling for locality and a corresponding feeling, amounting to a prejudice, against anything that makes light of its value. Welty is even ready to disapprove of fairy stories because "once upon a time" is not this time, that place; and she relegates the historical novel to the pathos of being just another fairy tale. "Fiction is properly at work on the here and now, or the past made here and now; for in novels *we* have to be there" (*Eye,* 117). To understand a character in a story, we must see him in relation to his place,

11. Davenport, "That Faire Field," 268.

"we must see him set to scale in his proper world to know his size" (*Eye,* 122).
Place defines a character by confining him to his place. A story would be another
story if its setting were changed. "Imagine *Swann's Way* laid in London, or *The
Magic Mountain* in Spain, or *Green Mansions* in the Black Forest." Further:

> The very notion of moving a novel brings ruder havoc to the mind and affec-
> tions than would a century's alteration in its time. It is only too easy to conceive
> that a bomb that could destroy all trace of places as we know them, in life and
> through books, could also destroy all feelings as we know them, so irretrievably
> and so happily are recognition, memory, history, valor, love, all the instincts of
> poetry and praise, worship and endeavor, bound up in place. From the dawn
> of man's imagination, place has enshrined the spirit; as soon as man stopped
> wandering and stood still and looked about him, he found a god in that place;
> and from then on, that was where the god abided and spoke from if ever he
> spoke. (*Eye,* 122–23)

In "Some Notes on River Country" Welty is so attentive to each genius loci that
she nearly sets place against time, provided it is a social place, rich in density and
texture:

> A place that ever was lived in is like a fire that never goes out. It flares up, it
> smolders for a time, it is fanned or smothered by circumstance, but its being is
> intact, forever fluttering within it, the result of some original ignition. Some-
> times it gives out glory, sometimes its little light must be sought out to be seen,
> small and tender as a candle flame, but as certain. (*Eye,* 286)

It is not entirely true: there are lost places. In Ireland, a community called Bally-
kilcline no longer exists that was a living place before the Famine of 1847. But it
is touching that Welty has made a claim for the perpetual flame of a place,
knowing that in her love of this value she sins a little by excess. A few pages later
it turns out that her authority in the excess is the Natchez tribe who attributed
the decline in their numbers to "the fact that the fire had once been allowed to
go out and that a profane fire burned now in its place" (*Eye,* 295).

But the highest claim for the value of place is made in "Place in Fiction,"
where Welty makes something like a moral distinction between place and people:

> Hemingway in our time has sought out the formless and ruthless territories of
> the world, archaic ones often, where there are bullfight arenas, theatres of hunt-
> ing and war, places with a primitive, or formidable, stripped-down character,
> with implacable codes, with inscrutable justices and inevitable retributions. But

whatever the scene of his work, it is the *places* that never are hostile. People give pain, are callous and insensitive, empty and cruel, carrying with them no pasts as they promise no futures. But place heals the hurt, soothes the outrage, fills the terrible vacuum that these human beings make. It heals actively, and the response is given consciously, with the ardent care and explicitness, respect and delight of a lover, when fishing streams or naming over streets becomes almost something of the lover's secret language—as the careful conversations between characters in Hemingway bear hints of the secret language of hate. The response to place has the added intensity that comes with the place's not being native or taken for granted, but found, chosen; thereby is the rest more heavily repudiated. (*Eye,* 131–32)

It is a theory of pastoral. Place offers even cruel people the paradigm of a new beginning, in which they learn a language not the vernacular, not native but chosen, a lover's secret idiom. It is as if a place not only forgave the outrages committed on its land but existed in order to do so, making forgiveness its reason for being as it is. In "The Rock," Wallace Stevens writes of "a cure of the ground and of ourselves," and of

> *an illusion so desired*
>
> That the green leaves came and covered the high rock,
> That the lilacs came and bloomed, like a blindness cleaned,
> Exclaiming bright sight, as it was satisfied,
>
> In a birth of sight.[12]

I am sure that Welty thinks of place not in the abstract but in its particularity, of places in which the ground is cured and rocks are covered with green leaves because of someone's desire that they should be so covered. These places are for some of us nothing but their names—China Grove, Dexter, Dulcie, Farr's Ginn, Larkin's Hill, Beulah, Morgana, Bigbee. If they heal the hurt and soothe the outrage, we have only Welty's word for it, and her photographs, but these are enough for belief and conviction.

IV

To do so much, a place must not only have qualities, it must be—or become— a character, according to one's conceit of it. It may not speak for itself, but it

---

12. Stevens, *Collected Poems* (London: Faber and Faber, 1955), 526–27.

must seem to be present, however silently, in many conversations. So it is in "No Place for You, My Love," which was first published in the *New Yorker* in 1952 and then reprinted in *The Bride of Innisfallen and Other Stories* (1955).

The scene is, to begin with, New Orleans. A businessman, married, from Syracuse meets a woman at a luncheon party in Galatoire's. She is from Toledo, Ohio, and is probably involved in a love affair with a married man. We don't know any names. The man from Syracuse invites the woman from Toledo to take a drive with him—it is a Sunday in July—in his rented Ford convertible. They drive south and keep going, not stopping even when they have crossed the Mississippi on a ferryboat. There is still more South. They see a graveyard, a church, a priest removing his vestments from a clothes hanger, an old man walking south, a shack with a beer sign on it, "Baba's Place." They go into Baba's Place, and the man orders a beer and a ham sandwich. There are men playing cards; a dog, asleep; a goose waddling about. Someone plays the jukebox. The man and the woman dance. After a while they leave and drive back. There is little conversation. The journey is mostly heat, mosquitoes, moths, gnats, the speed of the car. Approaching New Orleans, he stops the car and kisses her. Nothing is said. They drive on till they reach the city and he drops her off at her hotel. They shake hands. He says "Forgive," knowing that she expects it of him. She goes into the hotel lobby, "and he thought a figure in the lobby strolled to meet her." The story ends: "As he drove the little Ford safely to its garage, he remembered for the first time in years when he was young and brash, a student in New York, and the shriek and horror and unholy smother of the subway had its original meaning for him as the lilt and expectation of love" (*Stories*, 579–80).

Welty has written of "No Place for You, My Love" in "Writing and Analyzing a Story." I have little to add to her account of it, except to bring together a motif in the story and another one in the commentary which she has separated. In the story, the man is thinking:

> Had she felt a wish for someone else to be riding with them? He thought it was more likely that she would wish for her husband if she had one (his wife's voice) than for the lover in whom he believed. Whatever people liked to think, situations (if not scenes) were usually three-way—there was somebody else always. The one who didn't—couldn't—understand the two made the formidable third. (*Stories*, 568)

"Who is the third who walks always beside you?" Eliot asks in "The Waste Land." Welty's story has nothing more to say about the third, but in the commentary she notes another image of it. She has been explaining that in the first version of the story she had sealed the woman—a southerner at that stage—inside her own world and given the story over to her. She decided that she must get outside the woman's mind by making her a woman from the Midwest and by inventing a new character, "a man whom I brought into the story *to be* a stranger." She must keep out of his mind, too. Soon she came to see that the real point of view was neither the woman nor the man but the journey itself, south and back again:

> That country—that once-submerged, strange land of "south from South"— which had so stamped itself upon my imagination put in an unmistakable claim now as the very image of the story's predicament. It pointed out to me at the same time where the real point of view belonged. Once I'd escaped those characters' minds, I saw it was outside them—suspended, hung in the air between two people, fished alive from the surrounding scene. (*Eye*, 111)

The logic of the structure of the story now presented itself, and the scene of the little drama became an agent of it, more than a context for it:

> As I wrote further into the story, something more real, more essential, than the characters were on their own was revealing itself. In effect, though the characters numbered only two, there had come to be a sort of third character along on the ride—the presence of a relationship between the two. . . . This third character's role was that of hypnosis—it was what a relationship *can do*, be it however brief, tentative, potential, happy or sinister, ordinary or extraordinary. I wanted to suggest that its being took shape as the strange, compulsive journey itself, was palpable as its climate and mood, the heat of the day—but was its spirit too, a spirit that held territory, that which is seen fleeting past by two vulnerable people who might seize hands on the run. (*Eye*, 111–12)

At the end of the commentary, Welty sees her two characters, man and woman, become one—and that one is the place of their predicament. "The vain courting of imperviousness in the face of exposure," she says, "is this little story's plot." The characters attempt it "as a mutual feat," while admitting nothing to each other "except the wicked heat and its comical inconvenience." Nevertheless "it happens that they go along aware, from moment to moment, as one: as my third character, the straining, hallucinatory eyes and ears, the roused-up sentient being of that place" (*Eye*, 113).

Does the place heal the hurt, soothe the outrage, promise man and woman the imperviousness they courted beyond exposure? That would be too much to hope for from this south of South. There are no pastoral consolations in this story. Welty does not yield to those "good Americans" who feel obliged, as Irving Howe said, to show "unconsidered respect" for "nature." She does not imply that "a special wisdom is to be found, and found only, among tight-lipped farmers, village whittlers, and small-town eccentrics."[13] Or among the cardplayers in Baba's Place. The landscape does not provide even local gratifications. But the journey south and back again is imagined as taking on the quality—"roused-up sentient being"—of the imperfect man and woman it subsumes.

---

13. Howe, *Selected Writings, 1950–1990* (San Diego: Harcourt Brace Jovanovich, 1990), 181.

Part

IV

EXPLORATIONS 2

PLACE IN MODERN FICTION
OUTSIDE THE SOUTH

St. Paul Boy

Scott Donaldson

It needs a complex social machinery to set a writer in motion.
—HENRY JAMES, HAWTHORNE

I

A good deal has been made of F. Scott Fitzgerald's hometown by commentators on his work, but the fact is that he spent precious little time there. He was born in St. Paul in September 1896 and left eighteen months later. The next decade was spent in Buffalo and in Syracuse. The Fitzgeralds did not return to St. Paul until the summer of 1908, shortly before Scott's twelfth birthday. From 1908 to 1911 the family lived in St. Paul and Scott attended St. Paul Academy. Then he was sent east, first to the Newman school in Hackensack, New Jersey, and afterward to Princeton. During this period (1911–1917) Fitzgerald ordinarily spent his summers and Christmas vacations in St. Paul. This was followed by a two-year absence during his service in the U.S. Army and his brief career in the advertising business in New York. Fitzgerald did not come back to St. Paul until the summer of 1919, when he rewrote *This Side of Paradise* (1920) in a burst of activity and so won the hand of Zelda Sayre. He and Zelda stayed in the East after they were married in New York in the spring of 1920; but, when their child was to be born, they "played safe and went home to St. Paul." Scott and Zelda arrived in St. Paul in August 1921. Scottie was born in October. A year later they left the city permanently.

After infancy, then, Scott Fitzgerald lived in St. Paul for three years in prep school, half a dozen summers thereafter, nine months in 1916–1917 when he was sent home from Princeton for academic reasons, nine months in 1919–1920,

An abbreviated version of this essay was presented as the opening talk at the F. Scott Fitzgerald Society International Conference in St. Paul, September 2002.

and fourteen months in 1921–1922: about ten years of his life, altogether. In one sense, of course, the amount of time is immaterial. Scott Fitzgerald's mother's family was based in St. Paul; his father moved there to seek his fortune; he himself was born there. Stay away as he assuredly did for the last half of his life, St. Paul was always the place he came from. But there is more to it than that. The city itself, his family's position within its particular social structure, and his own interaction with others there played an essential role in shaping his life and career.

St. Paul had its unprepossessing start in 1837, when the Canadian Pierre ("Pigs Eye") Parrant built the first birch-roofed cabin, uncorked his jug, and began to sell whiskey to the Indians. The town grew rapidly, in good part because of its location at the head of navigation on the Mississippi River. By the late nineteenth century St. Paul had become a thriving community that inspired the admiration of famous visitors. In *Life on the Mississippi* (1883), Mark Twain declares it to be a very "wonderful town" constructed in "solid blocks of honest brick and stone" and having "the air of intending to stay." The Mississippi and the railroads made it an ideal site for commerce, and like most outsiders Twain was struck by the physical beauty of the place, with its high bluffs offering a wide view of the river and the lowlands. Twain also celebrated the growth of the bustling twin city of Minneapolis on the western side of the Mississippi, which though developed later than St. Paul had already surpassed it in population. And he called special attention to White Bear Lake, which was to play an important role in Fitzgerald's early life. White Bear "is a lovely sheet of water, and is being utilized as a summer resort by the wealth and fashion of the state," Twain observed. There were several summer resorts around St. Paul and Minneapolis, he went on, but White Bear Lake was "*the* resort."[1]

Twain's contemporary Charles Dudley Warner—they were coauthors of *The Gilded Age* (1873)—also singled out St. Paul for praise. St. Paul and Minneapolis were both fast-growing cities inhabited by handsome, vigorous, and active people, he reported in a March 1887 article for *Harper's Magazine,* but his personal preference was for St. Paul because of its picturesque location on the bluffs. Warner was especially impressed by Summit Avenue, another setting that was to play a significant role in Scott Fitzgerald's life. Located high above the city and offering splendid views of the winding river below, Summit was "almost literally a street of palaces," Warner wrote.[2]

---

1. Mark Twain, *Life on the Mississippi* (New York: Harper and Row, 1951), 486–93 passim.
2. Quoted in Henry A. Castle, *History of St. Paul and Vicinity* (Chicago and New York: Lewis Publishing, 1912), 126–28.

It may be that Edward Fitzgerald, who was born in Maryland and descended from some of its oldest colonial families, read these or other encomiums about St. Paul and so decided to move there. At any rate, Edward did come west to join the flood of newcomers that tripled the population between 1880 and 1895. He married St. Paul's Mary (Mollie) McQuillan in 1890. Mollie was the eldest child of Philip Francis (P. F.) and Louisa McQuillan. An immigrant from Ireland, P. F. journeyed upriver to St. Paul from Galena, Illinois, in 1857 and launched a successful wholesale grocery business. When he died twenty years later, at forty-three, he left behind a fortune of more than $250,000.

Only two of the five children Mollie gave birth to survived their early years. She was twenty-nine and Edward thirty-seven at the time of their marriage. They had two little girls in the first few years of marriage, but both of them died in an 1896 epidemic—at the very time that Mollie was pregnant with her only son. Francis Scott Key Fitzgerald, named for a distant relative on his father's side of the family, was born September 24, 1896, and assumed the burdens of the replacement child. Much was expected of him. He was, in effect, to make up for the loss of his dead older sisters.[3] Scott's mother overprotected her baby boy and become "half insane with pathological nervous worry" at the least hint of illness. Even after he was joined by his sister Annabel in 1901, she continued to pamper and spoil her clever and handsome son.

Mollie "just missed being beautiful," her husband once said of her, but that was southern gallantry. In photographs she faces the camera with a forbiddingly dark gaze and looks somewhat dowdy. She seemed to one of Scott's contemporaries to have "worn the same dress all her life." Sometimes her shoes did not match. When she walked by on her way to daily mass, she invariably carried an umbrella and wore a gloomy countenance. Aside from church-related functions, she and her husband had little involvement in the social life of the community. In his first novel Fitzgerald invented a mother for his autobiographical hero, Amory Blaine, who in her elegance and charm stands sharply in opposition to his own mother. But at least he usually provided his fictional characters with mothers. Often, with the notable exceptions of Jimmy Gatz and Dick Diver, they are given no fathers at all.

Along with good looks and good manners, Edward Fitzgerald bequeathed to his son a taste for romantic poetry and lost causes. Born near Rockville, Maryland, in 1855, he glorified the Confederacy in the stories of the Civil War he

3. Jay Martin, "Biography and Humanity," *Humanitas-Communitas: Occasional Papers on Humanities and Public Affairs* 3 (Winter 1999): 53–54.

told his son. Scott, who delighted in these yarns, admired his father's graceful ways. But Edward lacked the drive required to achieve success and, apparently, was an alcoholic. In St. Paul he started a business manufacturing wicker furniture—the American Rattan and Willow Works—but this venture failed in the wake of the panic of 1897. Edward then took a position with Procter and Gamble that moved the family to Buffalo and Syracuse. He lost his job in the spring of 1908. The event traumatized young Scott. "Please don't let us go to the poorhouse," he prayed, but there was no danger of that. Instead the Fitzgeralds limped back to St. Paul to live on the largesse of the McQuillans. His father was given a desk and a title in the family business, but nothing much to do. At fifty-five, Edward Fitzgerald was a defeated man.

Scott Fitzgerald was thus burdened with a father who had twice failed in business and an eccentric mother who—despite her inheritance—did not move comfortably in the social circles she yearned for her children to occupy. In a much-quoted letter written to John O'Hara in 1933, Fitzgerald summed up the situation. "I am half black Irish and half old American stock with the usual exaggerated ancestral pretensions. The black Irish half of the family had the money and looked down upon the Maryland side of the family who had, and really had, that certain series of reticences and obligations that go under the poor old shattered word 'breeding.'" As a result, he "developed a two-cylinder inferiority complex." If he became king of Scotland tomorrow, Fitzgerald insisted, he "would still be a parvenu."[4]

In *F. Scott Fitzgerald and the Art of Social Fiction*, Brian Way aptly links Fitzgerald with such predecessors as Henry James and Edith Wharton as keenly observant "historians of manners" who wrote "social fiction."[5] In his writing, as in his life, Fitzgerald repeatedly confronted the gulf between the middle-class boy and the upper-class girl he falls in love with. That social class matters is a dirty little secret most Americans are inclined to deny. Motivated by democratic sentiments and the myth that in this nation more than anywhere else on earth it is not only possible but very nearly obligatory to make one's way from rags to riches—hence realizing the American dream—we confidently tell each other that there are no significant barriers between the classes. Fitzgerald knew better, for unlike Wharton and James and some of the English novelists who created the novel of

4. Scott Donaldson, *Fool for Love: F. Scott Fitzgerald* (New York: Congdon & Weed, 1983), 2–5 passim.
5. Way, *F. Scott Fitzgerald and the Art of Social Fiction* (New York: St. Martin's, 1980), vii–viii.

manners, he had looked around him, seen the social barriers, and tried to sur-
mount them.

Some revisionist interpreters of Fitzgerald's life and work maintain—as
Lloyd C. Hackl puts it—that "the McQuillan family and their grandson [Scott]
Fitzgerald were very much insiders, a part of St. Paul society." By way of evidence
they cite the McQuillans' generous contributions to the Catholic church and the
fact that Mollie's younger sister was maid of honor at the wedding of railroad
tycoon James J. Hill's daughter. In 1873 P. F. McQuillan was one of a group who
brought the Sisters of the Visitation from St. Louis to St. Paul. Mollie and her sisters attended the school these nuns founded, and so did Scott's sister, Annabel.
Later Mollie showed off Scott at the Convent of the Visitation, bringing him
along to recite poetry or sing songs for the nuns. So extensive was the family's
support that when Scott and Zelda went to Europe in the spring of 1921, Archbishop Dowling of St. Paul tried to arrange an audience with the pope. "None
have merited more of the Church in this city" than the McQuillans, he wrote.[6]
This evidence seems impressive but depends entirely on the presumed promi-
nence of the McQuillans among the city's lace-curtain Irish families. Scott himself was hardly impressed. As he put it, his mother's family was "straight 1850
potato famine Irish," and hence at a significant remove from the top of St. Paul's
social hierarchy. Few Irish Catholics were among Scott's boyhood companions.
Some of his friends, in fact, seemed to believe that Catholics were secretly plot-
ting to overthrow the government. During their boyhood years Fitzgerald and
his companions who lived atop the bluffs fought mock battles with the "micks"
from Lower Town—the descendants of the Irish immigrants.

In *The Far Side of Paradise* (1951), the first biography of Fitzgerald, Arthur
Mizener discourses upon the makeup of St. Paul in the early years of the twentieth century. The city at that time had both "a great deal of the simple and quite
unselfconscious democracy of the old middle-western cities" *and* "its wealth and
its inherited New England sense of order. The best people in St. Paul are admirable and attractive people, but they are, in their quiet way, clearly the best
people. They do not forget their Maine or Connecticut 'connection': they send
their children to Hotchkiss or Hill or Westover, to Yale or Princeton, to be educated; they are, without ostentation or affectation, cosmopolitan." Mizener's comments may grate against our latter-day sensibilities; the remark about "the best

6. Hackl, *"Still Home to Me": F. Scott Fitzgerald and St. Paul, Minnesota* (Cambridge,
Minn.: Adventure Publications, 1996), 14–15, 62–63.

people," in particular, sounds offensively snobbish. But that does not mean that he was wrong about St. Paul. In several observations of his own, Fitzgerald describes in detail that "sense of order" Mizener observes.[7]

St. Paul felt "a little superior" to such other midwestern cities as Minneapolis, Kansas City, and Milwaukee, Fitzgerald wrote in reviewing Grace Flandrau's novel *Being Respectable* (1923). The other cities were but two generations old, while St. Paul was a "three generation" town. St. Paul was hence considered more settled, more conservative, more "complacent" (Flandrau's word) than the brash and bustling younger cities. It also was significantly more eastern in its outlook. In the 1850s, Fitzgerald points out, the climate of St. Paul was reputed to be exceptionally healthy, and consequently "there arrived an element from the East who had both money and fashionable education. These Easterners mingled with the rising German and Irish stock, whose second generation left the cobbler's last, forgot the steerage, and became passionately 'swell' on its own account. But the pace was set by the tubercular Easterners."[8]

Five years later Fitzgerald elaborated on the social structure established by these settlers. "There were the two or three nationally known families—outside of them rather than below them the hierarchy began. At the top came those whose grandparents had brought something with them from the East, a vestige of money and culture; then came the families of the big self-made merchants, the 'old settlers' of the sixties and seventies, American-English-Scotch, or German or Irish, looking down upon each other somewhat in the order named.... After this came certain well-to-do 'new people'—mysterious, out of a cloudy past, possibly unsound." "Like so many structures," Fitzgerald concludes, "this one did not survive the cataract of money that came tumbling down upon it with the war." But it was the hierarchy in place during his prep school and college years when he sought to climb his way up the city's ladder. Fitzgerald understood precisely where he belonged—on his mother's side, among the respectable Irish "old settlers" who were generally looked down upon both by the cultured easterners and by the Scotch-English and the Germans, and, on his father's side, at best among the "possibly unsound" newcomers.[9]

The Fitzgeralds' position in St. Paul's social hierarchy was nicely symbolized by their places of residence. Scott was born in an apartment at the San Mateo

7. Mizener, *The Far Side of Paradise: A Biography of F. Scott Fitzgerald* (New York: Random House, 1959), 16.

8. *F. Scott Fitzgerald in His Own Time: A Miscellany*, ed. Matthew J. Bruccoli and Jackson R. Bryer (Kent: Kent State University Press, 1971), 141.

9. Mizener, *Far Side of Paradise*, 16; Donaldson, *Fool for Love*, 10–11.

Flats, 481 Laurel Avenue, a short walk from Summit Avenue. The next year, his grandmother Louisa McQuillan built a substantial (if not particularly imposing) home on Summit, but she sold it two years later. When the Fitzgeralds returned to the city from Buffalo in 1908, Scott and his sister Annabel moved in with their grandmother at 294 Laurel. During the succeeding decade, the family occupied at least five different domiciles, the first three of them on Holly Avenue, like Laurel close to "the Summit Avenue area," or "the Summit Avenue section" or "the Summit Avenue neighborhood," as biographers have termed it. But not *on* Summit. In one sense, as St. Paul historian John J. Koblas observes, these various homes—all of them within a twelve-square-block area near Summit—offered young Scott "the relative stability of residing within a single definable community and having a secure circle of friends." But at the same time the boy could not help being conscious of his family's precarious position as renters rather than owners of homes, living on the fringes of St. Paul's best street: a circumstance that differentiated him from that circle of friends who grew up—like Nick Carraway in *The Great Gatsby*—in a community "where dwellings are still called through decades by a family's name."[10]

According to one architectural historian, "St. Paul's Summit Avenue stands as the best-preserved American example of the Victorian monumental residential boulevard." Blight and economic downturns have diminished its luster, but even today Summit remains the city's "high street"—characteristically a street rising above the rest of the community, both in physical location and in social stature.[11] Electric trolleys and a tunnel made the elevated setting available for building in the 1880s, when the empire builder James J. Hill (greatly admired by Jay Gatsby's father and by Rudolph Miller's father in the story "Absolution") built his huge mansion near the eastern end of the avenue. Other leading families followed suit.[12] By the time Fitzgerald was born, Summit Avenue ruled.

A character in *Being Respectable* takes a Sunday afternoon walk along the most fashionable stretch of Summit, strolling unhurriedly up one side "past the opulent houses he knew so well" and down the other side "past more opulent houses he knew equally well." Between the houses on the south side "sudden dreamy prospects" of the gray, winding river came into his view, "composed" by the walls of the houses and the trees. In the little park at Summit and Western, he sat and

10. Matthew J. Bruccoli, *Some Sort of Epic Grandeur: The Life of F. Scott Fitzgerald* (New York: Harcourt Brace Jovanovich, 1981), 23–24; John J. Koblas, *F. Scott Fitzgerald in Minnesota: His Homes and Haunts* (St. Paul: Minnesota Historical Society Press, 1978), 10–11.

11. Donaldson, *Fool for Love*, 12–13.

12. Hackl, *"Still Home to Me,"* 50–51.

looked for a long time at the river and the green pastures and groves of trees beyond. Then it grew dark and the lights came out: "sparkling yellow stars in the
gray," moving lights on the river, and the bridges like "necklaces, glittering ten-
derly." So did the novelist Flandrau, Fitzgerald's friend, also a native of St. Paul,
celebrate her city's most elegant street.[13] There is no closely comparable passage
in Fitzgerald's writing, although, in "Winter Dreams," his character Dexter Green
does wax rhapsodic as he drives Judy Jones home one summer night. The street,
given no name, is undoubtedly Summit Avenue. "The dark street lightened, the
dwellings of the rich loomed up around them, he stopped his coupé in front of
the great white bulk of the Mortimer Joneses house, somnolent, gorgeous,
drenched with the splendor of the damp moonlight. Its solidity startled him."[14]

The mansion's solidity, Dexter explains, stands in striking contrast to Judy's
young beauty, its sturdiness accentuating her slightness and, perhaps, the fragility
of the dream he has invested in her. The Jones house, like Nick Carraway's, was
one that would be known through the generations by the family name, a dwelling
as assuredly permanent as Fitzgerald's own domiciles were shakily temporary.
Edward and Mollie Fitzgerald did finally achieve an address on Summit Avenue,
moving into a brownstone-front row house at 593 Summit in 1915, when Scott
was at Princeton, and then to 599 Summit in 1918, the house where Scott rewrote
This Side of Paradise. It has been officially designated a National Historical Land-
mark. As landmarks go, this one has singularly little to do with the famous figure
associated with it. He lived at 599 Summit less than a year. It was a rented house—
neither Scott nor his father ever owned a home of his own—and, worse, a mere
row house rather than one of the sprawling free-standing houses that dominate
the avenue, and, worse yet, located at the wrong end of Summit. When he wrote
Alida Bigelow the news that Scribner's had accepted his novel for publication, he
headed the letter

<blockquote>
(599 Summit Avenue)
In a house below the average
Of a street above the average
In a room below the roof.[15]
</blockquote>

That there was never to be a Fitzgerald house in St. Paul set Scott and Annabel
apart from their companions. So did his family's lack of a summer place at White

13. Flandrau, *Being Respectable* (New York: Harcourt Brace, 1923), 18–19.
14. *The Short Stories of F. Scott Fitzgerald*, ed. Matthew J. Bruccoli (New York: Scribner's,
1989), 232.
15. Donaldson, *Fool for Love*, 13; Mizener, *Far Side of Paradise*, 16.

Bear Lake. By the 1880s St. Paul's wealthiest citizens were building summer cottages at the lake, and in his youth Scott rode the electric streetcar out to spend evenings or weekends in those cottages, but it was hardly the same as going to a place of one's own at White Bear, or—once there—sailing in a boat of one's own.[16] Sensitive as he was to social gradations, Fitzgerald knew he faced considerable handicaps when he came back from Buffalo and tried to establish himself as a boy who *belonged.*

Mollie Fitzgerald did what she could to advance her son's campaign to conquer St. Paul. "Her great hope was her son, whom she loved extravagantly as a woman will when her husband has in some way disappointed her," as Andrew Turnbull observes.[17] She could not eradicate her husband's failure, but she could and did use the McQuillan resources to enroll Scott in St. Paul Academy, the community's leading private preparatory school, and to send him to Professor Baker's dancing school with the children of the city's most prominent families. The three years Scott spent in St. Paul, beginning in the summer of 1908 after his father's dismissal by Procter and Gamble and ending with his departure for Newman school in the fall of 1911, constituted by far the longest period he was to live in the city of his birth. They were also supremely important years in shaping the way he looked at the world around him.

II

Scott was a precocious lad in many ways. He was extremely good-looking after the model of his father. He had a quick and retentive mind. He liked participating in neighborhood games and took a leading role in organizing them. He learned how to attract girls and took an uncommon interest in how he stood vis-à-vis other boys in their affections. His mother cosseted him, dressed him up, and showed him off but rarely imposed any discipline. Hence she encouraged what he called "my first childish love of myself," an egoism that led him to repudiate his unsatisfactory parents and imagine himself a foundling, the son of "a king who ruled the whole world."[18] He had rejected this fantastic notion by the time he came back to St. Paul in 1908 but continued to regret the progenitors fate had saddled him with. "My father is a moron and my mother is a neurotic," he wrote his editor, Maxwell Perkins, in 1926. "Between them they havn't . . . the

16. Carol Irish, "The Myth of Success in Fitzgerald's Boyhood," *Studies in American Fiction* 1 (1973): 180.

17. Turnbull, *Scott Fitzgerald* (New York: Scribner's, 1962), 27.

18. Ibid., 28.

brains of Calvin Coolidge."[19] Ashamed of his heritage, he was throughout his life particularly sensitive to social slights. Such snubs rankled the more because he felt, himself, that after all they were probably deserved.

At St. Paul Academy (S.P.A.), where the city's elite sent their sons to be prepared for college, it is safe to say that Scott Fitzgerald was the only boy whose father had twice failed in business and had no occupation. And probably the only boy without a substantial family home. And one of the very few Irish Catholics. Saddled with these social handicaps, he made matters worse by letting his ego run unchecked: bragging, showing off in class, posing too many questions about money and class to his bewildered and annoyed school companions. *Now and Then,* the school newspaper, offers conclusive testimony that he struck his fellow students as insufferably cocky. By and large the paper described events at the school, and participants in them, in highly favorable terms. The watchword was much the same as that at S.P.A.'s rival school in Minneapolis: Boost, Don't Knock. Nonetheless, *Now and Then* printed several gibes directed at Fitzgerald during his first year at S.P.A. "Young Scotty is always bubbling over with suppressed knowledge" was the initial barb, followed by the accusation that he was the author of a book called *How to Run the School.* The severest criticism of all came in Sam Kennedy's "Personals" item for the Easter 1909 issue: "If anybody can poison Scotty to stop his mouth in some way, the school at large and myself will be obliged."[20] Fitzgerald at twelve obviously talked too much and knew (or pretended to know) too much to satisfy his schoolmates. He wanted desperately to be popular but managed to alienate those he most desired to please. The root of the problem was the overweening sense of self-importance his mother had instilled in him. As he was to write his daughter when she was about to enter prep school, "I didn't know till 15 that there was anyone in the world except me."[21]

The principal road to success at St. Paul Academy led through athletics, especially football. When the school was founded in 1900, the coprincipal C. N. B. Wheeler—himself a college athlete at Harvard—established the tradition (bor-

19. *Dear Scott/Dear Max: The Fitzgerald-Perkins Correspondence,* ed. John Kuehl and Jackson R. Bryer (New York: Scribner's, 1971), 134–35.

20. For quotations from *Now and Then* and for succeeding information about Fitzgerald's boyhood educational experiences—including letters from Clifton Read and Alida Bigelow Butler, and an audiotape of the NBC Radio Biography in Sound—I am indebted to the staff at the library of St. Paul Academy, which maintains a Fitzgerald archive, and to Caroline Lazo, who let me know about their holdings.

21. *The Letters of F. Scott Fitzgerald,* ed. Andrew Turnbull (New York: Scribner's, 1963), 5.

rowed from Groton) that every boy, whatever his size or age, was required to play football. Fitzgerald tried gamely to make himself into a football player but was ill equipped to excel at the sport. Although quite fast, he was rather slight and not particularly well-coordinated. Scott did not earn good grades at S.P.A., either, for he lacked disciplined study habits. In class, his mind was often occupied with stories rather than with his daily lessons. In the back of notebooks he scrawled plot summaries and tried out characters' names. Wheeler, who taught English and history, recognized his inventive bent and encouraged him to write these juvenile adventures. *Now and Then* printed four of Fitzgerald's apprentice stories, and it was through them that he distinguished himself at St. Paul Academy. One of the stories celebrated the triumph of "Reade, Substitute Right Half," the improbable tale of "a light-haired stripling" who comes off the bench to make a saving tackle and intercept a pass for the winning touchdown. At which point the crowd cheers "Reade! Reade! Reade!"—the final words of the story. For young Fitzgerald, eager to prove his worth, victory did not count so much as recognition.

This football story was the second that Scott published in the school newspaper. The first was called "The Mystery of the Raymond Mortgage" despite the fact that the thirteen-year-old author neglected to mention the mortgage in his story. When it appeared in the September 1909 *Now and Then*, the fledgling author read his story "at least six times" and hung around the school corridors to ask other boys, as casually as he could, if they chanced to have read it.

Fitzgerald's other two stories in *Now and Then* both dealt with the Civil War. In "A Debt of Honor" a Confederate soldier falls asleep on guard duty, is pardoned by Gen. Robert E. Lee, and redeems himself by his bravery—which costs him his life—at Chancellorsville. In "The Room with the Green Blinds" Fitzgerald rewrote history by imagining that John Wilkes Booth escapes after assassinating Lincoln. Booth is eventually captured and killed in this revisionary account.[22] Murdering the president may have been going too far, but Scott was enough the son of his father to inherit his southern sympathies. During his first public debate at S.P.A., he and two other lads upheld the negative on "Resolved: that the South was not justified in seceding," and their team was awarded the decision. (And one of his high school plays, as we shall see, adopted a favorable view of the Confederacy.)

22. Fitzgerald's juvenile stories are available in *The Apprentice Fiction of F. Scott Fitzgerald, 1909–1917*, ed. John Kuehl (New Brunswick: Rutgers University Press, 1965).

Fitzgerald's boyhood stories established that he was different, but they did not make him popular with his schoolmates. What popularity he achieved during his formative years in St. Paul came through the games and clubs he organized among the neighborhood children and through his youthful encounters with girls. Scott was forever forming secret clubs among youngsters in the neighborhood. He was secretary of the White Handkerchief Club, chief scout of the Boys' Secret Service of St. Paul, and founder and president of the Cruelty to Animals Society, the Gooserah Club, and the Scandal Detectives. Among the boys who joined these clubs were Cecil Read, Paul Ballion, Bob Clark, and Mac Seymour, all of whom attended Central High School, not S.P.A. Fitzgerald recalled the initiation rites for one of these short-lived organizations. "Paul and I subjected [Cecil] to ... eat[ing] raw eggs and ... operat[ed] on him with saw, cold ice, and needle." Read, one of Scott's closest friends (note the similarity of his name to the fictional halfback Reade), later looked back on these shenanigans without animosity. Scott was "a great leader and organizer," he reported for an NBC Biography in Sound about Fitzgerald. During the summers he often invited Scott to visit him at his family's place on White Bear Lake. His mother would put half a dozen cots on the sleeping porch, where Scott, Cecil, and other boys lay awake and talked about their future plans. On one of those nights, Read recalled, Fitzgerald told him that (1) he wanted to go to Princeton, (2) he wanted to join University Cottage Club, and (3) he wanted to write a play for the Triangle Club. He also revealed that he hoped to write a great Catholic novel. Fitzgerald accomplished all three of his college goals, but the novel went unwritten.

A fine reminiscence of Fitzgerald during this period comes in a letter that his lifelong friend Alida Bigelow Butler wrote in 1970 responding to an inquiry from students at St. Paul Academy. Soon after his return to St. Paul in 1908, Scott— "quite short, blond, sharp nose, eager darting blue eyes," as she remembered him—developed a crush on Alida. In good weather he would come over in his knickerbockers to sit on her porch and talk. "Scott must have asked questions because that was his habit. He wanted people's reactions in those days, reactions about other people. There was a 'character' book phase.... Scott engineered the project, which was for each one of us—boys and girls—to make headings in the notebook: favorite girl and boy (choices 1, 2, 3), favorite sport, book, game, blond or brunette [preference]. Then more personal: what boy would I like to kiss, etc.? ... When we had once written in the notebook and had by any method tried to read the other persons' notebooks, the fun died down. The fun was in the organization of the project, not the project itself." And Scott was invariably the organizer.

When they were twelve and thirteen, Alida and Scott and the other children in the neighborhood went to dancing school together. On Saturday afternoons, approximately twenty boys and twenty girls walked down Grand Avenue to Ramaley hall, the girls carrying their slippers and the boys their patent leather shoes. "Professor" William H. Baker, a sometime bartender at White Bear Yacht Club, conducted the dancing lessons. An apple-shaped man with a bald head, Baker was impeccably dressed in tails and white kid gloves as he guided his young charges through the waltz and two-step. Until the music began, the girls sat on one side of the room and the boys on the other. The orchestra consisted of "a tinkling piano, played by a not very young lady."

At dancing school, Alida observed, Scott demonstrated little sense of rhythm, no particular feeling for music, and not much grace of movement. In her recollection he was awkward physically and knew it. Invited to summer outings at the Bigelow home on Manitou Island (in White Bear Lake), he participated in such childhood games as beckons wanted but was regularly beaten in high-jump contests by Eleanor Alair and didn't even try to play tennis. Unathletic though he may have been, however, "all the girls wanted to dance with Scott because he was Scott the instigator, the ringleader, the boy who asked questions, the boy who was handsome."

As was to be the case throughout his life, Fitzgerald was far more successful in attracting females than in making friends with males. "When he had been in St. Paul only a month, five girls confessed that he was their favorite boy," Turnbull wrote in his biography. His favorite girl that summer was Violet Stockton, a visitor from Atlanta. In his "Thoughtbook," fourteen pages of notebook paper he kept locked beneath his bed, he described the girls he had crushes on and— most important—how he ranked in their affections. Violet, for example, was a year older than Scott, "very pretty with dark brown hair and eyes big and soft" and a soft southern accent he found entrancing. The "Thoughtbook" describes in some detail their juvenile lovers' quarrel and the conversation in which they ironed out the misunderstanding and made up. As a piece of dialogue, very much to the life, it surpasses anything in Fitzgerald's S.P.A. stories.

> "Violet," I began, "Did you call me a brat?"
> "No."
> "Did you say that you wanted your ring and your pictures and your hair back?"
> "No."
> "Did you say you hated me?"
> "Of course not, is that what you went home for?"

"No, but Archie Mudge told me those things yesterday evening."
"He's a little scamp," said Violet indignantly.[23]

The reference to wanting "your hair back" probably refers to Scott's habit of collecting samples of girls' hair, which he wound carefully around toothpicks and pinned for safekeeping. At Alida Bigelow's he would produce his collection of hair swatches and ask those assembled to identify what girl each had come from.

In the pages of his "Thoughtbook," Fitzgerald was beginning to be a writer, someone caught up in the emotions awakened by his experiences yet capable of describing them in objective detail. The repeated references to his ranking with girls—was he first, or second, or third, in the affections of the girl of the moment?—demonstrate his obsessive concern with gradations in status. At the same time, each particular girl was becoming more than a name on a list. "For the first time in his life," like his fictional counterpart Basil Duke Lee, he was learning to realize "a girl as something opposite and complementary to him, and he was subject to a warm chill of mingled pleasure and pain."[24]

"It is not necessary to send a boy away to school in order to have him properly prepared for college," proclaimed an S.P.A. advertisement in the 1910 Twin City Bluebook. "Our graduates are just as well prepared as those of any school in the country." In the ten years since the school was founded, the ad pointed out, the school had placed "sixty boys at Yale, Harvard, Princeton, University of Minnesota and other colleges." Despite such assurances many boys transferred to eastern prep schools during this period. The lower forms at S.P.A. customarily enrolled about sixteen boys at this time, but the graduating classes averaged only five or six.[25] Fitzgerald joined the eastward-bound students in the fall of 1911 when his parents, with financial aid from his devout aunt, Annabel McQuillan, decided to send him to Newman, a Catholic school in Hackensack, New Jersey, for his junior and senior years

Pleased to start fresh at an eastern prep school, Fitzgerald unfortunately repeated the mistakes he'd made at St. Paul Academy, with the difference that without a second social universe of home and neighborhood to escape to, his unpopularity mattered more. "All one can know," he once observed, "is that somewhere between thirteen, boyhood's majority, and seventeen, when one is a sort of counterfeit young man, there is a time when youth fluctuates hourly between

23. Turnbull, *Scott Fitzgerald*, 19–20.
24. Ibid., 30.
25. Fitzgerald Archive, St. Paul Academy.

one world and another—pushed ceaselessly forward into unprecedented experiences and vainly trying to struggle back to the days when nothing had to be paid for."[26] At Newman he paid.

Evaluating himself at fifteen with remarkable candor, Fitzgerald admitted to a dominating philosophy of "aristocratic egotism." He thought himself "a fortunate youth" capable because of his "facility and superior mentality" of doing a great deal of good or evil. *Physically,* he marked himself "handsome, of great athletic *possibilities,* and an extremely good dancer." *Socially,* he was convinced that he had "charm, magnetism, poise," so that he could dominate others and exert "a subtle fascination over women." *Mentally,* he was vain of his quick mind and ingenuity. On the other hand he thought himself "worse than most boys" *morally* because of a "latent unscrupulousness and the desire to influence people in some way, even for evil." In addition he was selfish, lacked a sense of honor, and could be cold to others. *Psychologically,* he had "a curious cross section of weakness" in his character and could easily be thrown off his "poise into a timid stupidity." He knew he was "fresh" and not popular with older boys. *Generally,* and worst of all, he "lacked the essentials" and "had no real courage, perseverance or self-respect."

In this account a solipsistic Fitzgerald takes as much delight in his faults as in his virtues. "There seemed to have been a conspiracy to spoil me and all my inordinate vanity was absorbed from that," he wrote. That self-love could "be toppled over at one blow by an unpleasant remark or a missed tackle," and yet "underneath the whole thing lay a sense of infinite possibilities that was always with me whether vanity or shame was my mood."[27]

Thinking so much of and about himself, Fitzgerald was a prime candidate to fail in the adolescent competition for acceptance at his boarding school. Once again he showed off his "rather extraordinary fund of general information in class" and pointed out others' mistakes. On the football field he immediately annoyed his companions by telling them what to do. To make things right he offered a boastful untruth: "Excuse me for bossing everyone around, but I'm used to being captain of the teams in St. Paul." Football counted for a great deal at Newman, and, during the game against Newark Academy, Scott disgraced himself by avoiding a head-on tackle. "Do that again," the quarterback Charles (Sap) Donahoe warned, "and I'll beat you up myself." He tackled bravely thereafter, Fitzgerald claimed as he told this story, because he was more frightened of

26. Quoted in Mizener, *Far Side of Paradise,* 27.
27. Quoted in Turnbull, *Scott Fitzgerald,* 34–35.

Donahoe than of any opposing ballcarrier. And, surely, though he did not say so, because he wanted desperately to please Donahoe. In due course Donahoe became his good friend, but during his first year at Newman he made no real friends at all.[28]

The only bright moments of that desolate year came when he was allowed off campus to see Broadway shows. "When I was fifteen," he later recalled, "I went into the city from school to see Ina Claire in *The Quaker Girl* and Gertrude Bryan in *Little Boy Blue*." Together they blended into "one lovely entity, the girl."[29] Then during Christmas vacation he saw a production of *Alias Jimmy Valentine*, which, together with his reading of Arsene Lupin stories, prompted him to write a play called *The Captured Shadow*. It was performed in St. Paul in August 1912 by the Elizabethan Dramatic Club, a group of young people recruited by Fitzgerald and directed by Elizabeth Magoffin (hence the "Elizabethan" club). An audience of more than two hundred turned out for the play, which raised $60 for the Baby Welfare Association and generated favorable notices in the local newspapers. "Much comment was elicited by the young author's cleverness," a reviewer noted. "ENTER SUCCESS!" Scott wrote in his scrapbook next to the clippings. At last, he was beginning to receive the kind of recognition he yearned for.

From early boyhood on Fitzgerald demonstrated a theatrical bent. When he was ten, he was making up shows about the American Revolution, in which he wore a red sash in the role of Paul Revere. In Buffalo he and his friend Hamilton Wende regularly took in Saturday stage matinees. Afterward they would reenact scenes, in which Fitzgerald showed a remarkable capacity to repeat long sections of dialogue. Back in St. Paul, he often went to the vaudeville shows at the Orpheum theater, again rushing home to reenact what he had seen. He organized and put on plays at the homes of his companions—in Teddy Ames's living room, Alida Bigelow's basement, Cecil Read's attic. At thirteen he perfected a routine to entertain and/or shock streetcar passengers, in which he reeled around, pretending to be drunk. "I imagined he would become an actor of the variety type," his S.P.A. teacher Wheeler said of him years later.

Actually, Fitzgerald's initial exposure to the Elizabethan Dramatic Club came in August 1911—*before* he left for Newman. He wrote and played the leading role in a brief one-acter called *The Girl from Lazy J*, which was performed at the Magoffin home during the club's organizational meeting in August 1911. The plot involves a wicked Mexican cowpuncher, a masked heroine who is his undoing,

28. Ibid., 35; Mizener, *Far Side of Paradise*, 28–29.
29. Bruccoli, *Some Sort of Epic Grandeur*, 33.

and an excessively proper hero. The dialogue is stilted and the characters beyond credibility, as one might expect of a fourteen-year-old playwright. It is interesting, however, that this improbable play demonstrates an awareness of the way that social class has its impact on true love—a theme that was to be pervasive in Fitzgerald's mature fiction.

The Captured Shadow involves a gentleman burglar (one of Fitzgerald's youthful preoccupations) who is so much the gentleman that he returns everything he steals. The drama borrows heavily from its sources and tries for humor throughout, introducing a well-bred alcoholic who falls out of chairs and a number of gags lifted directly from joke books. One of the characters laments that she has lost two watches in ten years. "Yes, it's terrible the way time flies." Yet *The Captured Shadow* is far more carefully plotted and five times as long as *The Girl from Lazy J.* "For all its grotesqueries," Fitzgerald was to say of it, "the result was actually interesting—it was a play."

During his senior year (1912–1913) Scott improved as a football player, wrote three separate stories for the *Newman News,* and became less desperately unpopular than he had been the previous year. But he achieved his greatest public success during the summer, with another play for the Elizabethan Dramatic Club. *Coward,* a Civil War melodrama, is built around the slowly awakening resolve of a young southerner to join the Confederate Army in order to protect his home and loved ones. *Coward* outdrew *The Captured Shadow* and made more money for charity. It was presented first at the St. Paul YWCA and then, on demand for an encore, at White Bear Yacht Club. Fitzgerald not only wrote and acted in the play but also served as stage manager. "THE GREAT EVENT," he noted in his scrapbook. The following summer brought another great event with his play called *Assorted Spirits,* a farcical exploration of the ghost world that was his last production for the Elizabethan Club. "Scott Fitzgerald, the 17-year-old playwright . . . turned out a roaring farce and is clever throughout," one reviewer commented.[30]

During 1911–1914, while away at Newman and Princeton, Fitzgerald continued to write stories, poems, and short humorous pieces. But it was the plays he wrote and acted in and stage-managed during the summers in St. Paul that brought him the kind of attention and applause he was never able to earn at St. Paul Academy. For his career the theater proved to be a false start. After his prep school and college days, Fitzgerald went back to fiction almost entirely. When

---

30. The account of Fitzgerald's early interest in the theater and the references to the plays he wrote are drawn from *F. Scott Fitzgerald's St. Paul Plays, 1911–1914,* ed. Alan Margolies (Princeton: Princeton University Library, 1978). See especially Margolies's introduction, 3–10.

he next came back to St. Paul for an extended stay, it was to rewrite *This Side of Paradise.*

Like his father before him, Scott returned home in the summer of 1919 an apparently defeated man, with the difference that at twenty-two Fitzgerald had plenty of time to recover. His prospects for success did not seem promising. Because of ill health and/or poor grades, he had not been graduated from Princeton with the class of 1917. In the army he completed a draft of his first novel and, when stationed near Montgomery, Alabama, met the beautiful and reckless Zelda Sayre—the girl he was to marry. But he did not distinguish himself as a soldier and never got overseas to see action. Fitzgerald's novel was turned down by Scribner's, although Perkins encouraged him to make some changes and try again. After the war he secured a job as an advertising copywriter in New York, work that he neither liked nor devoted himself to wholeheartedly. His heart remained in Alabama, where Zelda was taking her time making up her mind. In June 1919 she broke off their engagement; Scott simply did not qualify as good husband material. Then he went on a bender in New York, quit his job, and took the train to St. Paul in order to reshape his novel. If he had a publishing contract, he felt sure, Zelda and her parents would be ready to accept him.

He worked hard over the summer of 1919, writing in an attic room at 599 Summit every day and of an evening drinking Cokes and smoking cigarettes with Father Joe Barron, the writer Donald Ogden Stewart, and his boyhood companion Richard (Tubby) Washington. In September he shipped his manuscript off to Scribner's and waited. Then the postman rang with Maxwell Perkins's special-delivery letter of acceptance, and Fitzgerald was ecstatic. "He ran up and down Summit Avenue stopping cars and telling all his friends and a good many mere acquaintances" that *This Side of Paradise* had been accepted for publication. Fitzgerald "was in a sort of trance all day," as he wrote to Perkins.[31]

Scott and Zelda were married in New York in the same week that *This Side of Paradise* was published. The book made an immediate success, attracting readers with its depiction of a young hero in revolt against the received values of the time. The Fitzgeralds stayed in the East and became somewhat scandalous public figures for their partying and outrageous behavior. They returned to St. Paul in August 1921, seeking a setting where Zelda could have her child and Scott could write free of their hectic social life in New York. Neither childbirth nor geography changed their ways, however. During the fourteen months Scott and

31. Mizener, *Far Side of Paradise*, 95.

Zelda spent in St. Paul, from August 1921 to October 1922, they succeeded in scandalizing the community. As a boy Fitzgerald had been eager to impress St. Paul with his considerable talent. In young manhood, with his career as a writer well underway, he (and Zelda) seemed determined to shock his hometown instead. It was as if he was thumbing his nose at a place that was loath to accept him as among its elite.

The Fitzgeralds were twice evicted from dwellings during their brief sojourn in St. Paul. On arrival they rented a cottage in Dellwood, the most exclusive section around White Bear Lake. Unlike most of the neighboring homes, the cottage was equipped for winter use, and Scott and Zelda signed a lease for a year's stay. Less than two months later, they were asked to leave. The Fitzgeralds organized a number of all-night parties in their rented home. During one of them the furnace went out, and Fitzgerald—not noticing—let the water pipes freeze and burst. So, in early October, Scott and Zelda packed up and moved to the Hotel Commodore, an apartment hotel. They were living there when, on October 26, their daughter Scottie was born.

Their friend Xandra Kalman next found the young family an in-town residence at 626 Goodrich Avenue. "New Address/Permanent!" Scott scribbled to Max Perkins. The house provided the Fitzgeralds with their most comfortable and sensible living arrangement in St. Paul. Scott rented a small office downtown where he revised the page proofs of his second novel, *The Beautiful and Damned* (1922), and wrote his story "The Popular Girl." But neither Scott nor Zelda was prepared to settle down to a conventional domestic life or to give up partying. They continued to offend the proprieties, and almost always drinking was involved.[32]

On December 1, Fitzgerald gave a talk at the Women's City Club of St. Paul. His friend Tom Boyd wrote an account of that talk for the *St. Paul Daily News* that may not be accurate but probably captured the spirit(s) of the occasion. "Just before my first novel came out," Boyd reported Fitzgerald as saying, "Mr. Perkins . . . told me that he thought it would be a very nice thing if I spoke. . . . It was quite a remarkable speech. Several children were carried out screaming." In other remarks, Fitzgerald denied that he knew anything about flappers. "The flapper is interested in shocking people. None of my heroines ever cared enough about people to know whether they were shocking them or not." He provided a few items of information about himself. "I am 25. Married, white, and I have never been in jail—voluntarily. I have no political opinions. I don't know how

32. Koblas, *Fitzgerald in Minnesota*, 35–41.

to play the piano and I can't hammer brass." The tone throughout Fitzgerald's talk, it seems safe to speculate, ran counter to that of most speeches delivered at the Women's City Club.[33]

Scott and Zelda combined talents to compose a mock front page of the "St. Paul Daily Dirge" for the "Bad Luck Ball" held at the University Club on Friday the thirteenth of January. "Cotillion Is Sad Failure" read the headline, followed by the subhead "Frightful Orgy at University Club." In this parody of society reporting, the town's leading lights are castigated, by their real names, for supposed misbehavior. Two of them, for example, are described as engaging in a "sordid fist fight" at the ball, exactly the sort of thing that might be expected of St. Paul's "vain frivolous peacocks."[34] Scott and Zelda obviously delighted in making fun of the socially prominent, adopting the attitude of observers rather than insiders.

By June 1922, Zelda had grown restless at their Goodrich Avenue home, and the Fitzgeralds moved to the White Bear Yacht Club for sunshine, relaxation, and a change of pace. Summer parties naturally gravitated to the club, and the Fitzgeralds joined in the merriment. They were alike in believing that "if you were good enough you not only could live according to the hedonistic code of the twenties but would probably turn out better for doing so," as Mizener observes.[35] The club disagreed, and for the second time in a year the Fitzgeralds were asked to leave their place of residence. At the end of August they went back to the Commodore. In the middle of October they headed east again, to rent a house in Great Neck, Long Island. Fitzgerald never lived in St. Paul again, but as a setting it was to figure prominently in his fiction.

III

In "The Ice Palace" (1920), a story written before he and Zelda were married, Scott Fitzgerald drew sharp lines of demarcation between the climate, the culture, and the people of Montgomery, Alabama, and those of St. Paul, Minnesota, communities disguised as "Tarleton, Georgia" and a "Northern city" in the story. "The Ice Palace" had its origin in two separate incidents of late 1919. In November he was in St. Paul, coming home from a motion-picture show, when "a scattering of confetti-like snow blew along the street" and he thought of the long and bleak winters he had spent there. A few weeks later he was visiting Zelda in Mont-

33. H. Alan Wycherly, "F. the Lecturer," *Fitzgerald Notes* 24 (Winter 1964): 1–3.
34. Mizener, *Far Side of Paradise,* 149.
35. Ibid., 163.

gomery where everything seemed warm and comfortable. She took him to a graveyard and told him he would never understand how she felt about the Confederate graves. He responded that he understood so well that he could put it down on paper. The next day, riding the train north, it came to him "that it was all one story."[36] He wrote the graveyard into "The Ice Palace," and the snow as well.

The story opens on a languid September day in Tarleton, with Sally Carrol Happer resting "her nineteen-year-old chin [exactly Zelda's age] on a fifty-two-year-old" windowsill. Sally Carrol raises herself upright "with profound inertia" in order to go swimming with her friend Clark Darrow, who has been "dozing around the lazy streets" of his hometown since graduating from Georgia Tech. On their drive to the swimming hole, it seems that everything and everybody they pass has been drugged. Downtown, "the population *idled casually* across the streets and a drove of low-moaning oxen were being urged along in front of a *placid* street-car; even the shops seemed only *yawning* their doors and *blinking* their windows in the sunshine before retiring into a state of utter and finite *coma*." Out in the country they encounter "a *drowsy* picturesqueness" as the heat flowed down, "never hostile, only comforting, like a *great warm nourishing bosom for the infant earth*." Sally Carrol is sound asleep by the time they reach the swimming hole.[37]

Acculturated though she is to sleepy southern ways, Sally Carrol wants "to go places and see people," wants her mind to grow, wants to live where things happen on a big scale. So she becomes engaged to Harry Bellamy, who is tall, broad, brisk, and energetic—very much a Yankee. She takes him to the graveyard, where she romanticizes the lost cause of the Confederate soldiers. There were "streaks of strange courtliness and chivalry in some of these boys," she maintains, and they "died for the most beautiful thing in the world—the dead South." He understands, Harry says. And in mid-January when she comes up north to his city (of St. Paul), he promises to show her the enchantments of a different landscape. "There's a winter carnival on, and if you've never really seen snow it'll be like fairy-land to you."

"Will I be cold?" she asks, and he reassures her. She may freeze her nose, but won't be shivery cold. "It's hard and dry, you see" (54). Sally Carrol has her doubts, for she doesn't like cold in any form, and as it turns out St. Paul in winter proves to be anything but fairyland. Like a child she is eager to hitch her sled to a grocery

---

36. Hackl, *"Still Home to Me,"* 53.
37. *Short Stories*, 48–52 passim (italics mine). Subsequent parenthetical references are to this edition.

wagon or to build a snowman (56–57), but otherwise she is overcome by the chill in the air and the coldness in the people she meets. Again Fitzgerald evokes the effects of the weather. During Sally Carrol's train ride north, it is very cold in her Pullman berth and the porter has no extra blanket to give her. In the morning, the snow has filtered into the vestibules between cars, and she stumbles her way to a cup of coffee in the dining car. "Sometimes a solitary farmhouse would fly by" outside the window, "ugly and bleak and lone on *the white waste;* and with each one she had an instant of *chill compassion* for the souls shut in there waiting for spring" (55, italics mine).

In St. Paul, Sally Carrol finds the weather too cold for satisfactory kissing. Harry encourages her to "feel the pep in the air," but she feels instead the frozen ambience of the place. Unlike her home, this northern city has no real past to celebrate. The library in the Bellamy house is full of rows upon rows of books and is furnished "with a lot of fairly expensive things" that look "about fifteen years old." She cannot help contrasting it with "the battered old library at home," with its huge medical books and oil paintings of her great-uncles and an old but still luxurious couch that showed the scars of its mending forty-five years ago (56). Northerners make no concessions to her southern ways. Harry's mother insists on calling her "Sally" instead of "Sally Carrol" and disapproves of her smoking. His Scandinavian sister-in-law seems incredibly listless, and it remains for a college professor—a newcomer from Philadelphia—to explain why. The people of St. Paul are "freezing up," he thinks, gradually becoming gloomy and melancholy like Swedes (59–60). Sally Carrol is never able to get warm in St. Paul and in a final climactic scene nearly freezes to death in the maze of the winter carnival's ice palace. Harry finds and rescues her, but now she is determined to go back home to the golden sunlight with its "quite enervating yet oddly comforting heat" (69). The story comes full circle at the end, with Sally Carrol resting her chin on the windowsill and Clark Darrow stopping by in his ancient Ford to take her swimming.

The ice palace Sally Carrol got lost in was based on the actual palaces erected for St. Paul's winter carnival. The largest of these was built in 1886, "three stories in the air, with battlements and embrasures and narrow icicled windows," and with a maze, just as in the story.[38] Fitzgerald may have seen photographs of that palace, and he certainly knew about the ice palace erected in 1916, when the winter carnival was resumed after some years of inactivity. "The Ice Palace" was faithful to the past in this sense and proved uncannily accurate as a prediction of

38. Koblas, *Fitzgerald in Minnesota*, 54.

the future. Zelda Sayre did not come to St. Paul before she and Scott were married in the spring of 1920. When she did arrive there, a year and a half later, her response to the weather precisely followed the lines her husband had sketched out in the story. Zelda stuck it out through one St. Paul winter, but she and Scott were gone before the first snows of the next one.

To judge by his various writings on the subject, Fitzgerald himself was of two minds about the wintry weather of his hometown. In "Winter Dreams" his protagonist Dexter Green skis across the Sherry Island golf course at Black Bear Lake "when the days became crisp and gray, and the long Minnesota winter shut down like the white lid of a box." At such times the country made Dexter feel "a profound melancholy.... When he crossed the hills, the wind blew cold as misery, and if the sun was out he tramped with his eyes squinted up against the hard dimensionless glare" (217). As well as anything Fitzgerald wrote, "Winter Dreams" captures the difficult situation of the poor boy (or, really, middle-class boy) in love with the rich girl. During the long fallow days of winter Dexter dreams of the glittering things he aims one day to possess. But the most glittering prize of all, the wealthy and beautiful Judy Jones, would remain beyond his grasp. Fitzgerald surely had in mind his own rejection by Ginevra King, a girl every bit as desirable as Judy Jones, and just as inaccessible to him. Ginevra came from Lake Forest, the exclusive enclave north of Chicago, and Scott met her during a Christmas party at St. Paul's Town and Country Club, when she was visiting her school friend Marie Hersey. Scott fell deeply in love with Ginevra and courted her throughout his college years. Losing her was one of the great disappointments of his life. Although he was married and a new father at the time he wrote "Winter Dreams" at the White Bear Yacht Club during the summer of 1922, the story is perhaps his most poignant expression of that loss.

Some of Fitzgerald's memories of winter contradicted the bleak views presented in "The Ice Palace" and "Winter Dreams." He fondly remembered the sleigh rides of his youth, for example. "It would be three when we set out in thick coats and sweaters, the girls flushed and consciously athletic, the boys slightly embarrassed but rakish in jumping off and on with complete abandon, to a chorus of little shrieks of simulated anxiety. At a dusky five o'clock we'd reach our destination, usually a club, and have hot chocolate and chicken sandwiches and a dance or two by the gramophone."[39]

In *The Great Gatsby,* Fitzgerald's narrator recalls taking the train home from prep school and college at Christmastime. When it pulled out of Union Station

39. Ibid., 41–42.

in Chicago into the winter night heading northwest to the Twin Cities, "and the real snow, our snow, began to stretch out beside us and twinkle against the windows, and the dim lights of small Wisconsin stations moved by, a sharp wild brace came suddenly into the air. We drew in deep breaths of it as we walked back from dinner through the cold vestibules, unutterably aware of our identity with this country for one strange hour, before we melted indistinguishably into it again."

"That's my Middle West," he continues in celebration, "the thrilling, returning trains of my youth, and the street lamps and sleigh bells in the frosty dark and the shadows of holly wreaths thrown by lighted windows on the snow."[40] Unlike Sally Carrol Hopper, Nick Carraway can take in deep drafts of the frigid air and find them bracing rather than chilling. The cold, like the snow ("our snow"), was part of him. Eventually Fitzgerald came to renounce those "damn Minnesota winters,"[41] while he continued to look back on certain events in St. Paul with nostalgia.

The adventures of Basil Duke Lee, written in 1928–1929 and later collected in *The Basil and Josephine Stories,* closely track Fitzgerald's youthful experiences in St. Paul and at Newman school. All of the stories present recognizable people and places from his boyhood and can be traced to their origins in the yearly ledger he kept. Two ledger entries of his fourteenth year directly link to "The Scandal Detectives," for example: "March 1911—the founding of The Scandal Detectives" and "April 1911—the Scandal detectives go after Reuben." Similarly, the September 1911 entry—"Attended state fair and took chicken on roller coaster"— helped form the basis of "A Night at the Fair." One story, "The Captured Shadow," even borrows its title from Scott's second boyhood play.[42] But the perspective Fitzgerald adopted in writing these stores makes them succeed in going beyond a mere recounting of the rare triumphs and frequent humiliations of his fictional protagonist.

Writing in his early thirties, Fitzgerald looked back at himself in the guise of the teenager Basil Duke Lee (a name whose aristocratic southern overtones remind us that Scott himself was named for Francis Scott Key). The Basil stories display the "double vision" Malcolm Cowley notes in Fitzgerald's writing. The

---

40. *The Great Gatsby* (New York: Scribner's, 1995), 183–84.
41. *F. Scott Fitzgerald: A Life in Letters,* ed. Matthew J. Bruccoli (New York: Simon and Schuster, 1994), 271.
42. *The Basil and Josephine Stories,* ed. Jackson R. Bryer and John Kuehl (New York: Scribner's, 1973), xxiii. For the ledger see *F. Scott Fitzgerald's Ledger: A Facsimile* (Washington, D.C.: NCR/Microcard Editions, 1973).

calamitous things that happen to Basil are so poignantly moving that a sensitive reader cannot help empathizing with him. Yet these disasters are at the same time depicted with ironic detachment. The author occupies a position both within and without the action, as if he were simultaneously the emotionally involved participant and the philosophical observer.[43] Occasionally Fitzgerald regards his autobiographical protagonist as if he were another person entirely. After depicting Basil's disastrous first year at St. Regis, the authorial voice reflects on his hero's present situation and future prospects. "[Basil] believed that everything was a matter of effort . . . and his fantastic ambition was continually leading him to expect too much. He wanted to be a great athlete, popular, brilliant, and always happy. During this year at school, where he had been punished for his 'freshness,' for fifteen years of thorough spoiling at home, he had grown uselessly introspective, and this interfered with that observation of others which is the beginning of wisdom" (78).

Basil struggles to succeed despite his undue egoism and his precarious position as "one of the poorest boys in a rich boys' school" (59). Unreasonable expectations lead him to embarrassing defeats at every step. Yet he sloughs off these setbacks and slogs along on his journey through adolescence, for he possesses that essential *vitality* whose loss Fitzgerald was to lament less than ten years later in *The Crack-Up* essays of 1936. At the end of "He Thinks He's Wonderful," Basil realizes that he has lost his chance to travel west with the enchanting Minnie Bibble by bragging about himself too eagerly and too long in a conversation with her father. "He lay on his bed, baffled, mistaken, miserable but not beaten. Time after time, the same vitality that had led his spirit to a scourging made him able to shake off the blood like water" and to go on, although wounded, "to new disasters and new atonements" (97–98).

In the earliest Basil Duke Lee stories, the protagonist exhibits this vitality by functioning as neighborhood organizer and inventor, just as Fitzgerald had. The characters in the stories are modeled on Fitzgerald's St. Paul companions. Margaret Armstrong becomes Imogene Bissel, Marie Hersey is Margaret Torrence, Cecil Read is Riply Buckner, Reuben Warner is Hubert Blair, the Ames's yard with its treehouse becomes the Whartons' yard, and the Scandal Detectives derive from the club of the same name that Scott himself dreamed up. Basil like his creator is blessed with imagination, "a shining-eyed, brown-haired boy of fourteen, rather small as yet, and bright and lazy at school" (17).

---

43. *Basil and Josephine*, xxiii–xxiv. Subsequent parenthetical references to the stories and quotations from the ledgers are to this edition.

His imagination led Basil/Scott to create "THE BOOK OF SCANDAL," containing dubious revelations about a neighboring businessman's criminal past and a local lad's attendance at the burlesque show. As a scandal detective Basil attempts to emulate the suave example of Arsene Lupin, the gentleman burglar in the Maurice Leblanc stories Fitzgerald had been reading. In another story Lupin segues into "that elusive gentleman, Basil Lee, better known as the Shadow" (55). Whatever the name, the important thing is that this most admired literary figure is a "*gentleman* burglar" (43), a romanticized character who moves smoothly in the highest social circles and by his bravado manages to control and dominate them.

The theme of sexual competition pervades the Basil Duke Lee stories. Basil, who takes a precocious interest in the courtship games of preadolescence, is persistently confronted by a rival in the person of Hubert Blair/Reuben Warner, an acrobatically graceful lad who "possessed the exact tone that all girls of fourteen, and a somewhat cruder type of grown women, find irresistible" (50). "It was at a Saturday night party in [Ben Griggs's] house in 1911," according to Koblas, "that Scott lost his childhood sweetheart Margaret Armstrong to his old friend and nemesis Reuben Warner."[44] Even in fiction Basil/Scott cannot defeat his rival. In "A Night at the Fair," a story that takes place at the Minnesota State Fair, Hubert seems to have lost the game when he strolls by the assembled crowd in the company of a "chicken" (a "common girl," as Fitzgerald explains) he has just picked up. The Van Schellingers, in their box, are properly horrified and invite Basil—who, luckily, has just abandoned his "chicken"—to sit with them in their box as they watch a reenactment of the Battle of Gettysburg. (These reenactments were in fact presented at Minnesota State Fairs of the time.) Later, he rides home with the socially desirable Gladys Van Schellinger. There is a tender touching of hands, and Gladys—who like Basil is going east to school—urges him to come see her the next day. Then she turns to him, her breath warm against his cheek. "Basil—Basil, when you come tomorrow, will you bring that Hubert Blair?" (57).

That putdown at the end of "A Night at the Fair" is but one of many that Fitzgerald's hero suffers in the nine Basil Duke Lee stories. Usually Basil deserves the blow for letting his outsize ego run out of control. "Hubert Blair is the nicest boy in town and you're the most conceited," as Margaret Torrence tells him "with deep conviction" (25). When he goes east to school from St. Paul, it is with a hopeful feeling that he will shake off his unpopularity in a romantic new environment. "Beyond the dreary railroad stations of Chicago and the night fires of

44. Koblas, *Fitzgerald in Minnesota*, 22.

Pittsburgh, back in the old states, something went on that made his heart beat fast with excitement" (147). But Basil has not yet grown up enough to recognize that other people exist. So he continually boasts about himself, offers unasked-for advice, and achieves at St. Regis (Newman) the same sorry status he'd earned at Country Day (S.P.A.): that of "the freshest boy in school." The headmaster, who has seen many students come and go, is bewildered by Basil's immediate and extraordinary unpopularity, among schoolmates and teachers alike. "It was most probably one of those intangible questions of personality," he concludes (60).

After an unhappy year at St. Regis, Basil comes home for the summer, having learned "that others had wills as strong as his, and more power" (92). He affects a winning posture of consideration for others, and it looks as if he will finally conquer St. Paul after all. During a game of Truth on Imogene Bissel's veranda, Gladys Van Schellinger (the only young person present who arrived in a limousine) confesses that Basil is her favorite boy in St. Paul, if not in the East, and Imogene declares Basil her favorite boy, period. But these public victories turn Basil's head, and soon he is expanding on the subject of popularity to his new friend Joe Gorman. He himself had been unpopular at school for a while, Basil admits, "because I was fresh, I guess. But the thing must be that some boys are popular with boys and some are popular with girls." Joe should be more polite to older people, Basil advises him. He should stop wearing those white ties of his, for nobody who went east to school wore them. It would be even better if Joe himself went east to school. On and on Basil goes, as if to transform Joe Gorman from "little more than a Midwestern bumpkin to an Easterner bursting with *savoir-faire* and [like himself] irresistible to girls" (83–85). Joe does not appreciate being informed of his shortcomings and converts Basil's ramblings into one brief damning sentence: "Joe said you told him that all the girls thought you were wonderful." "I never said anything like that," Basil indignantly insists, but the damage has been done (90). Once again he has talked too much and must suffer the painful consequences.

Most of these humiliations Basil brings upon himself, but Fitzgerald also makes it clear that his boyhood hero is socially disadvantaged. The issue of social class runs like a subcurrent through the course of the stories, quietly revealing Basil's insecure standing on the edge of the city's aristocracy. Basil like Scott is stigmatized by not having a father worth talking about. Mr. Lee is pointedly omitted in several places. The Van Schellingers introduce Basil as "Alice Riley's boy" (51), with no mention of his father. Basil happily reflects that "this summer he and his mother and sister were going to the lakes and next fall he was starting away to school" (21). At St. Regis he gets a letter from his mother with the news that "Grandfather is going abroad to take the waters and he wants you and me to come too" (69). It is as if Basil's father did not exist.

Like his creator, Basil is fully aware of his economic dependence on his mother's family. "Where would we be," Mollie Fitzgerald used to remark at the dinner table, "if it wasn't for Grandfather McQuillan?"[45] In response to a letter from Basil's mother, the St. Regis headmaster calls him on the carpet for poor grades. "I believe you have been sent here at a certain amount of—ah—sacrifice" (59), he harrumphs, while Basil writhes in shame at such a blunt statement of his family's financial inadequacy. These circumstances are forcefully brought home to him in "Forging Ahead," when his mother loses a great deal of money in the stock market and tells Basil that she cannot afford to send him to Yale, the college he's long dreamed of attending.

In the early 1910s, driving an automobile represented a way of establishing one's standing among the rich. Fitzgerald's ledger for July 1912 contains two possibly related entries: "Began to feel lack of automobile" and "growing unpopular" (xxiii). Both of these apply to the adventures of Basil Duke Lee. In "A Night at the Fair," Basil is too young to drive but not too young to recognize the connection between possession of an automobile and sexual power. What he yearns for most of all in that story is a pair of long pants to wear to the State Fair, trousers that will announce his graduation from childhood once and for all. At the fair, he and his friend Riply are transfixed by the sight of a Blatz Wildcat (Stutz Bearcat), small, red, low-slung, and "for the next five years . . . the ambition of several million American boys." A blonde, baby-faced girl reclines on the sloping seat of the car, which is driven by a pink-faced, pink-haired young man in a yellow suit. This is Speed Paxton, son of a local brewer. Speed is "dimly terrible," and his fancy automobile will not purchase him an invitation to St. Paul's coming-out parties. But Basil and Riply envy him for the chariot he drives and the provocative girl at his side (38). The next day, having decided he will not go to the fair without his new long pants, Basil thinks of the girls he will not meet as a result—the most desirable girls imaginable, riding off in Blatz Wildcats without his having kissed them (47).

The next year Basil, now old enough to drive, feels increasingly frustrated by the lack of a family car. He rides the train back from the East with Margaret Torrence, who announces that "we're going to get an automobile . . . and I'm going to learn to drive." "That's fine," Basil lamely replies, while wondering if his

45. Donaldson, *Fool for Love,* 6.

grandfather (again, there is no father in sight) might let him drive his electric (79). The lack of an automobile figures most prominently in "He Thinks He's Wonderful," a story set during the summer of 1912. "An element of vast importance had made its appearance with the summer; suddenly the great thing in Basil's crowd was to own an automobile. Fun no longer seemed available save at great distances, at suburban lakes or remote country clubs. Walking downtown ceased to be a legitimate pastime. On the contrary, a single block from one youth's house to another's must be navigated in a car. Dependent groups formed around owners and began to wield what was, to Basil at least, a disconcerting power" (86). The extent of that power is brought home to Basil when he must more or less beg a ride to a Saturday night dance at the lake.

In this story, Basil's fortunes swing wildly between the poles of joy and despair. In three separate incidents his unfortunate habit of boasting brings him down from the heights. Several girls choose him as their favorite boy in the Truth game, so from his position of eminence he decides to set Joe Gorman straight. Imogene Bissel is attracted to him at the dance, but when she leads him to a private spot at the end of the pier he cannot stop talking about himself long enough to seize the opportunity. Conspicuously uninvited to a party Joe has organized, he is lucky enough to meet the visiting Minnie Bibble instead. They get along wonderfully until he bores her father with a long recitation about himself. Yet even that final disappointment vanishes in a rather contrived ending. It so happens that his grandfather will let him use the electric in the afternoons if he keeps the batteries charged and washes the car once a week. And it so happens that Imogene Bissel has not gone to Joe Gorman's house party after all and would love to go riding in the electric with him. As the story concludes, they are cruising down Crest Avenue at a heady fifteen miles an hour—Basil triumphantly at the wheel, the girl of the moment at his side.

His grandfather's electric hardly stacks up against the Blatz Wildcat, but Basil makes it serve in his ongoing entanglements with girls. Minnie Bibble comes back into the picture in "Forging Ahead," during the time Basil is working to help pay his way to Yale. They meet during a dance at the "Lake Club." Minnie, from New Orleans, will be staying three weeks and is eager to renew their romantic liaison. He could come out to the lake in the evenings to see her, she suggests. "It's only half an hour in a car." When he points out that he doesn't have a car, she is undeterred: "I mean you can get your family's car." But "it's an electric," he says, meaning *only* an electric and hence slower than a gasoline-driven car (156). Minnie boldly takes the initiative, presenting herself at *his* house one afternoon as he comes home from work. She has only an hour before she must rejoin her family in town. They could take a ride in her car, she suggests, but the chauffeur might get in the way. "He listens," she explains. So the electric is made to serve after all. The chauffeur drops them off at "grampa's house," and Basil steers the electric to a secluded spot on the bluffs, with a view of the Mississippi flats a mile away. "Suddenly she was whispering in his arms, 'You're first, Basil—nobody but you'" (158). Fade-out to bliss.

The Basil Duke Lee stories constitute Fitzgerald's closest fictional representations of his boyhood in St. Paul, particularly of his teenage years. At times he considered looking further backward into his origins. In June 1922 he wrote Perkins from White Bear that he was thinking about launching his third novel. "Its locale will be the middle west and New York at 1885 I think. It will concern less superlative beauties than I run to usually and will be centered on a smaller period of time. It will have a catholic element."[46] The third novel turned out to be *The Great Gatsby* (1925), Fitzgerald's masterpiece. *Gatsby* bears little resemblance to the historical novel with "a catholic element" that he proposed in the summer of 1922, except for its contrast between the East, as the locus of opportunity, and the Middle West, as the locus of morality. And although not so identified, Nick Carraway's hometown is clearly St. Paul. Fitzgerald wrote a good deal less about St. Paul, Minnesota, than Faulkner did about Oxford, Mississippi, and a good deal more about it than Hemingway did about Oak Park, Illinois. None of them could shake off the influence of the places they came from.

IV

A number of St. Paul people who knew Fitzgerald or whose parents and grandparents knew him deprecate any assertion that he had reason to feel insecure about his social position. The St. Paul where he grew up a generation later than Fitzgerald was not at all that hierarchical, according to Roger Kennedy, historian and director of the Smithsonian Institution. "Scott was a part of us," insisted Norris Jackson, who married Betty Ames and moved into the house that Fitzgerald commemorated for its spacious backyard in the Basil stories.[47] Kennedy and Jackson, like most others who share their conviction on this issue, felt quite comfortable and secure about their own social standing in the community. They accepted Fitzgerald without so much as thinking about it. If he was beset by worries about his status, it must have been because he let his overactive imagi-

46. *Dear Scott/Dear Max,* 61.
47. Hackl, *"Still Home to Me,"* 12.

nation transform reality. To a certain degree these St. Paulites are right. Fitzgerald, like his fellow Irishman John O'Hara, can fairly be called the master of the imagined slight. He repeatedly embarrassed and abased himself before those he considered his betters: Gerald and Sara Murphy, for example. In order to remember—or even, to cultivate—such incidents, he kept lists of where and by whom he had been snubbed. Undoubtedly Fitzgerald exaggerated the slights he suffered throughout his life and, in particular, during his youth in St. Paul. But his hometown was complicit to a degree in inspiring those feelings. Scott did not invent the social structure of St. Paul that he described in his nonfiction and dramatized in several stories and novels. In a very real sense, he drew from his boyhood in St. Paul the basic donnée of his fiction: the situation of the (relatively) poor young boy unable to win the love of the beautiful rich girl. It seems reasonable to conclude that St. Paul through its social hierarchy contributed to the sense of inferiority his parents bequeathed to Scott Fitzgerald.

A dream he had in the spring of 1931, shortly after his father's funeral, exposes the depths of Fitzgerald's insecurity. In the dream he is living with his clumsy old mother in an upstairs apartment. On another floor there is a group of rich and handsome young men, whom he would like to know better. He talks with one of them, who seems amiable but does not encourage the acquaintance—"whether because he considers me poor, unimportant, ill bred or of ill renown I don't know, or rather don't think about—only I scent the polite indifference *and even understand it*" (italics mine). Next he discovers there is a dance downstairs to which he has not been invited. He feels that if "they" knew how important he was, he would have been invited.

The dream circles back to his mother. They have been quarreling, possibly, Fitzgerald proposes, because of his "ill-humour at being neglected by the people downstairs." He mistakenly wanders into the party and stammers "something absurd" to one of the fashionable young men. As he escapes, his mother calls out "in a too audible voice from an upper story." He reflects: "I don't know whether I am angry with her for clinging to me, or because I am ashamed of her for not being young and chic, or for disgracing my conventional sense by calling out, or because she might guess I'd been hurt and pity me, which would have been unendurable, or all those things. Anyway I call back at her some terse and furious reproach."

Further gaffes by his mother follow. She complains that she is not being served an adequate portion of food, but those serving her decline to remedy the situation. Mother and son go home together, where she locates a book for Scott and pathetically asks him if it isn't a book he'd loved and lost in his childhood. It resembles that book but is not quite the right one. Later in the dream she calls out to him once more, and he again answers angrily.[48]

This dream suggests how closely Fitzgerald's sense of social insecurity is connected to his feelings about his mother. If only she had been richer, smarter, better bred, more attractive, the young men would presumably have welcomed Scott into their company and seen to it that he was invited to the dance. The dream itself he recorded for the psychologist Margaret Egloff, a close friend he met in Switzerland during the time that Zelda was institutionalized near Lausanne. After extended conversations with Fitzgerald, Egloff concluded that he yearned to identify with, and become one with, "the rich, powerful, and chic of the world. . . . The fact that he was not born into that society galled him, and he hated himself for his own and everyone else's snobbery."[49] He despised his mother for her upward aspirations for him and hated himself for adopting them. He understood how foolish it was to care so desperately about the good opinion of people he did not, at bottom, even respect, but he could not stop himself.

Fitzgerald had a hard time making up his mind about his hometown, and his hometown reciprocated the feeling. "I no longer regard St. Paul as my home any more than the eastern seaboard or the Riviera," Scott wrote Marie Hersey in 1934. After all, he pointed out, his father was an easterner, and he'd gone east to college, and he'd never really returned after the fourteen-month stay in 1921–1922. At the end of his life he was inclined to embrace the Maryland roots of his father's family, reaching back to early colonial times. "I belong here," he said of Baltimore in 1935, "where everything is civilized and gay and rotted and polite."[50] He chose to be buried in Rockville, beside the graves of his parents. Yet in another mood he wrote Xandra Kalman in the late 1930s that St. Paul was "still home to me" and told her that he planned to bring his daughter, Scottie, to St. Paul for the summer, so she could see where he'd been brought up—a plan that did not materialize.[51]

Writers are rarely honored in their own lifetimes by the places where they grew up. Like Fitzgerald, they are usually too bold in unmasking pretensions and challenging conventional mores to please genteel society. And often, like Fitzgerald, they rebel against their roots by one or another kind of overt misbehavior. Clifton Read remembers sailing at White Bear one summer when Fitzgerald was only beginning to publish stories and overhearing a prim young wife remark about

---

48. Donaldson, *Fool for Love*, 13–15.
49. Ibid., 15.
50. *Life in Letters*, 270–71, 291.
51. Xandra Kalman, letter of 1970, Fitzgerald Archive, St. Paul Academy.

him, "Well, he may have talent, but he's too racy for me."[52] Not even the revival of interest in his work during the 1950s and 1960s fully reconciled St. Paul to its wayward native son. Not, in fact, until a hundred years after his birth in St. Paul, and fifty-six years after his death in Hollywood, did his hometown fully unbend to honor Fitzgerald as an eminent citizen of St. Paul.

Garrison Keillor had much to do with this recognition. First he saw to it that the World Theater in downtown St. Paul, from which the *Prairie Home Companion* radio show usually emanates, was renamed the Fitzgerald Theater. For the centenary itself in 1996, he brought some of the nation's greatest writers together to pay homage to Fitzgerald and his work. Leading citizens in the community joined in the observances, commissioning a handsome statue of Fitzgerald for Rice Park, downtown.

At the end of his essay "Early Success" (1937), Fitzgerald looks back on the days when he was beginning his career and dreaming of success. Sometimes, he says, he can make his way back "into the mind of that young man with cardboard soles" in his shoes, "creep up on him, surprise him on an autumn morning in New York or a spring night in Carolina when it is so quiet that you can hear a dog barking in the next county."[53] As aftercomers we may catch a glimpse of the author in St. Paul when he was even younger, still a boy too full of himself, insecure about his social status, unpopular in his overeagerness to please, consumed by dreams of mastery, and wonderfully imaginative in conceiving dramatic situations that would remove him, for a time, from cold harsh reality.

To catch that glimpse, let us walk with Scott past the elegant homes of Summit Avenue—the street where he did not quite belong. It is Saturday afternoon, August 24, 1912, the day after the successful performance of his play *The Captured Shadow*. Before the performance Bobby Schurmeier's parents invited the cast to dinner, and afterward they celebrated with a hayrack party and a dinner at the Town and Country Club. During our walk, we pause at the bluff to gaze at the winding Mississippi and the bustle of the city below. The boy at our side has every right to be proud of himself, and for a time he does go on expansively about the play, and the old man who told him, "You'll be heard from one day," after the curtain came down, and the newspaper reporter who asked him if he was really only fifteen.[54] Then a mood of melancholy steals over him, mirroring the hint of fall in the late summer air. In part this comes from the hollowness

52. Clifton Read, letter of February 12, 1970, Fitzgerald Archive, St. Paul Academy.
53. *The Crack-Up*, ed. Edmund Wilson (New York: New Directions), 90.
54. *Basil and Josephine*, 119.

like fear that follows completing a work: the play was all over, done and gone. In part it is as if young Fitzgerald was beginning to understand that, no matter what he did, it would not alter the way most people in his hometown regarded him. A few weeks earlier, after all—in one of those incidents he would never forget—he had been conspicuously left out of a party that was organized right before his eyes.

We should not wish it otherwise. Lacking the heritage of disappointment and embarrassment and defeat that St. Paul bestowed on Fitzgerald, he would probably not have written the great stories, or *The Great Gatsby,* or *Tender Is the Night.* Had his old friend Edmund Wilson included Fitzgerald among the case studies in *The Wound and the Bow* (along with Dickens, Kipling, Hemingway, and Joyce), he might have shown how St. Paul hurt him deeply enough to convert him into an artist. More than anywhere else he lived, and he lived in many places, it was his hometown—the midwestern yet eastern-leaning city of St. Paul—that made Fitzgerald the great writer he became: ever sensitive to social mortifications, ever yearning after the uncapturable.

Purgatory in the Midwest
The White Martyrdom of Urban Roche

Robert Benson

Asked by an interviewer if he thought it mattered where a writer lives, J. F. Powers gave an evasive answer that sounded more like no than yes. "I would always look in the direction I have looked. I would not fly blind and write without regard to a body of philosophy."[1] But fiction gives the airy nothings of philosophy a local habitation and a name; of Powers's principal mode, satire, Eudora Welty advises that when "engaged in its most intellectual of exercises, [it] must first of all establish an impeccable *locus operandi.*"[2] His evocation of place is not the first thing Powers's readers admire about his work, but "to understand Powers," as Mary Gordon declares, "one must understand that he is writing about a specific locale: the Middle West." Chicago, Gordon reminds us, "is a thousand miles west of New York, a thousand miles further from Rome." "In the middle of the continent," she continues, Catholic "farmers, businessmen and their sons held to the faith, but the stuff of their dreams was manufactured in the New World. The self-made man, hearty, well-heeled, at home in first-class trains, in suites at the Palmer House, was the man they wanted their sons to be. Chicago was the focus of ambition and mythology."[3]

The Midwest, perhaps more clearly even than the Northeast, has shaped the images of the successful American—energetic, ambitious, self-sufficient, and at home in the great world of business. This is precisely the version of the American

1. Sister Kristin Malloy, O.S.B., "The Catholic and Creativity: J. F. Powers (An Interview with J. F. Powers)," in *J. F. Powers,* ed. Fallon Evans (St. Louis: B. Herder Book Co., n.d.), 1.

2. Welty, *The Eye of the Story: Selected Essays and Reviews* (New York: Random House, 1978), 126.

3. J. F. Powers, *Morte D'Urban,* with an introduction by Mary Gordon (New York: Washington Square Press, 1985), [vii], [viii]. Subsequent parenthetical references to the novel are to this edition.

ideal that the Agrarians and the English Distributists found morally corrupt and spiritually bankrupt. J. F. Powers, whose priests think and speak more like captains of industry than like princes of the church, thought the same.

The great midwestern cities such as Chicago and St. Paul are in Powers's fiction emblems of the world, the world of the tripartite formula that includes the flesh and the devil—three things that the Christian must reject; three things always tugging at the sinner's sleeve. Against the world ultimately stands celestial Jerusalem, the heavenly city, the Christian's hope. Between the two Augustinian cities there can be no compromise. As Didymus realizes at last in the short story "Lions, Harts, and Leaping Does," "in trivial attachments, in love of things, was death, no matter the appearance of life. In the highest attachment only, no matter the appearance of death, was life."[4]

In the stronger of Powers's two novels, *Morte D'Urban,* this is the central conflict, and since all stories set in this world can only present the way to the City of God by hints and indirection, by shadowy and imperfect models, Powers opposes to Chicago and St. Paul remote rural churches and monastic foundations where the bleak cold of winter offers the clearest view of the way of sanctification, a chill *via negativa* of discomfort and daily self-denial in such places as St. Clement's Hill, Duesterhaus, and Ostergothenburg. There is irony, of course, in the fact that shadows of the heavenly city are not urban but provincial; nor are these out-of-the-way places free from the world's temptations or the persistent sinfulness of fallen man. So at the end of *Morte D'Urban* Father Urban Roche, who became a priest because he wanted "to stay in the best hotels, to meet the best people, to live like a Protestant," Mary Gordon observes (*Morte* [viii]), becomes the provincial of his order, and in removal from the world he finds peace and his true vocation. The death of the novel's title is not literal death as in Malory's *Morte D'Arthur* but is the death of Father Urban's urbanity or the purgatorial death of the self that is every Christian's duty—daily mortification.

Known principally as a comic writer, Powers takes spiritual warfare seriously; he recognizes that it is now, as it has always been, a matter of ultimate importance. Powers's comedy is like Dante's or Chaucer's. It is a serious matter in which the soul's salvation is at stake, but the Christian view is fundamentally comic because of the Resurrection. Much of the humor in Powers's fiction results from the tension between his characters' attachment to the world and their obligation to be

4. *The Stories of J. F. Powers,* with an introduction by Denis Donoghue (New York: New York Review of Books, 2000), 54. Subsequent parenthetical references to the stories are to this edition.

saints following the examples of the apostles and martyrs, "on this foot a sandal and on this foot a custom-made shoe," as Powers said. His comic vision is tough and unsentimental, but it is not savage because it is hopeful. His fiction accepts the Catholic and Christian view of man's Redemption. Wylie Sypher suggests that "the comic hero and the saint accept the irreconcilables in man's existence."[5] In the character of Urban Roche, Powers has brought those figures together.

His fiction also gives us glimpses of the church as something more than its visible presence in our cities and towns. Our vision, like that of Powers's characters, may be myopic, but even as he delineates self-indulgent priests, slothful and time-serving, willful and ambitious, Powers has in his mind's eye the supernatural reality of the church through time and triumphant in eternity. The businessman's church, the church with drive and ambition and promotion as its goal, the church Father Urban likes to imagine as "second only to Standard Oil" (*Morte*, 107) in efficiency and visibility, would not be nearly so funny, so shocking, were it not set in the context of the church of the patriarchs and prophets, the church of the apostles and of all the heroic saints and martyrs. As the portraits of Chaucer's Monk and Friar depend on our understanding the ideal from which these fallible characters depart, so too does our understanding of Powers's worldly priests. The comedy, as with Chaucer's work, comes both from the author's charity and from the silliness of golf, color television, aged steaks, sports cars—trivial delights that bring all the deadly sins in their train. It comes from our notion, however vague, of how things ought to be. For all his worldliness, Father Urban is at times but dimly aware of this ancient and heroic church yet is, in the end, obedient to it.

The world encourages us to forget what's at stake, and the Catholic Church in the Midwest is far enough from Rome and close enough to what some like to call America's heartland to make the heroic life of faith seem quaint, if not a little mad. Faith like that of the apostles and martyrs makes little sense in the midst of our comfort; it seems excessive and far removed from our desire for approval and success. Even in a monastery the old Franciscan Didymus, the protagonist of "Lions, Harts, Leaping Does," questions the point of following St. Francis. "There was nothing of suffering in the poverty of friars nowadays. . . . Verily, it was no heavy cross, this vow of Poverty, so construed and practiced, in the modern world" (*Stories*, 35). Didymus recalls "with wry amusement" Frederick Barbarossa's statement regarding the obligation of princes to bring priests back "to the condition of the first Christian Church. In those days the clergy raised their eyes

5. *Comedy*, ed. Wylie Sypher (Garden City: Doubleday Anchor Books, 1956), 237.

to the angels, shone through miracles, made whole the sick, raised the dead, made Kings and Princes subject to them, not with arms but with their holiness. But now they are smothered in delights" (*Stories,* 35). In Powers's view, the prayers and miracles are the norm, and the modern church in the Midwest is like the twelfth-century church indicted by Emperor Frederick. Powers knows what the standard is. "A saint is not an abnormal person," he wrote in 1943. "He is simply a mature Christian. Anyone who is not a saint is spiritually under-sized—the world is full of spiritual midgets."[6]

Morte D'Urban begins with a paragraph summarizing a sermon preached by Father Urban Roche as he has tried to raise money for the Order of St. Clement. In the opening lines of the novel, Powers joins its principal conflict and shows us Father Urban's understanding of the choices before us. The good father had

> roared and whispered and crooned about Francis of Assisi and Ignatius of Loyola and Clement of Blois and Louis of France and Edward of England and Charles of the Holy Roman Empire—it was he who, you might say, owned and oper-ated Europe but who, in the end, desired only the society of monks—it was he who rehearsed his own funeral, lay down in his coffin, joined in the prayers for the repose of his soul, mingled his tears with those of his attendants—it was he who rose from his coffin in good health, retired to his chambers, and was seized by a fever from which he very soon died. (*Morte,* 1)

The summary that Powers gives us sounds like a sermon Father Urban would have preached. The notion that the Holy Roman Emperor "owned and operated" Europe suggests how deeply secular and American is Father Urban's vision of the church in the world; but, like Charles himself, Urban Roche will come in the end to desire the company of monks. He will reject the empty promises and de-lights of the world and learn to think of the Hill as home, "an abandoned sani-tarium in rural Minnesota" (*Morte,* 9), the Clementines' latest foundation. The sermon at the novel's beginning attracts the attention of Billy Cosgrove, a rich spokesman of the earthly city who becomes for a time a benefactor of the Clemen-tines, an evil benefactor whose generosity comes with many strings attached. Insofar as Billy has any religion at all, it is superficial piety and a deep conviction that the church exists for his comfort and that its teachings should conform to his narrow materialism. From the outset he spots Father Urban as a kindred spirit.

The central spiritual struggle of *Morte D'Urban* is clear in the novel's opening pages. Father Urban, who has been on the road for the Clementines, their most

6. John V. Hagopian, *J. F. Powers* (New York: Twayne Publishers, 1968), 26.

successful retreat master, mission preacher, after-dinner speaker, and recruiter, is looking for exceptional and ambitious young men, men of taste and discernment, men not unlike himself. Suddenly he is ordered off the road to St. Clement's Hill, a remote foundation in the middle of nowhere. In an interview Powers refers to Father Urban as a "poor man's Fulton Sheen."[7] He was trying to "raise the tone" of the order, although he had "overshot the mark on occasion—two of his recruits had proved to be homosexual and one homicidal" (*Morte,* 9). Undoubtedly he worked hard for the order, and "still he found the time and energy to make friends, as enjoined by Scripture, with the mammon of iniquity" (*Morte,* 10). That, of course, is Father Urban's problem, the center of his spiritual drama and probably the reason that Father Boniface, the provincial of the order, requires him to "report to the newest white elephant, the new foundation, as it was called in the letter, near Duesterhaus, Minnesota" (*Morte,* 19). Father John, a humble and obedient Clementine, has been reassigned in the same way at the same time. But, although Father Urban believes that "Jack should have been taken off the road long ago" (*Morte,* 15), he resents his own reassignment, regarding it as a waste of his considerable talents. Father John's dutiful acceptance Father Urban admits to himself is the proper attitude, but adds that such an attitude must "come easier for someone like him. What did *he* have to lose?" (*Morte,* 21).

Father Urban's rejection of the world takes place in stages and in at least four different sorts of places. Powers first shows us Father Urban's removal from Chicago, from the handsome downtown offices of the order, from the resplendent Pump Room to the barren remoteness of St. Clement's Hill in rural Minnesota and the life of unobserved duty inside the retreat house. Through much of the novel Father Urban tries to maintain his former life, clinging to such remnants of the great world as can be found in the city of Great Plains, St. Monica's parish, and the house of the Thwaites family on Lake Lucille. Great Plains is no Chicago, but it's the best place available to the worldly protagonist. As the action unfolds, the places, partly by way of the connections Powers makes between his story and Arthurian legend, become more obviously symbolic. At Lake Lucille and in the wilderness with Billy and especially at Belleisle with Sally Thwaites Hopwood, moral choices are presented with great clarity and simplicity, and Father Urban's desire to live as both priest and friend to mammon becomes demonstrably impossible.

The world that Father Urban loves and resists abandoning is presented clearly when he invites Father John to the Pump Room ("the idea had been to give Jack

7. Ibid., 123.

something to remember in their exile" [*Morte*, 23]), and this scene highlights Urban's sophistication and Jack's simplicity. Harvey Roche had heard God's call to the priesthood in the life and example of one Father Placidus, "every ounce a priest, a man better known than the order he represented." Father Placidus, Father Urban fondly recalls, "put up at the Merchants' Hotel, where bootblacks, bellboys, and waiters who'd never seen him before seemed to welcome him back" (*Morte*, 69). That's the world Father Urban finds irresistible, a world of physical comfort, financial success, and at least the appearance of admiring attention from the hotel staff. It was Father Placidus with whom "young Urban had ridden into the dark wood of the parish-mission circuit" (*Morte*, 71).

The novel's long good-bye to that world begins with the lunch at the Pump Room. Jack drinks too much and is as puzzled as a child might be by meat on a flaming sword ("You'd think they'd do that in the kitchen" [*Morte*, 23]) and by serving boys in turbans and white breeches and green hose. In spite of Urban's intentions to give Jack a meal to remember, he wonders if Jack would not have preferred a cafeteria. Dining on champagne and shish kebab, "one of Billy Cosgrove's favorite combinations" (*Morte*, 22), Jack enjoys making the simple connection, "We know Our Lord ate lamb" (*Morte*, 24); but this reflection does not interest Urban. He can only think that, in the Pump Room, "the spirit of Billy, powerful if not all protecting, seemed to watch over them" (*Morte*, 22).

After preaching his last mission before reporting to the retreat house, Father Urban catches a train, "the Voyageur, or Voyager, as it was called," and finds the country out of Minneapolis "empty, flat and treeless, Illinois without people" (*Morte*, 29). The name of the train suggests the double view Powers takes of Father Urban's passage through the world. On one hand the Voyageur suggests the rootlessness of the protagonist's life on the road, the road into the dark wood, a road away from what Urban views as the constraints of his vocation. The other suggestion is that, in setting out for the Clementine foundation outside of Duesterhaus, the place he will come to think of as home, Father Urban is becoming a pilgrim off on a spiritual journey that will become the means of his sanctification.

After showing us the delights of the Pump Room, the attraction of the luxury of membership, Powers takes us to the provinces. Receiving a chilly welcome in Duesterhaus, Father Urban begins the long walk out to St. Clement's, which the locals refer to as "The Home." Walking through the farm fields outside town, the urban priest fancifully imagines learning "the ways and habits of animals"— reading track, identifying trees and wildflowers. We learn later that he looks for wildlife but sees none and that he recognizes three groups of trees: "red oaks, evergreens, and trees." Father Urban's sense of danger in the country is ludicrously naive. He is afraid, for example, that walking faster, which would help him keep warm, "might be an invitation to the invisible dogs barking the news of his coming from farm to farm." He is so citified that he fears the dogs will attack him. He briefly considers fighting them with his attaché case and then imagines himself dead, "perhaps eaten. Anything could happen here" (*Morte*, 31). This urban fantasy is similar in its thematic burden to the scene in Robert Penn Warren's "Blackberry Winter" when the stranger pulls a pocketknife on a yard dog. Father Urban regards himself as a good city man, and he both resents and fears his reassignment.

As he approaches the incongruous buildings of the order's new foundation, Father Urban sees a muffled figure "moving slowly through the dead grass and weeds, through the haze" (*Morte*, 32). Father Urban signals his presence by coughing and is frightened to discover that the man who turns round to see him is carrying a rifle. Father Urban thinks "this was some half-witted yokel—who, having been given hunting privileges, and having killed a stranger, would get off scot-free at the inquest" (*Morte*, 33). That's the very essence of urban ignorance. The gun-toting yokel turns out to be the rector of St. Clement's, Father Wilfrid Bestudik, who was nicknamed Bunny at the novitiate and is Father Urban's superior. Father Wilfrid is trying to shoot gophers.

As Father Wilf shows Father Urban around St. Clement's Hill, it becomes clear to the reader that he is a decent and enthusiastic man, unworldly and inefficient, and that he is happy to be out in the middle of nowhere trying to do the order's work and God's. Looking around, Father Wilf proclaims this to be "a grand place." Father Urban agrees, but he gazes without pleasure or promise at "the bare trees and bushes, the dead fields, the trees in the distance like black whiskers on the winter horizon." When the rector asks if Father Urban is cold, he replies, "Just numb is all." Father Urban is a man in real spiritual difficulty who reminds himself on being shown the chapel to spend more time before the Blessed Sacrament and even at this early stage acknowledges that "it was all too easy to neglect prayer if you lived at the pace he had in the world" (*Morte*, 37). Removal from the world, from the city, and from the vanity of life on the road is essential. For a long time Father Urban will resent his new assignment, maintaining "a secret ascendancy over the life around him—up to a point, for he muttered some to himself" (*Morte*, 76).

The world is certainly not giving up Father Urban without a struggle, and, for his part, he tries for most of the novel to accommodate the world and to maintain his sense of autonomy. The world comes to St. Clement's Hill in two principal forms: color television and golf. Billy Cosgrove, the very embodiment of the dark spirit of concupiscence, breaches the cloister's wall first by sending a Christmas food hamper and an electrified crèche to St. Clement's. The hamper contains several bottles of liquor; although Father Urban is aware that "many a good city man had gone down that drain," he still accepts the world's way of keeping Christmas: "Let's open one of Billy's bottles" (*Morte*, 101). Billy also arranges to have a new color television set delivered to the Hill on Christmas morning. The intrusive presence of the television and its superficial version of human drama and slick advertising prove a Trojan horse of distraction and allure. None of the residents at the Hill has ever had the opportunity to watch TV regularly, and for a time they turn it on with "a faith, hope and charity that must have been rare at the time" (*Morte*, 111–12). By the time they realize that there is nothing particularly edifying being shown, they are hooked on the evening news, crime dramas, and westerns.

At St. Clement's Hill, the television quickly takes up all their free time in the evenings, and in the darkened room "it was no longer possible for Wilf to read the papers, for Brother Harold to do his homework, or for Father Urban and Jack to play checkers" (*Morte*, 113–14). Obviously these are not saints being distracted from prayer and contemplation. Only Father John regrets "the passing of their old way of life" (*Morte*, 114). And these imperfect men of the cloth begin going about their work routine with a banal image of themselves as "just a couple of average guys such as they saw in the evening on television" (*Morte*, 115). It's difficult under the best of circumstances to see the performance of dull duty as contributing to the greater glory of God, but television makes such otherworldly offering all but impossible.

Powers said that he wrote about priests "for reasons of irony, comedy, and philosophy. They officially are committed to both worlds in a way most people are not. This makes for stronger beer."[8] The rector at St. Clement's with his newspaper, childlike Brother Harold with homework to do, and Urban and Jack, the older brothers playing checkers, are figures in a domestic setting distracted from their duties, amusements, and one another by the mindless pleasure of television. In *Morte D'Urban*, as in many of Powers's stories, the close interior spaces of monasteries, sacristies, rectories, and convents suggest the discipline and regularity of religious life, but they are frequently described in mundane terms and through the domestication of what seem, to the average reader, odd and unfamiliar places. Father Eudex in "The Forks," having been rebuked by the monsignor for helping the overworked janitor, remembers the voice of his dead aunt

8. Malloy, "The Catholic and Creativity," 8.

and "translated the past into the present: I can't come out and play this after-noon, Joe, on account of my monsignor won't let me" (*Stories*, 101). In "The Valiant Woman" Father Firman and his housekeeper Mrs. Stoner play honeymoon bridge every night. She always wins. Occasionally mail comes to the rectory ad-dressed to "Rev. and Mrs. Stoner." A nun in "The Lord's Day" wants her pastor's permission to replace a stove. There are complaints about the food provided or not provided by housekeepers, arguments among keepers of the keys of the King-dom about who gets to keep the keys to the parish automobile or the church. Powers brings the private lives of priests vividly to life by rendering them in the ordinary terms of family life while not forgetting that these characters do not see the domestic analogy as the reader is allowed to see it. Nor does he forget that these domestic arrangements are peculiar precisely because the characters in-volved are celibate men whose lives are supposed to be centered on serving God. In "The Prince of Darkness," Father Burner plans to avoid the difficulties some housekeepers cause by having his mother become his housekeeper if he is ever given a parish. The common life of families and the religious is supposed to be beneficial for the individual's growth in virtue. Living together exposes weak-nesses of character that should be overcome with prayer and God's grace, but often in the lives of Powers's priests, curates, and housekeepers the revelation of character produces frustration and irritation that few rise above. Father Burner hates his room, "a fabulous brown rummage of encyclopedias, world globes, maps, photographs, holy pictures, mirrors, crucifixes, tropical fish, and too much furniture. The room reproduced the world, all wonders and horrors, less land than water" (*Stories*, 168).

Many of Powers's priests demonstrate their resistance to the strictures those closed places impose by spending as much time as they can out, usually driving automobiles. The monsignor's car in "The Forks" is "long and black and new like a politician's" (*Stories*, 93), and three times a day the monsignor goes driv-ing. Father Burner in "The Prince of Darkness" also drives to assert his indepen-dence. As he took a curve, "wheels parallel to the center line," and lit a cigarette, Father Burner "tugged viciously at both knees, loosening the binding black cloth, easing the seat" (*Stories*, 189). Father Smith, pastor at St. Monica's, Great Plains, and Father Urban himself show a similar devotion to motoring about. By con-trast, the pious Father Chumley, curate at St. Monica's, spends most of his time in church in the confessional.

In *Morte D'Urban*, Powers makes the connection between television and the sorrowful city clear in the situation of Mrs. Thwaites, a wealthy parishioner at St. Monica's who lives out in the country in a large house that reminds Father

Urban of the main building at St. Clement's Hill. A cruel and utterly self-absorbed woman, Mrs. Thwaites watches television on two sets, watching constantly the two available channels. When Father Urban first sees her, "the only light in the room came from the sets, a dead light, so that Mrs. Thwaites's face showed up like a photographic negative: a little old woman with the face of a baby bird, all eyes and beak, but with a full head of bobbed white hair" (*Morte*, 135). The old woman has a rosary in one hand and the TV remote in the other. The dark room with its equatorial temperature suggests Mrs. Thwaites's infernal connections. Even when she bows her head slightly for the priest's blessing, she continues to watch television. Mrs. Thwaites is the widow of a man whose "great work in life" was "making apostates, and making money" (*Morte*, 137). She is one of the Clementines' few benefactresses, and Father Urban is naturally disposed to make excuses for her, but Monsignor Renton says, "It all goes together. The television sets, the bomb shelter, and the religion." When Father Urban notes that she is a daily communicant, the monsignor simply responds, "God is not mocked" (*Morte*, 138).

Father Urban does his best to stay in touch with the world beyond the Hill. "He agreed to address the Great Plains Commercial Club at its annual Poinsettia Smorgasbord" (*Morte*, 85), where he uses the occasion to try to demystify Catholicism for his mixed audience. He wants the faith to sound normal and agreeable to Protestants, and he feels compelled to "shoot down" a woman who wants Father Urban to speak up on the idea of respecting the pope as Christ's vicar on earth. This is Great Plains, not Chicago or St. Paul, but it's the best Father Urban can do, and he regards his time away from the Hill and away from the rector as "a few hours spent with real people in real places" (*Morte*, 90). Father Urban is later given permission to fill in at St. Monica's in Great Plains while the pastor, Father Smith, takes a vacation. As a parish priest Father Urban is more interested in nightcaps in the upper room of the rectory and in parish census taking than he is in the cure of souls. It's in the upper room, with a scotch highball, that Father Urban writes to Billy about his idea for a golf course at the Hill. The upper room seems more like a boardroom or a men's club than the place to eat the Passover supper.

Father Smith dies while on vacation, and for a time Father Urban hopes that the bishop will ask him to stay on at St. Monica's as pastor. What the bishop does offer him, pointing to a marshy blank spot on a map of the diocese, is three Indian missions. The idea of going still further out into the middle of nowhere, a rural landscape of bogs, has no appeal, and in his unenthusiastic response we see again how attached to the world Urban Roche is. The North American Martyrs,

Jesuits in the seventeenth century, made it as far west as the eastern end of Lake Superior, and all suffered martyrdom further to the east, but by mentioning Indian missions and by giving vivid glimpses at the Hill and elsewhere of the bone-chilling cold and isolation of rural Minnesota, the author hints at the life of sacrifice and dedication that Father Urban runs from. Self-denial has no interest to him, and the idea of shedding his blood for the faith seems a romantic notion that has no relevance in the comfortable world of good food and fellowship. The faithful surrender of self goes against the grain of American self-determination.

Still trying to raise the tone of the Clementines as he attempts to attract the right sort of retreatants to St. Clement's Hill, Father Urban discovers that a small neighboring farm is for sale, and he conceives the notion of building a golf course. It is easy to interest Billy Cosgrove in the idea, and Father Urban goes to the novitiate to argue that a golf course would be a good way to draw the unchurched to the Hill. With the building of the golf course, the landscape of the novel becomes increasingly symbolic, and parallels between the modern Midwest and the world of medieval chivalry and piety become clearer. In medieval literature the construction of a stadium for tournaments—as described, for example, in Chaucer's Knight's Tale—suggests man's attempt to bring order and sanity to the chaos of war and irrationality. Similarly, Father Urban sees the golf course as a way of transforming the wilderness of rural Minnesota, a way of bringing the distractions of the earthly city to the Hill. His motive is not order but accommodation. The golf course is more intrusive than the television because it permanently reconfigures the natural world, reshaping creation for utterly frivolous ends. Powers does not work out the details of his comparison of the modern with the medieval world in a systematic fashion, but the invocation of medieval times obvious in the last third of the novel calls attention to the underlying seriousness of his comedy. In the Middle English romance, the Green Knight challenges Arthur's court to play a Christmas game the implications of which are of the utmost gravity.

When the dynamiting of stumps is finished, the course architect, Chub Robertson, leaves Father Urban in charge. Expert workmen come to do the greens, and Father Urban makes certain that "they were given their formula of fertilizer, were gently watered, mowed, and weeded—by young men in bare feet." This is a far cry from the pictures for the Hill's brochure of an agrarian Father Urban with a hoe in hand. He had never taken to proper gardening and resented the order's attempts to make a farmer of him, but his grooming of the course is a different matter. When Chub comes to inspect the course in June, he pronounces the greens playable and says to Father Urban, "You've done well here" (*Morte*, 199). Father Urban has labored well in the fields of mammon, and Chub has blessed the work of this faithful but misguided servant.

The golf course generally accomplishes the purposes Father Urban saw for it. "To the Hill had come a number of those better types who had never made a retreat before and whose support—and not just material support—was required if the place was to succeed as a spiritual powerhouse or oasis (Father Urban used both terms), although the less desirable types were still in the majority" (*Morte*, 200). But the success of the golf course causes the bishop to consider taking over the Hill for a diocesan seminary. Everything Father Urban has worked for is at risk when the bishop shows up with a Father Herman Feld to play a round of golf. The bishop is a lousy golfer and a bad sport, and "he wished to see done what he could not do himself, and . . . he had chosen young Father Feld to be the weapon of his will, his champion" (*Morte*, 234). Golf has become, as Father Urban recognizes, a form of judicial combat in which the outcome is believed to be the judgment of God. Having Father Feld beat Father Urban will give the bishop a comfortable feeling about taking over the Hill, which he has the authority to do, golf game or not.

Father Urban is on his game and preaches "a great sermon in golf" (*Morte*, 236). On the ninth green, however, on the verge of triumph, the order's gray champion is cut down when the bishop's ball hits him in the head and knocks him out. Father Urban is taken to the hospital in Great Plains, where he learns from Monsignor Renton that the accident has caused the bishop to abandon the idea of taking over the Hill. Father Urban does not like regarding the accident as an act of God, "since it made short work of him as a responsible instrument of God's will in an orderly universe" (*Morte*, 242). So Powers's worldly priest is removed from center stage in his own drama, and now gradually he must come to terms with his weakened condition.

Father Urban's conversion is not as simple as a miracle, but some things are noticeable at once. Wilf gives him permission to move out to Mrs. Thwaites's house at Lake Lucille. Katie drives him to the cathedral in Great Plains every morning so that he can say Mass, and at Lake Lucille "he could be seen moving slowly about the grounds, under the great oaks, reading his office, and wearing his cassock—he had decided against slopping around in slacks while there" (*Morte*, 244). Here Powers has already given us a new view of Father Urban by calling attention to his priestly duties as well as his traditional garb. The world, the flesh, and the devil are not through with Urban yet, but the novel is quickly moving toward its resolution. The golf-ball accident is climactic precisely because it is an act of God. According to Powers, "nothing else could have slowed up a man like Urban."[9] Father Urban begins to turn his thought beyond himself. He becomes aware, dimly at first, then with greater clarity, of the necessity of self-abnegation, of his utter dependence on God.

Cruising about on Lake Lucille with Mrs. Thwaites, Father Urban first sees Sally's castle on one of the lake's small islands, "a battlemented tower of rough red granite" that Sally's father had built for her when she was a child. The tower bears the name Belleisle "from some romantic tale" (*Morte*, 246), and it is there that soon Father Urban's chastity will be tried. Motoring around on the lake listening to Mrs. Thwaites's worries about her family, Father Urban has "a vision of life in late medieval times" (*Morte*, 247). He sees himself as a courtier in the presence of the old queen, and this fantasy provides him with some perspective on the difficulties inherent in his situation: how to be a priest and provide for Mrs. Thwaites's considerable spiritual needs without displeasing her.

When Father Urban learns that Mrs. Thwaites has been winning the earnings of her Irish maidservant at dominoes, he intercedes on Katie's behalf, announcing to Mrs. Thwaites, "I've just met a damsel in distress" (*Morte*, 249). The old woman's only response is to turn up the sound on her television sets. Father Urban later learns that Katie has been dismissed. He recognizes Mrs. Thwaites's unfeeling attachment to the things of this world and thinks, "Children, how hard it is for them that trust in riches to enter into the kingdom of God" (*Morte*, 250). This is not simply a pastoral judgment. It is a judgment also of Father Urban's life in the church, and the reader has a sense that the priest is beginning to see the double application.

After returning to the Hill, Father Urban is invited to go on a fishing trip with Billy in a remote area north of Duesterhaus near the Canadian border. Billy and his chauffeur, Paul, arrive at St. Clement's from Chicago, and Paul says, "I don't see no Indians." This is a coarse version of Father Urban's initial reaction to the rural landscape outside Duesterhaus, but this time it is the priest who gently remonstrates with Paul. "Spoken like a true Chicagoan," Father Urban says (*Morte*, 255). The fishing trip takes the three men into true wilderness, and there Father Urban rejects the devilish Billy in one of the funniest and most dramatic sequences in the novel. Spending two days and nights with Billy makes Father Urban realize "that Billy's character wasn't quite what [he] had believed it to be.

9. Ibid., 13.

A few spoons seemed to be missing" (*Morte*, 273). Trying, as he had with Mrs. Thwaites, to be both priest and courtier, Father Urban remembers the "thrilling sermons" he had preached "on saints who had really asked for the martyr's crown," but he also remembers with admiration Lanfranc, who must have dealt with William the Conqueror "with great finesse" (*Morte*, 276). Father Urban even thinks of writing a book on living for the faith instead of dying for it, a book he might entitle, "Lambs Who Lay Down with Lions and Lived" (*Morte*, 277).

Circumstances on the fishing trip, however, make diplomacy with Billy impossible. Out in an outboard motor boat with Paul and Father Urban, Billy spots a swimming buck. Declaring simply that "he'd look all right on your wall, Father" (*Morte*, 277), Billy urges Father Urban to steer the boat closer and tries to drown the deer by grabbing the antlers and pushing the head under. It takes Father Urban a minute or so to realize what Billy's trying to do. When he does, he throws "the motor into high" (*Morte*, 278), and Billy falls overboard. Back in the boat, Billy pushes Father Urban into the water and leaves him to be picked up later by the proprietors of the fishing camp. The rescued stag is another figure suggesting medieval narrative, and the stag can be seen as an image of the soul longing for living waters (see Psalm 42:1). Before leaving St. Clement's on the fishing trip, Father Urban had shown Billy the chapel, decorated in part by Brother Harold's rather primitive paintings, "not representational in the photographic sense." One of the pictures is of a stag "drinking from three wiggly lines." Father Urban tells Billy that this "was known as 'The Living Waters' and symbolized not only baptism but the other sacraments, and therefore, you might say, the Church" (*Morte*, 260). Billy's crude attempt to reduce the deer to a possession starkly demonstrates the depth of his wickedness. His willful destruction of the created order is satanic. The danger is not the gun-toting yokel that Father Urban feared upon his arrival in Minnesota; it is the savage and disordered urbanite whose will is law. Father Urban will continue to ponder the state of Billy's soul, but he does at last free himself from the notion of accommodating it in its unrepentant state. Father Urban left alone in the wilderness does not seem alarmed or greatly distressed. These north woods are even more remote and lonely than the Hill, but Father Urban is not resentful, nor does he now imagine himself being eaten by fierce dogs. The devil has left him.

The flesh of Sally Hopwood is Father Urban's last ordinary temptation. Mrs. Thwaites's married daughter lures Father Urban to Belleisle, plies him with very good scotch, and tries to seduce him, first by proposing that they take a swim and then, when Father Urban says that it's too cold and they've had too much to drink, by offering herself naked save for her golden calf high-heeled shoes. It's a bad moment, reminiscent of Sir Gawain's temptation in Bercilak's castle. Like his medieval counterpart, Father Urban preserves his chastity. He "took his eyes off her and kept them off, commending himself. It was like tearing up telephone directories, the hardest part was getting started" (*Morte*, 297). His resistance is undercut slightly by the revelation that he commended himself, but under the circumstances that seems as unimportant as Gawain's accepting the green girdle. What counts is that he has not entertained the temptation or fallen into serious sin. On her way to the water Sally throws her golden calf shoes at Father Urban, and "the second one struck him on the head. 'Hey!' he yelled, but did not turn around and look at her. The second shoe had hurt. It might have killed him. What a way to go" (*Morte*, 297–98).

Before Sally boldly offers herself to him, Father Urban sips too much scotch and imagines what his life might have been outside the church, "in some kind of business you could breathe in, perhaps heavy machinery, much of it going overseas, lots of travel, meeting fellows like Haile Selassie and Farouk's father, whatever his name was, and operating out of a spacious office on Michigan Avenue, high up, with a view of the lake, walnut paneling, Persian carpets, furnished with gifts from potentates and dictators of the better sort, a tree at Christmas, efficient rosy-cheeked girls in white-collared dark dresses, Irish girls hired for the purity of their vocables, and himself hardly ever there" (*Morte*, 292). This fantasy, in which he also imagines himself married and the author of a popular book called *When Saints Were Bold,* highlights all of the worldly ambitions Father Urban has tried to include in his priestly life. It is clear both to Father Urban and to the reader that this is a whiskey dream. He is brought back to dangerous reality by Sally's suggestion that they take a swim. In successfully resisting her, Father Urban rejects his fantasy life and all its empty promises as well.

Back at the Hill, Father Urban "went around with a numb feeling" (*Morte*, 302). The parts of his old life that once seemed most important to him—opportunities to preach, his contacts with important people, even golf—no longer seem to matter. He is physically weaker, but he joins Father John in the garden, not simply to have his picture taken for a brochure, but to work. With a persistent cold, he is not up to much gardening, but he does not quit until he faints and has to be placed in an oxygen tent in the hospital in Great Plains.

It has taken being struck in the head by a golf ball to bring Father Urban to his senses. Physical weakness brought to him against his will proves the means of his sanctification. When Dante encounters the penitent proud bearing heavy stones on their shoulders in Purgatory, Omberto Aldobrandeschi explains that he must "bear this burden here among the dead because [he] did not bear this load among the living."[10] Suffering and self-mortification are the life of this world, and, like most Christians, Father Urban tries to avoid such discomforts as long as he can. He is brought to his senses by being made to suffer involuntarily. What is crucial is his response to such suffering. Saint Thomas writes that it is in the nature of punishment to be against the will, but when the punishment is voluntarily accepted, "it loses somewhat the nature of punishment."[11] That is the essential character of the purgatorial way. Father Urban begins to see in his weakened condition an opportunity to imitate Christ, not in the dramatic fashion of heroic martyrdom, but in the white martyrdom of self-denial, of ordinary human suffering offered to God. Sitting in his room at St. Clement's Hill, Father Urban "wondered how many old paupers before him had watched the coming of winter from that window" (*Morte*, 304). No longer interested in special pleading, no longer insisting that he is an exceptional case, he claims fellowship with God's poor.

During this period of recuperation Father Urban spends time talking to Father John, who is trying to write a version of Malory's Arthurian story. That story ends with Lancelot giving up the life of chivalry and becoming a hermit priest in the company of the Archbishop of Canterbury; as Father John writes, when Lancelot's knight companions "saw Sir Lancelot endure such penance, in prayers and fastings, they took no force what pain they endured, for to see the noblest knight of the world endure such abstinence that he waxed full lean." The next paragraph begins with Father Urban's barber's remarking, "You've lost some weight" (*Morte*, 309). Like Lancelot, Father Urban gives up the world and takes himself to perfection.

The final section of the novel, which is very short, moves apace. Father Urban is elected provincial of his order for the Chicago Province. Powers uses the Latin writing of Saint Bernard of Clairvaux for the ritual of Father Urban's installation, and after that, in less than six pages, he describes Father Urban's life as the provincial head of his order. The rite requires Father Urban to say of the people who stoned Saint Stephen the Protomartyr, "those who are estranged from truth by passion and pleasure in sinning, and who are overcome by weakness and ignorance, must surrender their passion to regret, their pleasure to sorrow, and

10. Dante Alighieri, *Purgatory* 11.70–72, trans. Allen Mandelbaum (New York: Bantam Books, 1984), 99.

11. Saint Thomas Aquinas, *Summa Theologicae*, I.II^{ae}, q. 87, ad 7 (quoted by Dorothy Sayers in *The Comedy of Dante Alighieri: Cantica II, Purgatory* [Baltimore: Penguin Books, 1955], 59).

conquer the infirmities of the flesh with the fire of justice, and meet ignorance with liberality" (*Morte,* 318). And so it will be for Urban Roche.

Despite its brevity, much is accomplished and more suggested in the closing chapter. Father Urban returns to the novitiate outside Chicago, and Powers notes that "seldom had a new Provincial so badly disappointed the hopes and calculations of men" (*Morte,* 322). Father Urban does little, and what he does bespeaks an otherworldly inefficiency that irritates and puzzles those who knew the old Urban. Of this final chapter Powers said in an interview that he regarded it as vitally important. "I used an entirely different instrument there. The scene is hardly ever set, just touched upon, in and out, in and out; the threads are all tied together."[12] The setting is less important because here Powers is writing about the spiritual landscape. He notes that the new provincial, he who once groomed a golf course, has the infected trees in the Avenue of Elms cut down. The glory of the novitiate's grounds, at least in the world's eyes, must be pruned away. Father Urban's headaches grow increasingly severe, but he tries to "disguise his condition" by opening his breviary and closing his eyes when attacks occur, and "thus, without wishing to, he gained a reputation for piety he hadn't had before, which, however, was not entirely unwarranted now" (*Morte,* 324). The novel that has begun as a satire of a worldly and self-indulgent priest, his order's gray champion on the links, ends with a compassionate view of a latter-day Saint Paul, brought to his senses not by a blinding light and the voice of God but by a bishop's golf ball and simple obedience. Even this last view of Father Urban is tough-minded and unsentimental. The reputation for piety is not "entirely unwarranted." But clearly the new provincial, who "seemed to think of the Hill as home" (*Morte,* 326), bears the burdens he has in the world gracefully. He has accepted his infirmities and set aside his worldly ambition for himself and for his order. By the world's standards Father Urban is as dull, out of touch, and unpromising as he had once found Fathers Boniface, Wilfrid, and John, but in the surrender of his attachments to the world, "no matter the appearance of death," he has found life on the penitential road that ends in the New Jerusalem.

12. Malloy, "The Catholic and Creativity," 6.

"A Tyrannous Sense of Place"
Notes on Wallace Stegner's Lyrical Realism

Thomas Bontly

When I was teaching fiction workshops for a living, I often lamented the anorexic thinness of my student's work, nowhere more apparent than in their presentation of the story's setting. A bar, a coffeehouse, a campus pad—we usually didn't know much more than that. If I suggested that a little more development might be welcome, the indignant authors would very likely tell me that they *wanted* to leave the setting vague—they thought their story would have "more universality" if it could "happen anywhere."

I ran across a possible origin for this curious theory in the remarks of a minimalist writer then in vogue and immediately set about counteracting his pernicious influence. Yet the more I preached the doctrine of place, even designing assignments that would force my students to render places they knew well, the less some of them seemed to understand. I finally concluded that the students who failed to grasp the value of a well-rendered setting were generally those who simply didn't understand *fiction*—that is, that mysterious alchemy by which we find the general in the particular, the universal in the specific. They couldn't see that, only after readers have entered imaginatively into a work of fiction, can they begin to discover those Easter eggs of meaning the writer has hidden beneath every tree and bush.

Now that I can read purely for pleasure, I have noticed that the writers I most enjoy, and those I've learned the most from over the years, have all been masters of the fully realized setting—none more accomplished or more dedicated to the task than Wallace Stegner. In his foreword to *The Collected Stories*, Stegner discusses his short stories as the products of his own experience, which he describes as "quintessentially American, though it could not now be reproduced: childhood on a belated and benighted frontier, youth in a provincial capital, maturity with the whole confused world to run in." Despite, or perhaps because of this peregrine life, Stegner developed what he called "a tyrannous sense of place"—a sense, as his friend and former student Wendell Berry put it, that "if you don't know *where* you are, you don't know *who* you are."[1]

Much of Stegner's fiction and a fair amount of his nonfiction may be seen, I think, as an attempt to establish just who he is—his own identity and values— by rendering in full the places that had a major impact on his imagination. Because most of the places he wrote about were western places, and because he was closely associated with the effort to preserve the western environment, Stegner is sometimes described as a "western writer," or, even more limiting, a western *regionalist*. These are misleading terms, it seems to me, because they suggest that a writer's work merits attention chiefly as a document of some political or social reality not found elsewhere in America.[2] Stegner's work merits attention, I would argue, precisely *because* it has remained relevant for all thoughtful readers, and a source of great pleasure to those who value good writing. Furthermore, the "western regionalist" tag is simply too broad. As Stegner wrote, "There is no such thing as the West. There are only Wests, as different from one another as New Hampshire from South Carolina or Brooklyn from Brookline." Having lived in several western states, and traveled extensively through several others while researching his books, Wallace Stegner knew better than most that the fabled West was in fact "many regions, many states of mind, many ways of life."[3]

These days the regionalist label also carries with it the onus of obsolescence, because, with a few exceptions, the United States no longer consists of distinctive "regions." The internet, the interstate, transcontinental air travel, and the culture they have spawned have all diminished our sense of purely regional identities. We may be southerners or midwesterners, New Englanders or westerners, but the world we see when we hop off the airplane or coast down the freeway exit ramp in another part of the country is almost identical to the world we left back home—the same motels, the same franchise restaurants, the same mini-marts

---

1. Stegner, *The Collected Stories* (New York: Random House, 1990), ix; Berry quoted in Stegner, "The Sense of Place," in *Where the Bluebird Sings to the Lemonade Springs: Living and Writing in the West* (New York: Random House, 1992), 199.

2. According to Jackson J. Benson, *Wallace Stegner, His Life and Work* (New York: Viking, 1996), the first critic to describe Stegner as a "Western realist" was his Stanford colleague and rival, Albert Guerard (338). Guerard resented Stegner's tight control of the creative writing program, yet it can only be lamented that these two talented writers and scholars could not coexist amicably in their nearly ideal environment.

3. "Why I Like the West," *Tomorrow* magazine, 1950, reprinted in *Marking the Sparrow's Fall*, ed. Page Stegner (New York: Henry Holt and Co., 1989), 98.

and mega-malls. The more we travel, the more we obliterate the geographical isolation and cultural uniqueness on which a purely regional literature depends.

This was a phenomenon that Wallace Stegner understood very well. In his essay "The Sense of Place" he comments on the rootlessness of modern American society ("the American home is often a mobile home") and relates the condition to his own nomadic childhood. "I know about the excitement of newness and possibility, but I also know the dissatisfaction and hunger that result from placelessness." Many of Stegner's stories deal with children or adults who must cope with alien or hostile environments, and his diagnosis of the modern malaise pinpoints our lust for newness and change as an underlying cause:

> Indifferent to, or contemptuous of, or afraid to commit ourselves to, our physical and social surroundings, always hopeful of something better, hooked on change, a lot of us have never stayed in one place long enough to learn it, or have learned it only to leave it. In our displaced condition we are not unlike the mythless man that Carl Jung wrote about, "who lives 'a life of his own, sunk in a subjective mania of his own devising, which he believes to be the newly discovered truth.'"[4]

An acquired sense of place, Stegner seemed to feel, could serve as a corrective to this "subjective mania," but how does one develop such a sense in a culture like ours, where every place looks, sounds, and feels pretty much like every other, and where we can change our location on the planet with such ease and regularity? Stegner himself was helped, paradoxically, by his impoverished frontier childhood. "I was nearly twelve before I saw either a bathtub or a water closet," he wrote in 1962, "and when I walked past my first lawn, in Great Falls, Montana, I stooped down and touched its cool nap in awe and unbelief." Lest we consider such primitive conditions a deprivation, he assures us that "there are some advantages to growing up a savage, and to tell the truth I am not sure I would trade my childhood of freedom and the outdoors and the senses for a childhood of being led by the hand past all the Turners in the National Gallery."[5]

In later life, as a successful author, popular speaker, and environmental activist, Stegner made many trips across the country and abroad and commonly spent a part of each summer in Vermont. Yet the place he called home for forty-seven years was a suburban community on the eastern foothills of California's coastal

4. Stegner, "The Sense of Place," 204–5.
5. "Child of the Far Frontier," in *Marking the Sparrow's Fall*, 7. The essay originally appeared in *Horizon* in 1962 and was expanded in *Wolf Willow: A History, a Story, and a Memory of the Last Plains Frontier* (New York: Viking Press, 1963).

range, just south of San Francisco. Here, in an environment he both cherished (for its natural beauties) and abhorred (for its human-wrought changes), he honed to a fine degree, in short stories, novels, histories, essays, and memoirs, his tyrannous sense of place. Let us see what that sense was composed of, then examine a few samples, taken from his mature work, of its expression.

The sense of place, as Stegner tells us in his essay of that name, is composed of many elements. It is partly geographical (we can find ourselves on a map) and partly economic and political (we know how the people around us earn their living, and therefore how they vote on certain issues). It may involve accents, dialects, tastes, sensibilities, traditions, and even morals. Stegner employs all these elements of place in his writings, but for him the most important designators of a place are its *natural setting* and its *human history.* The underlying structure of the land—its geology—and the kind of weather it endures—its climatology—determine both the life-forms that can flourish there and the terms of existence that are imposed on them. How those inhabitants, especially the human ones, alter the place in turn, or are altered by it, becomes for Stegner one of the great dramas of human life—and therefore, of course, one of his major themes.

In our society places must have names, and the names themselves often reflect this ongoing drama—they tell a kind of story. "No place is a place," Stegner says, "until things that have happened in it are remembered in history, ballads, yarns, legends, or monuments. Fictions serve as well as facts." Thus the historian, the storyteller, contributes significantly to our sense of place. Expressing that sense is one of his major cultural tasks. In fact, Stegner adds a little later in the same essay, "No place, not even a wild place, is a place until it has a poet"—that is, until it receives "that human attention that at its highest reach we call poetry."[6]

As a fiction writer and essayist, Wallace Stegner tried to fulfill this dual role as both chronicler and poet of places he knew well. Responsive to the natural world and deeply moved by its beauties, he made the precise observation and sensuous evocation of nature one of the hallmarks of his prose. A realistic novelist by training and conviction, deeply skeptical of human ambition and the social forces it generates, he crafted a narrative style I call lyrical realism, chiefly to suggest its ability to engage the reader on two levels: the purely aesthetic (in which we celebrate the natural world) and the critical/analytic (in which we recognize and respond to social and environmental issues). I don't think there have been many writers in the past fifty years who have struck this combination as often, and done it as well, as Wallace Stegner.

6. "The Sense of Place," 202, 205.

• • •

The first of several places to make its impact on Stegner's imagination was the prairie of southern Saskatchewan, where his restless and ambitious father tried to homestead a wheat farm between 1914 and 1920. In the winter the family lived in "the raw new non-town of East End, where the Frenchman River flows out of the Cypress Hills." In the summer they lived on the homestead itself, "two days [from town] by lumber wagon with the cow tied behind, one day by buckboard . . . seven or eight excruciating hours by model T." Stegner called these years, between the ages of five and eleven, "the shaping years of my life" and added, perhaps hyperbolically, "I have never forgotten a detail of them."[7]

Several of Stegner's early fictions use the Saskatchewan borderland as a setting, most notably the epic *Big Rock Candy Mountain* (1943), but he found himself drawn back to the material again and again, enriching his presentation of this bleak semi-wilderness with each treatment. A piece entitled "The Making of Paths," first published in the *New Yorker* in 1958 and later expanded for *Wolf Willow* (1963), is one of several later essays in which Stegner explores the depths of his feelings for the barren land. Describing an incident in which his father struggles to replace the axle of their old model T, damaged while fording the creek that traversed their property, Stegner contrasts the man-made machine and the natural setting:

> I remember that square, high car, with its yellow spoke wheels and its brass bracing rods from windshield to mud guard and its four-eared brass radiator cap. It stuck up black and foreign, a wanderer from another planet, on the flat by Coteau Creek, while my father, red-faced and sweating, crawled in and out under the jacked-up rear end and I squatted in the car's shade and played what games I could with pebbles and a blue robin's egg. We sat there on the plain, something the earth refused to swallow . . . and with the prairie as empty as nightmare clear to the line where hot earth met hot sky.

From that episode, the boy derives "the essential feeling of the country for me—that sense of being foreign and noticeable, of sticking out." It is all the more acute because "we did not belong to the earth as the prairie dogs and burrowing owls and picket-pin gophers and weasels and badgers and coyotes did, or to the sky as the hawks did, or to any combination as meadowlarks and robins and sparrows did."[8]

---

7. "Finding the Place: A Migrant Childhood," in *Where the Bluebird Sings*, 5.
8. "The Making of Paths," in *Marking the Sparrow's Fall*, 12.

One should note the characteristic Stegnerian inversion: it is not the prairie itself that is alien and strange, but the human invaders and their machines. In the natural world each creature has its home, its niche in the environment; only man refuses to conform. And he stands out at his great peril, as the boy soon learns. The family was still living in a tent, just "unloading the lumber for the shack" they planned to build, when "a funnel-shaped cloud appeared in the south, moving against a background of gray-black shot with lightning-forks." Stegner evokes the terror of the approaching storm by focusing on his remembered impressions: "the air grew tense and metallic to breathe, and a light like a reflection from brass glowed around . . . we looked at the strangely still tent, bronzed in the yellow air, and felt the air shiver and saw a dart of wind move like a lizard across the dust and vanish again."

The boy takes shelter in a shallow hole, from which he observes a gopher across the coulee, looking out from his own hole. Then "the grass stirred; it was as if gooseflesh prickled suddenly on the prairie's skin. The gopher disappeared as if some friend below had reached up and yanked him into his burrow." In the next minute the storm strikes and the boy feels the wind "pluck at" his shirt and "wrench" his hair. The rain tramples his back "with a fierce rush," and he realizes that "to give the wind more than [his] flat back would be sure destruction, for that was a wind, and that was a country, that hated a foreign and vertical thing." The cyclone passes ("we got only its lashing edge") and the boy feels "better about being who I was, but for a good many weeks I watched the sky with suspicion; exposed as we were, it could jump on us like a leopard from a tree."[9]

This passage relates interestingly to another essay of the same period, in which Stegner remarks that "there is something about exposure to that big country that not only tells an individual how small he is, but steadily tells him *who* he is." He confesses that he has "never understood identity problems," because when he "lay awake at night and heard the wind in the screens and saw the moon ride up in the sky . . . I knew well enough who, or *what* I was, even if I didn't matter. As surely as any pullet in the yard, I was a target, and I had better respect what had me in its sights."[10]

I've quoted these passages at length because they go to the heart of Stegner's feeling for nature and the human place within it. Man is a "target" only because he has set himself apart, both by venturing into territories where he is ill-equipped to survive and by attempting to alter that environment to suit his needs. A wheat

---

9. Ibid., 12–13.
10. "Finding the Place," 10.

field, a model T Ford, a tent, a shack, even a shallow hole in the ground are all human marks on the face of the planet that, as it were, challenge nature. So much more, Stegner felt, were the dams and irrigation projects that "reclaimed" the desert (as if it had ever been ours to start with); so much more the over-populous cities on arid plains, or suburban developments on mountain slopes adjacent to still-active geological faults. These are all marks of human foolhardi-ness, or arrogance, which the planet may not forgive. Yet, though there is cer-tainly an environmental "message" in much of Stegner's writing, there is also the lyricism of an individual mind responding to the awesome beauty and haunting mystery of the natural world. It is one thing to preach, and quite another to re-create, an experience like the cyclone with such care and precision that one feels the authentic terror and awe of a natural cataclysm.

One should note also that Stegner does not entirely reject human markings. As a boy he loved the paths the family made around the homestead, because "they were ceremonial, an insistence not only that we had a right to be in sight on those prairies but that we owned a piece of them and controlled it." Not just any road or trail delighted him, but "our own trail, lightly worn, its ruts a slight, fresher green where old cured grass had been rubbed away." It "lifted my heart; it took off across the prairie like an extension of myself." Stegner concludes the essay by asserting, "Wearing any such path in the earth's rind is an intimate act, an act like love, and it is denied to the dweller in cities. He lacks the proper ma-nia for it; he is out of touch."[11]

Thus the humble path to the woodshed or privy is a human mark in tune with nature; it unites man to the land instead of alienating him from it. Simi-larly, a good deal of Stegner's later fiction and nonfiction seems to come from a desire to find and follow these paths that the mind has made through its experi-ence of the natural world. In what may be his finest and most original work, *Wolf Willow* (subtitled *A History, A Story, and a Memory of the Last Plains Fron-tier*), Stegner builds a prose rhapsody on a smell, "pungent and pervasive . . . as evocative as Proust's madeleine and tea," which he associates with his childhood. He has returned, "a middle-aged pilgrim," to East End, a "village [he] last saw in 1920." At first the homecoming is disappointing. "My memory gropes uneasily, trying to establish itself among fifty-foot cottonwoods, lilac and honeysuckle hedges, and flower gardens." He begins to suspect that he is "remembering not what happened but something [he] has written." And then, down by the river bathhouse he used as a child, he comes upon the gray-leafed bush, "the shrub we

11. "Making of Paths," 14–15.

called wolf willow, now blooming with small yellow flowers." He brings a handful of leaves to his nose, and "the present and all the years between are shed like a boy's clothes dumped on the bath-house bench. . . . reality is made exactly equivalent with memory, and a hunger is satisfied. The sensuous little savage that I once was is still intact inside me."[12]

Of course there is much more to the book than ocular nostalgia. *Wolf Willow* is a full-scale exploration of that "last plains frontier," its history and character, accomplished through several narrative genres, including one of the best cowboy sagas ever written, the Conradian "Genesis." Yet the entire project seems to start, as Stegner suggests in the above passage, with the recovery of the "sensuous little savage" that still lives inside his own mind. His literary and spiritual homecoming reminds one of Wordsworth's longing for that intuitive communion with nature he believed was the legacy of every human childhood—a legacy of joy and wisdom too easily surrendered by the civilized adult. Stegner would reject Wordsworth's optimistic view of nature (it can and does "betray the heart that loves her" in several of his stories), but he would endorse the poet's belief that only by forging a new link with the natural world, through observation, imagination, and reflection, can the civilized human being escape the maniacal deceits of modern society (Jung's "mythless man . . . sunk in a subjective mania").

Let us look now at a work that focuses on quite a different sort of place, the northern California community where Stegner spent the later half of his life— "in the main, happy, contented, and productive."[13] Stegner used his own home and the surrounding countryside in three novels and numerous essays, but the work I'd like to discuss, because it's seldom been analyzed, is a novelette called "A Field Guide to the Western Birds." Written in 1952, but not published until 1956, the story employs an implicit analogy between the natural order, which the narrator observes from his veranda and study windows, and the social order, which he reluctantly enters when he attends a local soiree in honor of an impoverished concert pianist.

Joe Allston is a retired literary agent who has found his earthly paradise on this California hillside with his wife of many years, the clever and sympathetic Ruth. He is supposed to be writing his memoirs, but he would prefer to sit on his veranda and enjoy the landscape. "It is a full-time job just watching and listening here. I watch the light change across the ridges to the west, and the ridges

12. *Wolf Willow*, 5–19 passim.
13. "Finding the Place," 4.

are the fresh gold of wild oats just turned, the oaks are round and green with oval shadows, the hollows have a tinge of blue." He is particularly taken by the birds: "I see a red-headed woodpecker working spirally around a trunk, a nuthatch walking upside down along a limb, a pair of warblers hanging like limes among the leaves." A serious birder would note the exactitude of those lines—each species does what it characteristically does do—but the narrator's sensuous delight in the natural world is evident as well. In his retirement, Joe is "beginning to understand the temptation to be literary and indulge the senses."[14]

This is important because, in spite of his former profession, he has never been an artistic sort of person. He is a practical man, skilled in contracts and deals, in getting things done, and he has little patience for arty pretension or even for the sensitivity of genuine artists. He is therefore predisposed not to like Arnold Kaminski, the Polish refugee pianist who is the guest of honor at the party of his wealthy neighbors, Sue and Bill Casement. Sue considers herself a patroness of the arts, and she hopes Joe can somehow help her protégé find his way to fame and fortune at Carnegie Hall. Despite the rampant philistinism of the Casements (their house is a study in Hollywood extravagance, exported to northern California), Joe would like to do the good-natured lady a favor, but he instantly spots Kaminski as a phony, and an arrogant and obnoxious one to boot. Not that he can't play the piano—one of the surprises of the story is that Kaminski proves to be quite an accomplished pianist—but his claim to be a survivor of the Nazi death camps is as bogus as his hosts' conception of true refinement and elegance. In fact, the entire party, from the moment Joe arrives to the moment he and Ruth make their escape, is a study in social hypocrisy, delusion, and deceit. The shallow vanities and crude pretensions of these West Coast Culture Vultures (only slightly more preposterous, perhaps, than their East Coast kindred) have seldom been skewered so adroitly, yet social satire is not the main dish Stegner has on the grill—it merely fires up the coals.

The real issue, as it turns out, is Joe Allston's tendency to judge his fellow human beings by their "field marks"—to classify them as types. Kaminski is rude and unattractive; he treats his hostess and an innocent young piano teacher with unforgivable contempt—in fact, he's the full-blown sexist pig, unmasked a good twenty years before the feminist movement put such fellows on notice. Yet, in the story's most striking irony, Kaminski turns out to be, not only a genuinely talented artist, but perhaps the most honest person at the party. "How could I

---

14. "A Field Guide to the Western Birds," in *Collected Stories*, 312–13. Subsequent parenthetical references are to this edition.

help insulting her?" he asks, when Sue rebukes him for whispering four-letter words in the piano teacher's ear. "If I didn't insult people like that I couldn't keep my self-respect" (352).

Self-respect, however, is something Kaminski sorely lacks. In the midst of lamenting the artist's plight in a materialistic society, he abruptly reveals his own imposture: he's from South Boston, not Poland, and his mother did not die in a death camp—in fact, she's still alive. Dropping his phony accent for the dialect of his old neighborhood, he reveals himself in a drunken rant:

> You wonner why people detes' me? Know why? I'm a fake, isn't an hones' thing about me. You jus' le' me go to Hell my own way, I'm good at it. I can lie my way in, and if I want I can lie my way out again.... Don't you worry about a starving kike pianist from Blue Hill Avenue ... [because] I can still play the piano. I can play the God damn keys off a piano! (354–56 passim)

And then, in rejecting the kindness of the Casements a final time, he blunders into their swimming pool. As Joe sees it: "For a moment he hangs in mid-air, his legs going like a cat's held over water, and then he is in the pool. The splash comes up ghostly into the moonlight and the fog, and falls back again" (356).

On one level, the story comments on the perverse, self-destructive nature of certain artists and asks, rather plaintively, why sensible, well-meaning people should have to put up with such nonsense. Yet, on another level, Joe recognizes that society needs misfits like Kaminski—birds it can't classify as easily as it would like—and that both their God-given talent and their self-imposed travail challenge our complacent assumptions about human character and social value. Joe would like to retreat to his veranda bird-watching, where the *Field Guide* makes identification a feasible task, but even in the bird world he is faced with anomalies, like the unidentifiable bird—"some kind of towhee"—that each day lands on the veranda "to challenge his reflection on the plate glass. He springs at himself like a fighting cock, beats his wings, pecks, falls back, springs again, slides and thumps against the glass, falls down, flies up, falls down, until he wears himself out and squats on the bricks, panting and glaring at his hated image" (312). Although Joe threatens to shoot the bird for disturbing his peace, he knows he won't. Instead, he will "watch the fool thing as long as I can stand it, and ruminate on the insanity of men and birds, and try to convince myself ... this behavior is not significant" (358). Nature, it seems, can't teach us how to deal with complicated human problems. At best it offers a respite from those problems, and a chance to see the mysteries that baffle us reflected in the natural order. One of the qualities a reader comes most to respect in Stegner's fiction is its refusal to opt for easy answers or pat solutions. Like a good realist, he looks always for complexity, complication, the individual case that defies generalization. And, like the lyric poet, he delights in discovering images from the story's natural setting that will help him crystalize the human dilemma he's portraying.

Nearly any of Stegner's later works would provide other good examples of his lyrical realism, but I'd like to conclude by looking at his deservedly popular last novel, *Crossing to Safety,* which Stegner called "a labor of love and bafflement, so close to the facts that at first I thought I would not try to publish it."[15] In tracing the friendship of two literary-academic couples, the Morgans and the Langs, over the course of thirty-five years, the novel develops three nonwestern settings: Madison, Wisconsin; Florence, Italy; and the Green Mountains of Vermont. Stegner's rendering of these locales is no less detailed, persuasive, and lyrical than his presentation of western scenes. Here, for example, is his description of early morning in a Vermont cabin:

> Standard summer cottage taint of mice, plus a faint, not-unpleasant remembrance of skunk under the house, but around through those a keenness as of seven thousand feet. Illusion, of course. What smells like altitude is latitude. Canada is only a dozen miles north, and the ice sheet that left its tracks all over this region has not gone for good, but only withdrawn. Something in the air, even in August, says it will be back.

For Stegner it is an easy jump from realistic description to philosophical reflection, accompanied as usual by a poetic metaphor. "Seen in geological perspective," Larry Morgan muses, "we are fossils in the making, to be buried and eventually exposed again for the puzzlement of creatures of later eras.... Here everything returns upon itself, repeats and renews itself, and the present can hardly be told from the past."[16]

It is appropriate, then, that in the second chapter the narrative leaps back in time, from 1972 to 1937, when Larry Morgan and Sid Lang first meet as lowly instructors at the University of Wisconsin. It is still the Great Depression in Academia, and seldom has the proud, impoverished, idealistic, yet often petty academic environment been portrayed with such clarity and conviction. Surviving tedious faculty receptions, Harvard-Yale snobbery, and a starvation budget, the

---

15. "The Law of Nature and the Dream of Man," in *Where the Bluebird Sings,* 227.
16. *Crossing to Safety* (New York: Random House, 1987), 4. Subsequent parenthetical references are to this edition.

Morgans are delighted to find themselves adopted by the generous, spirited, and much wealthier Langs. The friendship grows despite its many trials: a hazardous sailing expedition on Lake Mendota, a grueling childbirth at the hands of an incompetent obstetrician, adverse personnel decisions by a benighted executive committee. Later, the couples are confronted by more adversity: Sally Morgan's polio, which leaves her permanently crippled, Larry's meager income as a writer, Sid's failure to win tenure, and finally Charity Lang's terminal cancer. Through it all, the friendship endures, though not without its internal conflicts and periods of stress. The couples don't so much "like" each other as *need* each other, and that need, as Stegner shows us, generates the sturdiest kind of love. Ultimately, *Crossing to Safety* is about love of all types between man and wife, friends and colleagues, parents and children. It is about the pleasures and pains of love, its rewards and its often terrible price.

A minor theme of the novel is the influence of environment on human character and values—not only the places where we grow up but also the places we encounter on our pilgrimage through life. Larry Morgan is a westerner from New Mexico, a poor boy eager to make his mark in the literary world. Sally is the orphaned daughter of a Greek singer and was working her way through Berkeley as a librarian when Larry met her. Both Sid and Charity Lang are from blue-blooded New England families, graduates of Harvard and Smith, respectively. Among their distinguished relatives they count a Boston publisher, several Ivy League professors, and a former ambassador to France. The contrast in backgrounds couldn't be more marked, and the stresses and fractures these social differences cause are easily recognized.

Charity, though as loving as her name suggests, is proud and manipulative. An intelligent woman denied a career of her own by the conventions of the time, she is overly ambitious for her husband, who is the incurable amateur, the light-hearted poet manqué that his upper-class breeding has made him. Larry, on the other hand, is the epitome of the self-made man, who delights in playing the western primitive for his wealthy friends ("Rub-um sticks together," he says, when Charity asks how they will light a fire in the woods if they've forgotten to bring matches [142]).[17] Larry's rugged male individualism often butts head-first into Charity's aristocratic female arrogance, and he can't entirely avoid being jealous of Sid's manly attributes, both physical and social, though he often champions him against his headstrong wife. Only Sally, the orphan of foreign parents (though

---

17. Later, Larry explains his habit of early-morning typing: "If I'm going to set the literary world on fire, the only way to do it is to rub one word against another" (210).

her father, I believe, is never mentioned), remains calm, reasonable, and understanding throughout. Except for her disability, she is another of Stegner's loving
portraits of his own wife.

The natural world is richly described—a Vermont waterfall covers two lush
pages, and a wonderfully prolonged sunset orchestrates the somber final chapter—but the artistic and intellectual world—a world Stegner calls "the dream
of man"—is given top billing. Visiting Italy for the first time, Larry Morgan delights in the immediate accessibility of a great cultural tradition: "It was like
looking upriver into the pour of history, seeing backward toward the beginnings
of modern civilization" (207). He is particularly impressed with Florence:

> It thrilled me to think how the people of this little city had lighted mankind—
> both kindling and matches had been here in profligate plenty. It never ceased to
> amaze me to look across the river and see, small and sharp as if seen through a
> reversed telescope, a landscape of hills and cypresses cribbed from Leonardo....
> Every white American who wants to know who he is must make his peace with
> Europe. If he is lucky he can conduct the negotiations, as we did, in the valley
> of the Arno. (215)

It is interesting to note that, ever the resourceful backwoodsman, Larry begins
his tribute with the metaphor of a lighted campfire and, always a bit defensive
about cultural matters, concludes it in the language of military conquest. A master technician, Stegner never just "does" setting; he *uses* it to illustrate character,
theme, and drama.

The final great theme the novel takes up is the age-old question of how to die,
or how to incorporate the hard fact of death into one's philosophy of life. Facing
her own death, Charity rejects "religious gobbledygook" and tries to understand
her fate in biological terms:

> "It's as natural as being born," she said, "and even if we stop being the individ-
> uals we once were, there's an immortality of organic molecules that's absolutely
> certain. Don't you find that a wonderful comfort? I do. To think that we'll
> become part of the grass and trees and animals, that we'll stay right here where
> we loved it while we were alive. People will drink us with their morning milk
> and pour us as maple syrup over their breakfast pancakes." (237)

This Whitmanesque vision of immortality is not without its charms for Stegner,
who plays with it for a while, adding his own naturalistic detailing, but ultimately
it fails to answer the last hard question: what becomes of the individual will? Al-

ways a willful and supremely confident woman, Charity "masters" her husband even "from her deathbed," insisting that he attend a family picnic she has arranged while Sally escorts her to the hospital, yet her eyes reveal no triumph as she looks at her old friend and antagonist, Larry Morgan. "Her eyes . . . were like the eyes of Piero's gloomy Christ—a painting she had once . . . affected to repudiate" (260). The scene carries us back to Florence, to all the images of death and resurrection the younger couples absorbed and only half understood and the injured work-man whose stoic suffering brought their Etruscan idyll to a tragic close. Once again, Stegner has no sure answers, but no one could say he has not looked at the question with the unflinching gaze of the true artist.

Stegner's lyrical realism may be seen, in summary, as a dedication to technique that transcends mere technique, that enables the author to discover both the *facts* of place and the *mythos* of place, which, taken together, enrich and enlarge his vision of the world. If I could give my former students (and those I may yet en-counter) a prescription for improving their own sense of place, and thereby the overall quality of their writing, I couldn't do better than to recommend a strong dose of Wallace Stegner's major works. Not that they wouldn't notice weak links and blind spots. As Stegner himself wrote, "Ultimately there is no escaping the fact that fiction is only as good as its maker. It sees only with the clarity that he is capable of, and it perpetuates his astigmatisms."[18]

I seldom find Stegner's vision shortsighted, but there are times (as there will be with most authors as prolific as he was) when the inspiration itself seems to falter. At such times Stegner's fiction (less often, I think, his nonfiction) may strike us as merely "made," in the sense of cobbled together out of disparate ma-terials. When, however, Stegner's "tyrannous sense of place" has done the inte-grating and fusing, his narratives speak with the clarity and passion of great art.

18. "The Law of Nature and the Dream of Man," 217.

Early Updike
Wandering in the Fields of the Lord

Pat C. Hoy II

We are all exiles who need to bathe in the irrational.
—JOHN UPDIKE, *COUPLES*

More than thirty years ago, when I first read the stories in John Updike's *The Same Door* and *Pigeon Feathers*, I had just returned from war in Vietnam to begin a three-year teaching assignment at the U.S. Military Academy at West Point. That year, 1969, marked the end of the most turbulent decade of my life, a decade of continual displacements in and out of the country to Korea and Vietnam and back again. I was just past thirty. The forces buffeting me around during those years included the U.S. government, an inherited commitment to service, a sure sense of myself as a soldier, an unwary ignorance of my responsibilities as a new husband and father of two children, and a deep, aching need for love and stability.

When, in the aftermath of war, I read selectively among those two early collections of Updike's stories—"Ace in the Hole," "Dentistry and Doubt," "Snowing in Greenwich Village," and "Sunday Teasing" from *The Same Door,* along with "The Persistence of Desire," "Flight," "A Sense of Shelter," "Wife-Wooing," "Pigeon Feathers," "Home," "You'll Never Know Dear, How Much I Love You," "A & P," and "Packed Dirt, Churchgoing, a Dying Cat, a Traded Car" from *Pigeon Feathers*—I was caught unaware. I was not only reading literature for its own sake but also reading to recover vestiges of a lost life—one that I had passed through without savoring. Those stories and then the novel *Couples* (1968) spoke to me of a forbidden world just on the other side of reason and the laws of my southern upbringing. They taunted me.

Updike, 4F, had not seen war, but during those years he had re-created, often in telling detail, the America that soldiering had taken away from me and others. He did not put the war at the center of his fiction. He turned away from the protests and the turmoil, focusing instead on the lives of boys and young men making their precarious entry into adult life, struggling always between the need to be free and the need to be tethered (usually to a woman).

At West Point, with time on our hands, finally, we men could reflect on where we had been and where we were going with our own lives. Preparing for our classes, we often sat together laughing and joking about Updike's characters, but we were really talking about ourselves, rehearsing our own foibles, speaking out of our own desires and frustrations. Most of us were in our early thirties, our lives still ahead of us. But the idea of death had worn us down. We were anxious about ourselves and our commitments, suspended in a quiet interval, trying to regain our bearing. Updike teased us with a new landscape of forbidden, complicating possibilities. Escape was always on his mind—and never far from ours.

Now, the exquisite writing in that early work (1959–1968) compels me as much as the stories themselves. Updike may well turn out to be the best historian of the last fifty years of America's day-to-day life, but he is most compelling when America itself seems almost *residual,* when the stories become mythical— beyond a particular place and outside the precincts of time—when we recognize the characters as ourselves. Focusing on moments of dramatic intensity and human struggle, he crafts scenes of brief duration, but other chronological lines pass through these scenes—extended genealogical lines, especially—pushing us beyond the moments of conflict, beyond the confines of a given place, into the deeper wellspring of life. In *Couples* we are often carried forward from scene to scene, moving on the current of drama rather than narration.

As place recedes into the background, as it often does in Updike's fiction, his vision comes into the foreground, and we see instead of place the dramatic action of the scene itself. Eudora Welty reminds us that place is the "gathering spot of all that has been felt, is about to be experienced, in the novel's progress." She wants us to understand that in the best of fiction, the writer's "focusing becomes so intent and aware and conscious . . . as to amount to fusion." The details of place are there for us to observe, of course, but the importance of place lies in the power it bestows on the writer. Place "is for the writer writing simply *locus,*" and as the story extends itself in its own leisurely way, locus fades "off into the blue." Almost any place will do so long as the writer's roots (and ours) reach "toward . . . the deep and running vein, eternal and consistent and everywhere purely itself, that feeds and is fed by the human understanding." What arises out of place that matters most to the reader is a new vision, replete with feeling and experience and a sure sense that the writer has made "reality real."[1]

Shillington, Pennsylvania (and the farm outside it), and Ipswich, Massachusetts (and surrounding New England), certainly shape and inform Updike's fiction, but they slip easily into the background; having done their work for him, they anchor us, provide what seem to be authentic details, and make his vision hauntingly real. But the spirit of place turns out to be far more important than place itself. And even geographical place will not, in Updike's skillful hands, hold still. By a simple twist of his imagination, Pennsylvania and Puritan New England are transformed, sometimes through the agency of a woman's body, into a metaphorical landscape of salvation, yet that transfigured landscape is deeply rooted in the realities of Shillington and Ipswich.

In *Self-Consciousness* (1989), Updike writes of the primacy of Ipswich:

> I felt well located artistically . . . It was a community vivid but transparent to me, exotic but valid as a metaphor, and only I was there to tell its tale. . . . Other places I have lived (Cambridge, New York, Beverly Farms) have been too trafficked, too well cherished by others, or else, like the environment my mother created in Pennsylvania, need too much special explaining, and don't read simply as America.

He finds in New England "something flinty and dry, witty and reticent, complex and venerable, breathable and lucid that suited [him]." The people of the area have a tact that "wordlessly acknowledges another's right to an inner life and private strangeness."[2]

Out of that enclave in Ipswich, Puritan at its roots, Updike discovered that he could, from a distance, make use of the constricting influences of his native Pennsylvania while drawing on the excitement and promise of a community close at hand in New England. In Ipswich, despite the historical legacy, he could feel "light-hearted, desirable, healthy." The place itself seemed to relieve him of a number of "tics" or afflictions that had annoyed and limited him from childhood: skin problems, breathing difficulties, choking bouts, social dis-ease. "If Shillington gave me my life," he tells us, "Ipswich was where I took possession of it, the place where in my own sense of myself, I ceased to be a radically defective person."[3]

1. Eudora Welty. "Place in Fiction," in *The Eye of the Story: Selected Essays and Reviews* (New York: Random House, 1978), 122, 124, 129, 133, 128.

2. Updike, *Self-Consciousness: Memoirs* (New York: Ballantine-Fawcett, 1989), 266–67.

3. Ibid., 49.

If we pause now to look across the fictive landscape of *Pigeon Feathers* and *Couples,* we see that Updike's male characters—both young and old, struggling against fate and a Christian god, caught up in the midst of first one and then another existential crisis—turn for relief to various women, only to discover that these women, well-intentioned as they sometimes are, simply compound the burden of suffering. But in Updike's fictive world there seems to be no other way to salvation. His God sits back at a distance and watches the show.

"Flight" begins in a moment of self-consciousness with the seventeen-year-old narrator's confession that he thinks of himself often in the third person: "Allen Dow strode down the street and home."[4] The scene glides almost imperceptibly to an earlier moment when Allen was eleven or twelve. He and his mother are on a hilltop outside Olinger where they look out over a broad expanse of the Pennsylvania countryside. Allen tells us, "Suddenly she dug her fingers into the hair on my head and announced, 'There we all are, and there we'll all be forever.'" His mother lingers over the word *forever,* before she goes on to say, "Except you, Allen, you're going to fly" (52).

The central struggle between Allen and his mother is enclosed in a web of family disputes and disappointments that give this story range and timelessness. Allen bears the burden of his mother's suffering—an "inheritance," he informs us, "of frustration and missed opportunities that had descended from my grandfather to my mother to me, and that I, with a few beats of my grown wings, was destined to reverse and redeem" (57–58). But it takes more than a few beats of his grown wings; it takes a young woman to counteract the older one. Allen is there, more or less, for the ride.

When Allen and Molly meet, they are on a train, traveling to a high-school debating tournament. After the first day's debate, they spend most of the night in one another's company, enjoying the first blush of concupiscence. When Molly steps forward to kiss Allen, he feels as if he has been given "a face to eat, and the presence of bone—skull under skin, teeth behind lips—impeded me" (60). The next day, tired and self-conscious, he loses his debate and suffers humiliation. But on the train ride back to Olinger, he discovers "what it was to bury a humiliation in the body of a woman" (60). All he has to do is sit next to Molly, feel her body against his. Back home, struggling against his mother and her network of friends, Allen comes to realize that women, apart from their remoteness, can provide reassurance and relief from self-doubt and crippling anxiety. Molly does even more.

4. Updike, "Flight," in *The Early Stories, 1953–1975* (New York: Knopf, 2003), 52. Subsequent parenthetical references to this and other stories are to this edition.

"Flight" ends on the occasion of Allen's grandfather's death, an event that draws him, against his will, into alliance with his suffering mother. Yet struggling against the pull of death and the implicit demands for sympathy, he realizes "how hard [his] heart had become!" He resolves, with a "dry tone of certainty and dislike," that his mother will not win again (65). The story closes on a note of finality—as a defeated mother bids farewell to her son. Molly has dropped out of sight by story's end, but there is no doubt that she has fashioned the wings. It is she, not the mother, not even the father as myth would have it, who has stiffened Allen's resolve, made him stronger, hardened his heart—saved him temporarily from the fingers gripping "into the hair on his head."

We see the metaphorical seeds of this story brought to fruition several years later in *Of the Farm* (1965), where another male protagonist, well past his Pennsylvania youth, returns home from New England with a new wife (his second) and finds himself pinioned between her and his taunting mother. Mrs. Robinson's meddling, aimed mostly at her son Joey, seeks to elicit from him a declaration of loyalty and love. Instead, she creates resistance.

One night following a long, contentious discussion with his mother about his life, his wives, and his failures, Joey returns to his upstairs room to find his wife already stretched out in bed. He stands over her, meditating: "My wife is wide, wide-hipped and long-waisted, and, surveyed from above, gives an impression of terrain, of a wealth whose ownership imposes upon my own body a sweet strain of extension; entered, she yields a variety of landscapes." So powerful is Peggy at this moment that, in a subsequent dream, she manages for a while to "redeem with the sun of her presence, the years of dismal hours" Joey had spent on the farm as a child. Through her body the actual landscape of childhood confinement and displeasure is transformed into an imagined landscape of desire and redemption, and, beyond the power of Peggy's own knowing, Joey ends his nighttime meditation with a revelation: "Never had the farm been so gay."[5]

In a review of Denis de Rougemont's *Love Declared* (first published in the *New Yorker* in 1963 and collected two years later in *Prose Pieces*), Updike selects a phrase of de Rougemont's that "identifies a man's Iseult as 'the woman . . . of his most intimate nostalgia.'" As he ruminates about this phrase, Updike anticipates Joey's expansive metaphor of the body:

> While nostalgia does not create women, perhaps it does create Iseults. . . . A woman, loved, momentarily eases the pain of time by localizing nostalgia; the vague and irrecoverable objects of nostalgic longing are assimilated, under

5. Updike, *Of the Farm* (New York: Ballantine-Fawcett, 1965), 43, 45.

the pressure of libidinous desire, into the details of her person. Freud says she is our mother. But the images we hoard in wait for the woman who will seem to body them forth include the inhuman—a certain slant of sunshine, a delicate flavor of dust, a kind of rasping tune that is reborn in her voice; they are nameless, these elusive glints of original goodness that a man's memory stores toward an erotic commitment. Perhaps it is to the degree that the beloved crystallizes the lover's past that she presents herself to him, alpha and omega, as his Fate.[6]

We see those "elusive glints of original goodness" expressed in the mind of young Allen as he finds solace in Molly's body, and we see them again elaborated in Joey's lengthy meditation on the textures and contours of Peggy's body. We see too how clearly Peggy "crystallizes" Joey's past and relieves him of his anxiety about family complications and the burden of the farm itself. In each case the woman loved affords redemption for the suffering, nostalgic man.

Two other stories from *Pigeon Feathers* complicate these matters of redemption and bring into sharper focus a fictive world fueled by anxiety, sexual desire, and a remote but ever-present God. In these two stories we watch a single character, at two different moments in his life, struggle against a loss of faith and a fear of death.

"Pigeon Feathers," the title story of the collection, and "Packed Dirt, Churchgoing, a Dying Cat, and a Traded Car" highlight David Kern's inner turmoil over death. In the first story, David has just moved to the family farm outside Olinger, Pennsylvania; he is fourteen. In the second story, he is a married man with four children who, over the course of the story, resides in England, New England, and Pennsylvania.

In "Pigeon Feathers," displaced to the farm away from the comfort of town and the proximity of friends, David undergoes a crisis of faith that neither his family nor the church he regularly attends has prepared him for. Set in motion by his reading of H. G. Wells's demythologized "account of Jesus" in volume 2 of *The Outline of History,* David becomes prematurely anxious about his own death (14). Wondering about the nature of his soul, he tries to imagine what will happen to that soul from the moment he dies until the Judgment Day.

Books, family, and church fail David as he searches for answers to his dilemma, but his aging grandmother, with no apparent interest in theological matters, turns David's mind to the practical. For his fifteenth birthday, his parents have given him a Remington .22. His "Granmom," through the agency of her daughter,

6. Updike, "More Love in the Western World," in *Assorted Prose* (New York: Knopf, 1965), 286–87.

sends young David out to the barn to kill the pigeons who are fouling the stored furniture.

When David repairs to the barn to do his chore, he enters a space momentarily transfigured by the sounds of cooing pigeons and the play of light and shadow across the ladders and crossbeams of the barn's interior. David locks the door behind him and begins methodically to move about this sanctuary, up and down ladders, in and out of the light, killing first one and then another of the pigeons until he has six of them scattered over the barn's surface.

Caught up in the strange mystery of killing, David is himself transfigured. He "felt like a creator" as he shot the pigeons (31). Falling into the seductive rhythms of his job, his mind turns away from his own anxieties to the business at hand, and by the time his mother comes to investigate, David has acquired a confidence that allows him to meet her, out in the sunlight, with a smirk. She goes into the barn regretting her part in soliciting David's help and picks up two dead birds. She leads David across the road, giving him instructions to bury them, and leaves him to do the task alone: "They're your kill" (32).

As David eventually stacks the bird's bodies for burial, he becomes reflective, discovering in the intricacy of the varying patterns of each bird's feathers an answer to the riddle that has been troubling him. The designs have been "executed, it seemed, in a controlled rapture, with a joy that hung level in the air above and behind him" (33). As we read these words, we expect that David may be discovering a kind of old-fashioned comfort from the creator's work, that he is beginning to share in the rapture hanging in the air, perhaps beginning to see that a god who has created such grandeur might provide the solace he has been seeking.

But it turns out that David's way out of his dilemma is to align himself with the Creator in a very different way. He imagines himself a creature so much more magnificent than the "worthless" birds that this god, with whom he has just shared the power of life and death, will grant him immortality.

As David completed the gathering of the dead birds and "fitted the last two, still pliant, on the top, and stood up, crusty coverings were lifted from him, and with a feminine, slipping sensation along his nerves that seemed to give the air hands, he was robed in this certainty: that the God who had lavished such craft upon these worthless birds would not destroy His whole Creation by refusing to let David live forever" (33).

We see that David has rejected the traditional argument from design and has instead put himself on a par with this creator. It is a teasing ending that seems to subvert the story's design. We are led to expect that the killing will bring David to his senses. But as we puzzle out the negatives in that long, closing sentence—

"would not destroy his whole Creation by refusing to let David live forever"—
we see, finally, that David, through the auspices of his gun and his imagination,
has made of himself a god, a god who is indeed robed in the certainty that he
will live forever.

I sense here, behind this final scene, a god who will appear again in *Couples,* a
god Updike seems to favor in a review of Karl Barth's *Anselm: Fides Quaerens
Intellectum* (1962). At the beginning of this review, Updike quotes from one of
Barth's earlier works: "There is no way from us to God—not even a *via negativa*—not even a *via dialectica* nor *paradoxa.* The god who stood at the end of
some human way... would not be God."[7] Our understanding of this God, according to Anselm (and Barth and Updike) does not proceed from an act of intellec-
tion; understanding proceeds from an act of faith. We believe first so that we may
understand. Precisely what we are allowed to understand beyond the inaccessi-
bility of this God is not clear. We are apparently left to wander in his playground
working out for ourselves what we imagine to be our salvation. Certain in our
faith, we are, we must surmise, at the whim of forces beyond our understanding.

David Kern does not work his way *toward* this God in "Pigeon Feathers." His
is a faith built on destruction; whether false or not, the story conceals. We know
nothing of the Creator's judgment; we know only that David imagines himself
immortal. We surmise, nevertheless, that he has more to learn.

When next we see him in "Packed Dirt," David is away from Pennsylvania—a
husband, a world traveler, a father of four. But he is no less prone to bouts of
doubt and anxiety than he had been at fifteen. The terms of his struggle differ
now, however. So too does the *form* that Updike chooses for the story itself. Instead of focusing on a brief illuminating moment, he gives us four such moments,
all woven together to deepen and complicate our understanding of David's existential crisis and to extend the landscape of suffering beyond the confines of a
single place.

Within each of the first three scenes, David tries to locate himself comfortably in the concrete world of his senses, but he discovers both "radiance" and
"darkness" in the material world (106). The pleasure he finds in "the sight of bare
earth that has been smoothed and packed firm by the passage of human feet"
gives way to an anxiety about death, reminiscent of his experiences as a young
man in "Pigeon Feathers" (102). The churches he visits here in the new story eventually lead him to conclude that "we grow sated even with consolation" (172).

7. Updike, "Faith in Search of Understanding," in *Assorted Prose* (New York: Knopf,
1965), 273.

And his efforts, while in England, to save a dying cat leave him anxious because no one responds to his acts of kindness. Even his daughter's birth cannot attenuate his craving for appreciation, his need for confirmation.

It takes an eerie journey to his father's hospital bedside to wrest David from his battle with the senses. Before the journey begins, however, David and his wife attend a party where he dances again and again with another woman. They slither against one another's thighs, explore spines, kiss hands (he), finger chins (she), and are eventually "transposed . . . into a higher key" (109). Then off in "a sheltered corner of the room," they "stopped dancing altogether and talked," David tells us, "and what I distinctly remember is how her hands, beneath the steady and opaque appraisal of her eyes, in agitation blindly sought mine and seized and softly gripped, with infantile instinct, my thumbs. Just my thumbs she held, and as we talked she moved them this way and that as if she were steering me" (109).

Back home, when his wife turns to him in bed, he wonders whether she is motivated by the "loosening effect" of alcohol or whether she responds to him as if they are "a matched pair of tuning forks" (110). Whatever her motivation, "irritated by whatever illicit stimulations, [they] took it out on each other" in sexual congress—moved about as they were by currents beyond their understanding, as if *steered* by an invisible force (110).

David realizes, after his wife falls asleep and leaves him alone, that he has committed adultery in thought, but adultery turns out to be the least of his worries: "The universe that so easily permitted me to commit adultery," he tells us, "became, by logical steps each one of which went more steeply down than the one above it, a universe that would easily permit me to die." His brain "shouted about injustice, thundered accusations" as he railed about the unworthiness of a God who "permitted [him] this fear" (110). Jealous of the future and his absence from it, suspended in horror, he wakes his wife and tries to do with his fear what he had done with his lust—pass it "into her" (111).

The next day, his birthday, David's mother calls from Pennsylvania to tell him that his father has been hospitalized, and he is strangely "relieved," confident that his father will defeat death. David claims to be "restored to crisp health in the play-world of action" (111).

When he arrives in Pennsylvania, David learns from his mother that his father has "lost all his faith" (114). But in the hospital as David looks for signs of such loss on his father's face, he finds none, and he realizes, perhaps for the first time, that he needs his father between him and Heaven. "I was afraid," he says, "of being placed adjacent to that far sky" (115).

While there in the hospital room, David watches his father respond cordially to a young woman from the Luther Home Mission who has come to console him but who needs consoling herself. David sees that his father, even from hospital bed, continues to "shed faith upon others," and David tells us that for the "remainder of my visit with him his simple presence . . . reassured me, filled me with such a buoyant humor" (119).

Comforted by what he has learned, David returns to his own home in Massachusetts under the auspices of an unseen force:

> We climbed through a space fretted by brilliance and bathed in a monotonous wind. I had been driving forever; houses, furniture, churches, women were all things I had innocently dreamed. And through those aeons my car, beginning as a mechanical assembly of molecules, evolved into something soft and organic and consciously brave. I lost, first heart, then head, and finally any sense of my body. In the last hour of the trip I ceased to care or feel or in any sense see, but the car, though its soul the driver had died, maintained steady forward motion, and completed the journey safely. Above my back yard the stars were frozen in place, and the shapes of my neighbors' house wore the wonder that children induce by whirling. (121)

So we see that David, within this play world of action, is returned to the comfort of childhood. His soul momentarily dead, he rests behind the wheel of his car, relieved of all his senses, and submits himself to the force that moves him steadily forward along this seemingly endless journey. The car too has become bound up in a larger universe and will soon become (like his father) "utterly dissolved back into the mineral world from which it was conjured" (121).

But David's car will not be, as were those old cars of his father's, "dismissed without a blessing, a kiss, a testament, or any ceremony of farewell" (121). This is, after all, a story about those saving rituals that punctuate our endless journey within this smaller world that we inhabit. While here we leave our traces in the packed earth, in our acts of kindness and desperation, and in the stories we tell about ourselves and our fellow voyagers. This is also a story about acceptance, about submission—a willing surrender to a force powerful enough to steer us around, whether that force be a woman on the corner of the dance floor or "the stellar infinity of explosive sparks needed to drive" the car. It is a story that only a good father could lead a son to tell. If that father also be godlike, we know only of his power to console us and point the way.

Couples brings us to a geographical spot where these fictive developments come to fruition, to another stretch of God's playground—where his grown children play out an interval in their lives under his distant gaze. On the weekends and holidays, they frolic together. Day to day they go responsibly about their work as contractors, dentists, biologists, computer programmers, airline pilots, school-teachers, builders. But, in their free time, frolicking is their primary business.

At town center, in this fictive world of Tarbox, Massachusetts ("Sexpot," to one of the characters), we find a church steeped in history, beautiful in construc-tion, and crowned by a steeple topped with a weathercock—with a penny for an eye. Across the span of this intriguing novel, the watchful cock looks down on all the couples as they socialize, attend responsibly to their civic duties, create an unusual community, swap wives, and develop a tantalizing new religion.

At the end of the novel, the church burns down, but the cock is saved a few days after the fire, before the building collapses: "The old church proved not only badly gutted but structurally unsound: a miracle it had not collapsed of it-self a decade ago." When the weathercock, measuring five feet from beak to tail feathers, is presented by the salvage crew to the minister and two deacons, one a furry-haired satyr, the other a jeweler, we learn that "the clustering children made a parade, a dancing flickering field of color as they jostled and leaped to see better the eye their parents had told them existed." As these children swarmed around the minister and the deacons, they reached out to touch "the dull metal" of the weathercock. "The sky above was empty but for two parallel jet trails."[8]

The novel's central character, Piet Hanema, "affected by this scene of joy,... turned and realized he was standing where he had first glimpsed [his mistress] Foxy getting into her car after church, the spot where later they had met in the shadow of her mother's arrival, her tall body full, she in her pale turban; and he was glad that he would marry her, and frightened that he would not." Piet knows too, as he stands there amid the celebration, that "his life in a sense had ended" (457). He can no longer be in the "magic circle" of the community that he has helped form (451). He has broken the law of couples by breaking from his wife. The narrator tells us, "The Hanemas had become opaque to the other couples, had betrayed the conspiracy of mutual comprehension" (431).

That conspiracy of mutual comprehension lies at the heart of this taunting novel. To understand the novel we must understand the couples, their collective motivation, their interdependency. A failure to understand the terms of the con-spiracy leaves us supposing that the sinners have been punished, their church burned to the ground. Not attentive to the vision of the novel, we might just

---

8. Updike, *Couples* (New York: Ballantine-Fawcett, 1996), 457. Subsequent parenthetical references are to this edition.

think we are inhabiting the land of Hawthorne. But there are no scarlet A's in Updike's town, where adultery is the order of the day—any day. No stigmata.

As the novel opens, Piet and his wife, Angela, back from a party, are undressing. We get to know them in private, in the flesh, before we get to see them clothed in the community. From the outset, nakedness becomes a way of knowing in this fictive world. The Hanemas are recounting a conversation from the party. Someone had asked of the group what "we all see in each other." The town dentist, Freddy Thorne—the novel's most provocative truth teller—had suggested to Angela that all of them constitute a "magic circle of heads to keep the night out." There in the bedroom, Angela tells Piet that Freddy "thinks we've made a church of each other" (7).

Only Piet and Foxy and the Catholics in the crowd (three couples, one of them lapsed) go to church—the Catholics, of course, go out of obligation. But for Piet, the church is the source of his "amazing virility." He tells Angela that night that it provides for him "a stiffening sense of sin" (8). Making a punning play for her naked body, Piet puts himself at risk and loses. In bed, tumescent, he remembers former girlfriends, turns his mind to Foxy Whitman, the new wife in town, and recalls that earlier in the evening he had been on his back at the base of the stairs looking up her dress as she descended. "She had seen him peek and stared him down" (13). There in the bed on his back, "like a town suspended from a steeple," he prays to God for the relief he cannot get from his wife's body (15).

We do not see Piet in such a lonely state again until later in the novel, when he awakes from a dream of death. Lying in bed with his wife, in a panic, he remembers that there are "antidotes" to such panic. He tries to "lull himself with the bodies of women he knew," all of whom, except for the last in this series, are wives in Tarbox:

> Foxy's powdery armpits and petaled cleft simpler than a rose. The freckled boniness below Georgene's throat. Her factual nakedness and feather-cut hair full of gray, dulled his lust to see it, perhaps lovelessness let them come always together. Unlike Angela's ambrosial unsearchable. Carol's lissome waist and nerved-up dancer's legs. Bea Guerin's swarmy drunken breasts, nectar sweat between. The rank elastic crotch of the step-ins of Annabell Vojt who, though both were virgins, would allow him, in that rain-pattered cavity of a car parked amid nodding weedy hay, to kiss there, and exploringly tongue, applying mind to matter. (256)

Having no luck with the women's bodies, Piet turns to prayer and lapses into deeper despair: "He had patronized his faith and lost it. God will not be used.

Death stretched endless under him" (257). As his fear intensifies, he turns finally to Angela and pleads in an "alien" voice for her to put her arm around him. She "half-awoke and half-obeyed" (260).

We gain some sense of what motivates Piet and all the other characters in Tarbox by returning again to that review of de Rougement's two books on love. Updike finds de Rougement "dreadfully right in asserting that love in the Western world has by some means acquired a force far out of proportion to its assumed procreative aim." But, unlike de Rougemont, Updike does not believe that we need either a myth or a heresy to explain this phenomenon. He poses a question and offers his own answer to our human dilemma:

> Might it not simply be that sex has become involved in the Promethean protest forced upon Man by his paradoxical position in the Universe as a self-conscious animal? Our fundamental anxiety is that we do not exist—or will cease to exist. Only in being loved do we find external corroboration of the supremely high valuation each ego secretly assigns itself. This exalted arena, then, is above all others the one where men and women will insist upon their freedom to choose—to choose that other being in whose existence their own existence is confirmed and amplified. Against the claims of this mighty self-assertion, the arguments embodied in law and stricture for self-preservation appear trivial and base. The *virtus* of the choice is diminished if others would also have chosen it for us. The heart *prefers* to move against the grain of circumstance; perversity is the soul's very life. Therefore the enforced and approved bonds of marriage, restricting freedom, weaken love.[9]

The landscape of *Couples* is indeed a landscape of freedom where the men and women of Tarbox test this vexing proposition about love and marriage.

These couples seek relief from their parents' "rigid marriages and formalized evasions" (106). They seek "to substitute an essential fidelity set in a matrix of easy and open companionship among couples." Trying to "improvise a fresh way of life" where "duty and work yielded to truth and fun," they also seek "virtue," not in the marketplace and church but in their homes (106).

Late in the novel, as Piet walks along the beach alone, following his separation from Angela and his estrangement from Foxy, we learn that he "detected companionship in the motion of waves, especially those distant waves lifting arms of spray along the bar, hailing him. The world was more Platonic than he had suspected. He found he missed friends less than friendship; what he felt, remember-

---

9. Updike, "More Love in the Western World," 299.

ing Foxy, was a nostalgia for adultery itself—its adventure, the acrobatics its deceptions demand, the tension of its hidden strings, the new landscapes it makes us master" (429). At this point in the larger story, we have been a party to four of Piet's trysts, each of them a private affair, each of them, in the novel's terms, an adventure of the soul. He, like the other couples, goes about his fornicating in relative privacy. Others know, the gossip spreads, but there is, we must remember, a conspiracy of mutual comprehension at work in this community, a collective but undogmatic belief that what they are all trying to do is figure out what it means to be human—outside the confines of established law.

On the night of the Hanemas' breakup, Ken Whitman summons Angela and Piet to his house to hash out the details of Foxy's affair with Piet. Back home in the aftermath of that ordeal, Angela tells Piet that Foxy is not just another woman to him, that despite his expressed belief that the affair has ended, she doubts it. Piet objects, of course, but realizes even as he speaks that "he believed that there was, behind the screen of couples and houses and days, a Calvinist God Who lifts us up and casts us down in utter freedom, without recourse to our prayers or consultation with our wills." Piet senses at this moment that "Angela had become the messenger of that God" (415). But, if so, it is beyond her knowing.

Without consulting any God, without self-pity, without rancor, Angela decides to leave Piet. That decision to take charge of her life, like her earlier decision to remain monogamous while others frolicked, comes from *within*—not from law, not from her belief in a personal God. Like the others, she works out her own destiny. Only Piet frets over a God who will quell his anxiety and lift the burden of his suffering. When challenged by Foxy about his beliefs, he tells her, "God doesn't love us anymore. . . . We've fallen from grace" (200).

It is strange, then, that in this lighthearted conspiracy of couples the most appealing man would turn out to be Piet, the one "too thick in conscience." Foxy, strong in her own resolve throughout the novel, sheds light on Piet's attractiveness to her and the other women. She writes to him from her own self-imposed exile on an island in the Caribbean, explaining that the "weakness" others associated with him really signified that his "strengths weren't sufficiently used" (449). Bea Guerin, one of his mistresses, had described him as an "old-fashioned man." Foxy sees him as "a splendid red-headed squire, resourceful, loyal, living off the land, repairing armor with old hairpins, kidding [his] way into castles and inns, making impossible ideals work but needing their impossibility to attach [himself] to" (449). She knows that he is more "primitive" than the man she is divorcing and that the future belongs either to her rigidly scientific husband, Ken, or to chaos.

Foxy chooses Piet because she had felt "useful, and used" by him. So she decides that should she marry him, she would not try to "subdue" him. Her letter explains: "How much more generous it would be to let you wander, and suffer— there are so few wanderers left. . . . When you desire to be the world's husband, what right do I have to make you my own?" (449–50). Foxy would nevertheless "possess" him, she promises. In return for being "mastered" by his body, she would "tame" him with her mind. She loves him, she discovers, because he has a "genius for loneliness, for seeing [himself] as something apart from the world" (450). And she wants him to know, finally, that "after weeks of chastity I remember lovemaking as an exploration of a sadness so deep people must go in pairs, one cannot go alone" (451).

When last we see them making love, we learn that, with Piet, Foxy "could be as whorish as she wanted, that unlike most men he really didn't judge" (435). With her, during their reunion weekend, he enjoys a "blind pleasure tasting of infinity." He imagines the sacredness of mouths, proclaims them "noble," and opines that "to eat another is sacred." So there on that Sunday morning, "beneath the hanging clangor of bells," Foxy believes that she "had never felt so taken. No one has ever known me like this," she tells him (435). There in that suspended moment, lost in the abundance of one another's bodies, they corroborate their existence and enjoy a sustaining moment of blissful salvation.

The remarkable achievement of this novel, and the earlier stories, is that Updike compels us to believe in these men and women, compels us to understand that they, like us, are worthy—and to believe, if only for a long moment, that a man like Piet, so lucky with women and so vulnerable in life, might very well be the most *human* and exemplary of us all. Having broken the law of couples, he and Foxy are expelled from the "magic circle," but they, like Angela, go off to couple in other places.

In Updike's world men and women, young and old, cannot live comfortably alone. Seeking salvation apart from a God who has given them license—license to play, license to test the bonds of marriage and the complexities of love against the splendor and squalor of their own desiring—they seem destined, always, to wander together.

Running through this strange and compelling fictive landscape is a force both erotic and mysterious, a force that moves men and women around, vexes them, draws them compulsively together even as it pulls them into a realm where the boundary between lust and love is barely discernible. Like the rest of us, they wander in God's playground living out their lives against the press of an unknown fate.

Updike leaves us wondering whether the tranquillity his characters seek can ever be anything but fleeting, whether the characters themselves can ever know the value of their chosen sacraments. We know only that peace and consolation in this fictive world turn up in the strangest and most haunting of places—beyond the confining strictures of law and just beyond the reach of our own muddled sense of moral order.

Part

V

EXPLORATIONS 3

THE ACHIEVEMENT OF
WALTER SULLIVAN

Places and Spaces in the Fiction of Walter Sullivan

Martha E. Cook

I n three carefully crafted novels published over a span of nearly forty years, Walter Sullivan has created a fictional world from the Middle Tennessee region that claims his heart as well as his imagination. These novels, *Sojourn of a Stranger* (1957), *The Long, Long Love* (1959), and *A Time to Dance* (1995), are set in rural and urban places, on plantations and in city apartments, in times ranging from the years leading up to the Civil War to the 1990s. Their protagonists in turn are a young man attaining maturity and losing the prospects of marriage, a middle-aged man in successive marriages, and an old man and woman reaching the end of their lives in a loving, albeit stormy, marriage. Sullivan's fictional world opens in a historical time and place of possibility, in which the Civil War has not yet torn the nation apart, and moves through time to urban, late-twentieth-century spaces of both endings and beginnings. Likewise, his public themes of race and gender in *Sojourn of a Stranger* narrow to one man's personal struggle with the past in *The Long, Long Love* and the individual, yet universal battle for life in *A Time to Dance*. Throughout these novels, Sullivan literally and symbolically portrays the flora and fauna, the climate, the topography, the roads, the towns, the cities, and the houses of a region that is his actual and fictional home. However, *A Time to Dance* depends less on a sense of place and more on the placeless questions of mortality and faith that increasingly concern Sullivan, as we also see in a small but excellent body of short fiction, published primarily in *Sewanee Review*.

Sojourn of a Stranger is truly a southern story, with themes of race and gender that grow organically from the time and the places Sullivan has chosen for his setting. As Mark Winchell has noted, the elements of setting are "superbly well realized."[1]

1. Winchell, "The Whole Horse: Walter Sullivan and the State of Southern Letters," *Hollins Critic* 27.1 (February 1990): 7.

The novel begins in a historical time and geographical place of possibility, with a journey on a rural road between Memphis and Nashville in the era between the Indian Wars and the Civil War, and concludes with its central character, Allen Hendrick, trapped as the postbellum master of Cedarcrest, a plantation that has lost its signature house not to the ravages of war but to the hatred of one individual. Behind the events of the plot lies the War of 1812; beyond the Middle Tennessee setting lies the historically accurate, culturally unique Louisiana world of the *gens de couleur* that determines the fate of Allen Hendrick.

The first scene, like most subsequent ones, places the characters in a concrete terrain and climate, as they pass through "oak, hickory, hackberries with their top leaves curling and yellow in the July heat," and hints at the historical era, for they travel in a buggy and wagon.[2] They are aware of a crow, a flicker, a rabbit, squirrels; they observe "possum tracks"; they cannot see "the deer, the bear, the yellow-eyed cat" (12). They have come from Memphis and are approaching their destination of Gallatin and Sumner County. Marcus Hendrick, Allen's father, comments on the irony of the direction of their journey: "Nobody else in the history of our nation ever come East to run away." He continues: "When you run away you are supposed to head for Texas" (13). Almost immediately Sullivan reveals the potential conflict faced by the Hendrick family. As they approach Allen's paternal grandfather's land, which borders "General Jackson's plantation" (15), his mother, Lucy, points out, "My brother was with the army at Chalmette." She explains that, when Andrew Jackson marched through the square in New Orleans to celebrate his victory over the British, "behind him were the volunteers in fringed hunting shirts and the free men of color—*les gens de couleur libre*, his mother had called them—who had manned a battery under the moss-hung oaks" (16). Allen thinks that his mother is trying to compensate him for the burden of her mixed ancestry, "trying to give him something to live by. Something out of her past that he might be proud of, a token to compensate for the taint in her family's blood" (17). Subsequent events reveal that Allen has been made aware of his heritage when a stranger in Memphis tells him he "could pass for white" (19) and that his mother has determined that his future lies in being accepted by his white grandfather, General Hendrick. So his father, who has been estranged from his own father for twenty years, is retreating to his boyhood home east of Memphis, where he has made his own small fortune as a broker.

2. Sullivan, *Sojourn of a Stranger* (New York: Henry Holt, 1957), 11. Subsequent parenthetical references are to this edition.

Sullivan uses the climate of Middle Tennessee to mark the passage of time and to symbolize the change in attitude of General Hendrick and his rural community toward Allen. The seasons change; the forsythia blooms and the elms leaf out. Likewise, Allen Hendrick is gradually accepted in the community: "The taint in his blood was almost balanced out by the glory of the old general's name, made tolerable to the people in the town by all the general's land and slaves and money" (15). The general, who has rejected the marriage of Marcus and Lucy, believes he has the power to determine Allen's identity, declaring, "You are a Hendrick" (52). Allen also learns that his grandfather, who has fought in the Union Army, and his father agree in their opposition to the notion of secession and the establishment of the Confederacy. Marcus, in fact, is a nineteenth-century southern liberal. Married to a quadroon, he has published articles in abolitionist newspapers and made speeches in favor of emancipation. Later he reveals to his son that he once freed his only slave and bought other slaves so he could work to free them. He even seems to acknowledge that his attraction to Lucy Martineau was to some degree political, indicating that he found her in a house on the Ramparts in New Orleans and told her, "You will be one quadroon or octoroon who can forsake this life and place" (183). Now, though, he fears what will come to pass, telling his son of hearing from an old man, "In the world there is always meanness, and there is always a bottom rail to any fence" (58). For the old general and for his son, whose life has followed a different path, the division of the nation by war is heinous, but inevitable.

With Allen's growth to maturity, he is educated in the values of his agrarian society, learning about the significance of land: "whoever's got the land has got the money" (62). In this case, the land is the plantation Cedarcrest, a name Marcus pronounces to Allen "slowly, let[ting] it hang in the air between them as if the name itself held some pure value like money or an easy conscience" (22). When he has the opportunity to attend Transylvania College, Allen accepts the offer of his grandfather to remain near Cedarcrest, which will pass to him at the elder's death. When he goes to Nashville on an extended trip to conduct business for his father, Allen longs for the house and hills and fields of Cedarcrest. In Nashville he also continues to develop a relationship with Kate Rutledge, whose father owns the neighboring plantation, Roseneath, back in Sumner County. He imagines sitting with her "at night on the Cedarcrest veranda" (114). At the general's death, Allen recounts the history of his grandfather's life, concluding, "through it all there had been the land" (142). Although the land passes to Allen, his dream of being at Cedarcrest with Kate will never be realized. His grandfather may have declared him a Hendrick; but he is also a Martineau, and the mixed blood of his mother will always be the determining element in his identity in this society.

There is no romanticism in Sullivan's portrayal of setting or theme. The Hendrick family mourns the death of the general, but the plantation remains unaltered: "at Cedarcrest there was no desolation. For the trees still lined the gravel drive, and the water ran yet in the creek." Likewise, the house does not fall with its creator: "the general's house stood firm upon its hilltop. The things he had built and loved, he had left intact" (144). Allen has not lived in the house at Cedarcrest because of the presence there of his widowed aunt Valeria, only four years older than he. When she marries and departs for her new home, the general's heir quietly moves into place. But history has already determined that larger forces of war will disrupt this setting; and Sullivan skillfully blends the historical and the fictional, the public and the personal. Historically Tennesseans were divided by the issues of secession and emancipation, and the character Marcus Hendrick falls dead of a stroke after reading the news of the secession of South Carolina.

The failure of Allen Hendrick's hopes and dreams is inevitable. Lucy has never even visited Cedarcrest, nor does the general ever acknowledge her presence at Marcus's home in Gallatin. She refuses to attend the burial of her husband, secretly taking his gold and returning to her Louisiana family. On the eve of the war, Allen is pressured to enlist in a company of militia formed by his friend Houston Knott. Knott knows of Allen's heritage and has publicly proclaimed his own racist views. Yet he tells Allen: "You are a Hendrick and you own Cedarcrest and the public will all be watching you" (256). Allen has a personal motivation to fight, however. Although Captain Rutledge is General Hendrick's closest friend, he refuses to allow his daughter, Kate, to marry Allen because of Allen's mother. Finally he gives his permission on the condition that Allen fight against the North and that the South is victorious.

The concluding episodes of *Sojourn of a Stranger* are heavily ironic. Allen is promoted to lieutenant after leading "a charge against the colored troops" at Fort Pillow (280). Kate's father dies before the end of the war. When Allen returns to Cedarcrest, he finds a physical setting familiar in history and historical fiction: "No living soul, and no house either. Only a ruin. A shell of four jagged walls" (299). Yet the plantation has not been the scene of a battle or even on the route of retreating Federal troops. Ben Hill, a free black man who experienced a series of perceived betrayals by Marcus, has burned the house out of resentment and frustration at not finding Allen there. Kate has made her own home at Roseneath. Perhaps Allen might find a way to use the past experiences of his father and grandfather to discover how to move into the future, but Kate cannot. She flatly states, "I know only about the present" (316). Although all good historical fiction is firmly grounded in realism, often romance drives the plot—but not here. Kate has been educated at the Nashville Academy, but in her society she can see a future only as her father's daughter, not as Allen's wife. All the forward-thinking words and deeds of Marcus Hendrick cannot reform the hatred that a racist society has bred in Ben Hill, and Allen Hendrick cannot change the hearts and minds of his fellow southerners even by fighting against his own people at Fort Pillow.

The themes of race and gender that Sullivan develops in *Sojourn of a Stranger,* set in mid-nineteenth-century Middle Tennessee, published a hundred years later, recur in southern literature generation after generation. The subjects change, but the questions he raises are raised again in stories set in later times and other places. However, he chose in his next novel, *The Long, Long Love,* to move to a setting contemporaneous with its 1950s composition and to narrow his focus to the continuing question that defines twentieth-century southern literature: how does the modern southerner use the historical past to live in the present so that he can move into the future? *The Long, Long Love* moves back and forth in time through events in the life of Horatio Adams, from the loss of his parents on the *Titanic* to his second marriage and the marriage of his daughter, Anne, and in space from Horatio's Nashville home to the ancestral plantation Adams' Rest. In contrast to *Sojourn of a Stranger,* however, the actual passage of time is only a couple of years and the physical movement of the characters is confined to a much smaller geographical space. Within that limited sphere, Horatio must confront both political questions that stem from actions of his grandfather in the Civil War and personal issues of love and loss, from the death by suicide of his first wife to betrayal by his second, juxtaposed with the death of his only son. Yet, by the conclusion of *The Long, Long Love,* Sullivan has created not only hope for a younger generation but also reconciliation with the past and in the present for Horatio.

The opening setting for *The Long, Long Love* is a gingerbready Victorian house in the Edgefield section of Nashville, the former home of a couple who died on the *Titanic.* Their daughter dies in the influenza epidemic of 1918; their only son, Horatio, survives. A dreamy child, Horatio often wonders what his life would have been like if he had been born somewhere else, like Ohio. He chooses a wife from Ohio, and they build their own home in the fashionable Belle Meade section of Nashville. This desire to make a life for themselves in their own space seems admirable; yet Nancy Adams commits suicide on the night of their twenty-seventh wedding anniversary, unable to face death from cancer or a life with Horatio.

Nancy and Horatio's daughter, Anne, learns from her beau, Vanderbilt history professor Philip Holcomb, that there is some question about the historical accuracy of the family story regarding the circumstances of her great-grandfather's death in the Civil War. Less than a year after Nancy's suicide, Horatio elopes to Mississippi with Emily, a beautiful, sexy woman the age of his son, Tavean. The questions about the death of General Adams and the conflicts within Horatio's and Emily's marriage dominate the succeeding chapters of the novel.

The cultural significance of place in *The Long, Long Love* soon emerges. Emily does not fit into the Belle Meade society of Horatio and his friends:

> She did not know all the old gossip, all the old ramifications of family, the ancient glories and remembered scandals which were the folklore of the country club. . . . If Emily had been born somewhere else, no matter where, if only sufficiently far from Nashville, all would have been different. Her ignorance of the Nashville past would have been accepted and patiently, gleefully rectified, but being from Nashville and not knowing, Emily was suspect.[3]

The relationship of the past to the present as exemplified by place is also evident in the setting of the family plantation, Adams' Rest, located near the small town of Van Buren, the locale of a Civil War battle where General Adams supposedly died and the Confederate cemetery where his remains are believed to lie.

Sullivan cleverly uses the All Saints service at the Episcopal church in Van Buren to put into play a number of seemingly unrelated events. Anne and Horatio attend the service, in memory of Nancy, and return to an awkward scene in which Tavean refers to Emily as his "stepmother" (81). The next day, Tavean has an automobile accident, the recovery from which will place him in much too close contact with Emily as he recuperates at Adams' Rest. Coincidentally, the family learns that vandals have painted the Confederate monument on the square in Van Buren: "the marble shaft above Great-Grandfather Adams' bones was green" (89). When Tavean jokes about the statue, Horatio tries to make him aware of a lesson he has not fully understood himself: "We're what we are because of the past. And what we are will affect the future" (101). Although Emily wants to return "home" to Nashville (118), Horatio has become obsessed with solving the case of vandalism. He tells Anne, "This is home or ought to be more of a home for Emily" (119). Anne, fearful of the growing closeness between Tavean and Emily, responds, "But you keep on worrying about the past and future, and there

3. Sullivan, *The Long, Long Love* (New York: Henry Holt, 1959), 74–75. Subsequent parenthetical references are to this edition.

is nobody attending to the present" (120). After further vandalism, Horatio makes plans to have his grandfather's body moved to the family cemetery at Adams' Rest.

The attempt to dig up General Adams's bones becomes a central event in the plot of *The Long, Long Love*. First, the action draws an unwelcome crowd; no bones are found, but Horatio is more determined than ever to punish the vandals and locate his grandfather's remains. The character of historian Philip moves into a more significant role as he proposes to Anne. Then Horatio seeks his aid, and both Tavean and Philip begin to look into the general's papers at Adams' Rest. Horatio is obsessed with this matter from the distant past; but when Emily inquires about Nancy's suicide, he tells her ironically that she has no right to know about this incident from the more recent past. After Horatio arranges for the marker from his grandfather's grave to be moved to Adams' Rest, he returns to learn that Tavean and Emily are missing; then that they have had an accident; then that Tavean is dead. Anne has to carry the burden of informing her father of each subsequent disaster and making arrangements for Tavean's funeral. Eventually she learns from Philip that General Adams was not killed at Van Buren. From historical records Philip traces the story of the general to Alabama, where he learns that the general is actually buried at Elmview, in Columbia, Tennessee, where supposedly a young man whose mother he had raped killed him. Philip peels away the layers of the past and decides that, more than likely, the general had not raped the woman, who had apparently tended his grave. Major Pearson of Alabama, who was traveling with the general, had fabricated the tale of his death at Van Buren to protect his reputation.

At Adams' Rest, a place Horatio once described as seeming like "another time" (121), he is forced to deal with the death of Tavean, the truth about Emily's affair with his son, and the revelation from the past about his grandfather. At the hospital he tells Emily he never wants to see her again. After a quiet wedding, Anne and Philip move to their own apartment in Nashville, rejecting Horatio's offer to live in his Belle Meade home. Loneliness drives Horatio to retreat to Florida, where he gets drunk and picks up a woman who steals his wallet and his car; he refuses to press charges. Learning of Anne's pregnancy, he retreats to Adams' Rest once again. He resolves to forgive his grandfather and move his body from Elmview in Columbia to Adams' Rest. He now realizes, "I shared the guilt of all the past" (252). Using this hard-won insight, he makes a symbolic journey to Emily's mother's home in Nashville to free her from their marriage, yet discovers that he can forgive Emily, too. In the closing passage of the novel, he acknowledges his own and others' humanity, understanding that "nothing in the world is ever pure" (255). Only at Adams' Rest, a place that represents the past, can he come to terms with the historical past and his own personal past and learn how to move into the future. His first wife, Nancy, builds her own house and life but cannot accept Horatio for what he is. For Anne and Philip, though, a new place—their own space—modest though it may be in material terms, has given them an opportunity for a healthy future. And Philip's historical perspective has given Horatio the answers he could not find for himself. Through smaller places and spaces and a narrower time frame than in *Sojourn of a Stranger,* Sullivan has used his characters in *The Long, Long Love* to answer one of the central questions in the canon of southern literature. As Thomas Daniel Young reminds us in *The Past in the Present: A Thematic Study of Southern Fiction,* this necessity for finding meaning in the past in the present is central to fiction of the Southern Renascence. *The Long, Long Love* is a later novel than Robert Penn Warren's *All the King's Men,* which Sullivan himself sees as the end of this literary era; but it shares Warren's central thematic concerns.

Sullivan's fictional talents lay dormant for decades after the publication of *The Long, Long Love* in 1959, except for the publication of an occasional short story. The appearance of *A Time to Dance* in 1995 marked a change in his use of setting. His awareness of the powerful effects of sense of place in fiction is evident in a brilliant review-essay on Elizabeth Bowen that appeared in *Sewanee Review* in 1976.[4] However, Sullivan explains the diminishing emphasis of setting in his own fiction when he articulates his own deepening concern with the loss of traditional meaning in modern life, especially modern southern life, in an essay he entitled "Southern Writers in Spiritual Exile." There he expresses the need for the southern writer "to seek the transcendent outside the ambience of southern imagery, because the images of the South, familiar and beloved as they are, tempt us to believe that we have not lost our piety."[5]

Thus, in *A Time to Dance* Sullivan depicts his central characters, Max and Bunnie Howard, in a physical world that narrows from their rural home in fictional Nineveh, Tennessee, to an urban Nashville apartment with few distinguishing characteristics. Although the novel moves in memory over a period of about seventy years, it covers an even shorter span of actual time than does *The Long, Long Love.* In depicting this year of illness and death, Sullivan develops the themes

4. Sullivan, "A Sense of Place: Elizabeth Bowen and the Landscape of the Heart," *Sewanee Review* 84.1 (Winter 1976): 142–49.

5. Sullivan, "Southern Writers in Spiritual Exile," in *In Praise of Blood Sports and Other Essays* (Baton Rouge: Louisiana State University Press, 1990), 47.

of mortality and faith that also dominate his later short fiction. Juxtaposed with the story of Bunnie and Max is the account of the growth of love between their nephew, Julien, who helps care for them, and Shannon Marsh, a nurse. *A Time to Dance* opens at Max and Bunnie's home in Nineveh, which is subsequently revealed to be Bunnie's ancestral place, "her house, handed down to her through her family who had built it."[6] The house has been adapted to their lifestyle of alcohol and sexual adventures, with "a wet bar in the library" (24). The library has played a central role in their lives, as Max recalls when he replays the scene in which his friend John Ross chooses that space in which to tell him, "You never were a writer, Max. Nothing you ever did was worth reading" (112). But, with Max at age ninety and Bunnie at eighty-six, she suffers a stroke in Nineveh and they must move to a smaller apartment in Nashville. The urban setting and its culture are not alien to them, but they are confined to much smaller physical spaces than in the past.

As in *The Long, Long Love,* Sullivan uses the cultural significance of place, there to characterize Emily as an outsider, here to establish the Howards as insiders. Max recalls his years as a reporter in Nashville, when only members of the lower class would have become cadavers at the medical school. Times have changed: "It would have been unheard of in the old days for somebody like Jimmy Lucas— who was a member of Belle Meade Country Club and Saint George's Episcopal Church and lived on Chickering Road and drove a Jaguar— to have given his body to be dissected, but Jimmy did exactly that, and insofar as Max could determine he had escaped all criticism" (102–3). Through the recollection of Max and Bunnie's second wedding and reception and in the culminating events of the novel—Julien and Shannon's wedding at the cathedral and Max and Bunnie's sixtieth wedding anniversary celebration—their positions within this society are codified.

While Max and Bunnie are socially and culturally part of a larger world, their present lives in Nashville are highly circumscribed. Bunnie is virtually confined to the apartment by her physical weakness and incontinence. In contrast to her present life, she recalls fleeing to Rome when Max made a pass at her niece Susan, Julien's mother, or traveling to a literary event in New Orleans. Max can move about the city more freely; but his disastrous trip to attempt to purchase a lot at the Catholic cemetery in Nashville, to assure his and Bunnie's burial in consecrated

---

6. Sullivan, *A Time to Dance* (Baton Rouge: Louisiana State University Press, 1995), 43–44. Subsequent parenthetical references are to this edition.

ground, is evidence of his growing loss of independence. He tries to follow a map. He still remembers that Hillsboro Pike becomes Twenty-first Avenue as it approaches downtown Nashville, but he cannot keep the car on the road. As Bunnie's mind "darted from past to present, paused and darted back again" (21), Max struggles to continue to live in the present. Often, however, he is unaware of his position in regard to time or space.

The party room of the apartment complex where the Howards have been forced to move serves as the setting for the climactic scene of Max's death at their sixtieth wedding anniversary celebration. The party seems to be a success, bringing together generations of friends and family and serving in addition as a celebration of Julien and Shannon's marriage earlier in the day at the cathedral. Max and Bunnie have a tender moment of lucidity in which they recall their love for each other. Later, Max makes his way through the crowd to the men's room, "a long, narrow room that looked more like a corridor," where he dies on the toilet (184). The space symbolizes both the confinement of the coffin in which Max will be buried and a passage to his next life. After a funeral at the cathedral, his body is taken to the Howards' home in Nineveh for a wake. Bunnie attempts to have his casket "in the library, close to the windows with Max's head toward the bar" (190), but is persuaded to allow his remains to rest in the more socially appropriate, but less symbolic, living room.

The final scene is set primarily in Bunnie's own space, with comforting sights and sounds. The next morning she awakes "in her own bed at Nineveh. Beyond her open window, a mockingbird sang; there was a patch of sunlight on the familiar wallpaper" (189). Shannon visits Bunnie in her room, and they plan future visits to Nineveh. Not only have Shannon and Julien married; Shannon has deliberately gotten pregnant before the wedding, not to trap Julien, but as a sign of her commitment to family and future. Shannon and Julien become family and future for Bunnie, too; she is childless after two abortions because her pregnancies would have interfered with Max's professional life. Shannon is even able to reconcile herself with her mother in Bunnie's house before she and Julien leave on a honeymoon trip to Paris. Their joyous journey serves as a symbolic contrast to Bunnie's flight to Rome; however, the concept of forgiveness and reconciliation is embodied in that journey as well, because Max followed her and they resumed their life together. Although *A Time to Dance* is firmly grounded in its Middle Tennessee settings, they serve primarily to convey the potential charm and grace of lives so fully realized. Likewise, the theme of the struggle through time to attain and hold on to a life of meaning and happiness is profoundly important. Through concrete details created with wit and cleverness, Sullivan has given his readers a story of the twentieth century, one set in specific southern places and spaces that assumes universal significance.

As one reviewer noted of *Sojourn of a Stranger,* these novels are written "by one who knows his Tennessee."[7] *Sojourn of a Stranger* is the quintessential Tennessee novel. In it Walter Sullivan uses historical research and his own knowledge of Tennessee's places and spaces, her geography and topography, her politics and culture, to develop powerful themes of love and loss that are determined by historical conditions of race and gender. This novel exemplifies Blair Rouse's view in "Time and Place in Southern Fiction" that ideally "setting is so completely embodied in the very fabric of the work that if it were removed the whole structure would collapse and the novel would cease to exist." While the specific Middle Tennessee setting of *The Long, Long Love* is not as organically related to plot and theme, Sullivan has skillfully put to use believable times and places to create the theme that Rouse describes as "characteristically Southern," "the pastness in the very present existence of a central figure or group."[8]

While the Nashville and Nineveh spaces in *A Time to Dance* might be transformed to other settings without losing their thematic significance, they effectively contribute to the mood of this novel and no doubt to the pleasure felt by its readers. More important, however, *A Time to Dance* is related to Sullivan's body of short fiction, which he has continued to publish into the twenty-first century. The stories are virtually placeless. Occasionally the setting is identifiable as Middle Tennessee, perhaps Nashville, but houses small or large, nursing homes, churches, cemeteries lack that "ambience of Southern imagery" that Sullivan has rejected. Likewise, in most of the stories there is an overriding concern with mortality and a search for faith, though there is rarely much hope. When the past figures thematically, it is the characters' personal past; there is little concern with the historical past.

In two stories from the 1970s, religion seems to offer some hope to characters suffering from loss. Mr. Hood in "The Penalty of Love" senses the presence of his dead wife, who at the conclusion of the story seems to be leading him into the church where he has gone seeking answers.[9] "Elizabeth," a more complex and challenging story, opens with the title character recognizing a strong image of the past in the present: "The first thing she saw when she awakened was a relic

7. John Cournos, "Circle of Hate," *Commonweal,* October 11, 1957, 53.

8. Rouse, "Time and Place in Southern Fiction," in *Southern Renascence: The Literature of the Modern South,* ed. Louis D. Rubin Jr. and Robert D. Jacobs (Baltimore: Johns Hopkins University Press, 1953), 139, 132.

9. Sullivan, "The Penalty of Love," *Sewanee Review* 79.1 (Winter 1971): 53–69.

out of her past, a carved figure of the Virgin Mother of God."[10] This relic links Elizabeth to her family and its religious foundation, but only at the conclusion of the story does Sullivan indicate that perhaps this past may give meaning to Elizabeth in the present. In the arms of the character Leah Greenspan, Elizabeth has a powerful memory of her mother praying in a cemetery. As Mark Winchell explains, "She is able to . . . reach far enough into her past to recover a faith that is almost literally childlike."[11] A place represents this concept of faith, though it is not a specifically southern space.

Sullivan's more recent stories vary in the degree of hope that the characters experience. In "Sunset and Evening Star," set in an indistinct nursing home and hospital, the aged main character seeks meaning in religion, only to realize there are "no certainties."[12] "Mortmain" is even bleaker. The character Lucy, forced to confront a secret from her past when her brother-in-law dies, cannot find solace in religion. She throws a sack containing a rosary out her car window, and the story concludes with the following hopeless image: "the rosary fell out and the sack, caught in the light breeze, climbed briefly before it twisted and dipped and fell fluttering to the pavement."[13] In the foreground is the fate of the meaningless sack, rather than the rosary that might give meaning to Lucy's life. The space of the car is one that might symbolize Sullivan's recurring theme of the loss of firmly grounded faith.

Some of Sullivan's stories hint at more positive themes related to religion, but never with certainty. "Only the Dance," one of his few works with a young protagonist, closes with images of rebirth as the character Cecilia swims joyfully in the family pool after a transforming experience with a supernatural figure in another generic cemetery. Yet any real meaning for Cecilia's future lies beyond the scope of the text.[14] On the other hand, in "Love's Mysteries," another story in which secrets of the past emerge with a character's death, Sullivan more fully articulates the hope for healing that religion might provide. The physical world of the protagonist, Dolores, is in flux: she learns that her brother has bought their family home from her father's estate and given it to his lover, who once ran a brothel there. Yet the cathedral of her past seems unchanged. Finally Dolores

---

10. Sullivan, "Elizabeth," *Sewanee Review* 87.3 (Summer 1997): 345–73. Rpt. in *Revelation and Other Fiction from the Sewanee Review: A Centennial Anthology,* ed. George Core (Louisville: Harmony House, 1992), 204–26 (quotation from 204).

11. Winchell, "Whole Horse," 10.

12. Sullivan, "Sunset and Evening Star," *Sewanee Review* 102.3 (Summer 1994): 375.

13. Sullivan, "Mortmain," *Sewanee Review* 106.4 (Fall 1998): 570.

14. Sullivan, "Only the Dance," *Sewanee Review* 107.2 (Spring 1999): 170–86.

acknowledges that her family's own "atonement" must begin with forgiveness: "Living or dead, peace was what they needed now. From the beginning that is what they had all been seeking."[15] But Sullivan reminds us of the difficulty of attaining peace in his most recent story, simply entitled "Losses." In this work a young girl, Addie, is raped after her grandmother's funeral by a mortuary employee. She seeks refuge at a church, but realizes: "What was done was done. No prayer that was said now could change it."[16] Finding no solace in this place of religion, she runs toward home but does not anticipate that she will find the comfort she needs in this domestic space either. Her physical world symbolizes the loss of faith in her spiritual world.

Walter Sullivan's body of criticism is an important means of understanding his vital contribution to the canon of fiction produced in the American South over the second half of the twentieth century and into the twenty-first. His sense of the growing difficulty of finding meaning in history or religion has led him away from the strong sense of place in his novels of the 1950s, *Sojourn of a Stranger* and *The Long, Long Love*. In his most recent novel, *A Time to Dance*, he does not depend on setting to admit the possibility of finding meaning through the context of the personal past and of religion. His small but significant body of short fiction is set in a region with little sense of history or place; freed from the temptation to find meaning in the surface images that characterize the South of his heart, Sullivan has in this fiction opened up spaces to confront the timeless and placeless themes that engage his intellect and integrity.

15. Sullivan, "Love's Mysteries," *Sewanee Review* 109.4 (Fall 2001): 510.

16. Sullivan, "Losses," in *The Cry of an Occasion: Fiction from the Fellowship of Southern Writers*, ed. Richard Bausch (Baton Rouge: Louisiana State University Press, 2001), 189.

Walter Sullivan
A Profile

George Core

—the Muse's judge and friend,
Who justly knew to blame or to commend;
To failings mild, but zealous for desert;
The clearest head, and the sincerest heart.
—ALEXANDER POPE, *ESSAY ON CRITICISM*

W alter Laurence Sullivan, who was born in Nashville in 1924, has lived there all his life save for two periods in the 1940s when he served in the U.S. Marine Corps as a lieutenant during World War II and, later, when he earned an MFA in English at the University of Iowa. A graduate of the college at Vanderbilt University (1947), he joined the faculty there in 1949 and taught in the English department with great distinction until he retired in 2000. During that time he taught chiefly the modern British and American novel and fiction writing. Professor Sullivan is a superb lecturer who varies his presentation depending on the complexion of his audiences. "In his concluding lecture on a novel . . . Sullivan would deliver a peroration, hitting a spellbinding rhetorical height I had not heard outside a Southern Baptist church," Robert Buffington has written of Sullivan's demanding but popular course on the novel.

The man of letters, like the woman of letters, is a threatened species with no game wardens to protect it. Like the mule it cannot reproduce itself, and there is little more call these days, in or out of the academy, for such a writer than for a mule, no matter how crafty and hardworking either breed may be. Walter Sullivan, a man of letters as well as a professor, is best known as a critic. He has written essays and reviews for *Southern Review, Georgia Review, Sewanee Review,* and other periodicals; and many of the best of these pieces have been collected in *Death by Melancholy* (1972), *A Requiem for the Renascence* (1976), and *Blood Sports* (1990), two of which, like all of his novels, have been published or reprinted by Louisiana State University Press. He is also a fiction writer and a memoirist. He has published three novels, and well over a dozen of his stories have appeared in *Sewanee Review* and elsewhere; the best of these stories should be collected in a book. Among the strongest are "Elizabeth" (1979), which was reprinted in the O. Henry yearbook the next year; "Sunset and Evening Star" (1994); "Mortmain" (1998); "Only the Dance" (1999); and "Love's Mysteries" (2001)—all published in *Sewanee Review*. "Only the Dance" first appeared in *Southern Excursions,* a collector's item published by the Fellowship of Southern Writers, of which Sullivan is a founding member. He was elected chancellor in April 2001, a post in which he served through the spring of 2004.

His other honors include a Ford Foundation fellowship, a *Sewanee Review* fellowship, and an appointment as a Lamar lecturer at Mercer University (which resulted in *Requiem for the Renascence*). In addition to Mercer he has lectured at many colleges and universities: Davidson, Louisiana State, the University of North Carolina, Emory, Nicholls State.

Sullivan has written a book-length memoir about Allen Tate (1988), and he has struck many tributes to writers recently deceased—among them Robert Penn Warren, Peter Taylor, Andrew Lytle, Graham Greene, and Donald Davie. As a memoirist he brings to bear his affection and admiration for the person involved, his sharply etched recollections, and his graceful style. Of Warren's painful last days he declares: "The poetry and fiction and criticism were finished, but by facing it with courage and fortitude, he was making the long act of his dying an example for his friends." Of Greene he observes: "He could set a scene in a sentence, bring to life an already dead character by describing the room he lived in, bridge the gap between sequences with a repeated line of conversation, and show, better than any writer of his generation, fear in a handful of dust." Of Davie he remarks: "Embellishment of life in general was a part of his gift to those who knew him—embellishment not by exaggeration, but by the depth of his perceptions—by his knowing more than the rest of us know and by his saying it better in sentences that were almost as well formed as his written prose." In concluding his account of Allen Tate with a scene that unfolded at the house of Frances and Brainard Cheney, Sullivan mentions Tate's "capacity for monstrous behavior," explaining: "He was a complicated man, but without his complications and complexities, he perhaps could not have written his criticism and his poetry. I thought that night, not for the first time, that much of the little understanding I have of literature had come from him, and I was grateful. Whatever small agonies his bad temper had caused me were nothing when weighed against the benefits of his friendship. I had been lucky to know him."

This cast of writers and characters—southerners and Englishmen—represents many of the figures who have absorbed Walter Sullivan as a teacher and a critic. He has often written about such modern British writers as Conrad, Greene, Evelyn Waugh, Elizabeth Bowen, and William Golding and such southern writers as Faulkner, Warren, Tate, Lytle, Welty, Peter Taylor, and Flannery O'Connor. In addition to writing about these novelists he has regularly reviewed new fiction throughout his career, considering such writers as Walker Percy, Cormac McCarthy, and George Garrett over a long period and reviewing novels by such hands as Anne Tyler, Bobbie Ann Mason, Madison Smartt Bell, John Updike, and William Maxwell.

For the most part the writers who have most engaged Sullivan have been Christian, many of them deeply religious. In pondering this matter, Sullivan has quoted Jacques Maritain: "'Only a Christian, nay, a mystic, can be a complete novelist.' The subject of fiction, Maritain went on, is 'the conduct of human life itself,' and only the mystic 'has some idea of *what there* is in *man.*' Maritain refers here, I think, to our almost limitless capacities for good and for evil."

So it is the religious dimension of art, its spirituality, that has most engaged Walter Sullivan as a critic; and it is also an element in his fiction, especially in the short story "Elizabeth," to which I shall return. This distinctive emphasis undergirds and fortifies and enlivens his criticism, especially *Death by Melancholy: Essays on Modern Southern Fiction,* a book that is by no means a random collection. In the title essay that ends the book, he states: "In the exacerbations and polarizations of our time, good and evil are manifesting themselves in terms at once more subtle and more flagrant than ever before. Disorder, which is a final confirmation of evil, is everywhere, and we must encompass this fact in our work without disordering the world itself or suffering an accompanying disorder of our spirits. . . . We must avoid the temptation to portray evil for its own sake. . . . We must find images that will convey the full scale of the battle, and nothing less than the stake for which the struggle is being joined, which is the spiritual survival of mankind." Such a sacramental way of looking at the world and conveying human experience appears in a writer so indifferent to religion as Joseph Conrad—"not in the ordinary way a pious man," as Sullivan says. He quotes Greene on Conrad: "All he retained of Catholicism was the ironic sense of an omniscience and of the final unimportance of human life under watching eyes." This ironic view "conveys the absurdity of the world as Conrad saw it and the moral frailty of those that inhabit it," Sullivan concludes.

In his story "Elizabeth," Sullivan discovers and reveals a universal image that embodies the suffering of the protagonist and her staunch Catholic faith in the face of adversity. At the end of the action, after Elizabeth has left and then lost her petty, abusive husband (who has been murdered in a barroom brawl), the husband who caused her to lose their baby, she weeps in a city morgue and wonders what will become of her. Then she recalls going to a cemetery as a child to pray with her mother and other women "for the poor souls in purgatory." She thinks of that bright autumn day long ago when she was innocent and hopeful, remembering "the praying voices of the women." And suddenly she sees "a statue of the Mother of God rising above her."

In his novels Walter Sullivan has progressed from historical fiction in *Sojourn of a Stranger* (1957) to a novel of the contemporary world in which the action is deeply affected by the dead hand of the past, *The Long, Long Love* (1959), to a comedy of manners of the present day. *A Time to Dance* (1995) chiefly concerns the lives of an ancient couple, Max and Bunnie Howard, who are heading toward eternity without ever having grown up. Their childless marriage has been fitful and promiscuous. This novel, as Robert Buffington puts it, "is written in the vein of Muriel Spark's *Memento Mori*." There are many hilarious sequences, especially one that involves a funny and pathetic odyssey when Max sets out for the cemetery. He causes a traffic jam, general pandemonium, and near mayhem. Max infuriates various drivers, including a trucker who pushes Max's old Chevrolet with reckless abandon. Having narrowly avoided catastrophe, Max thinks to himself: "The son of a bitch . . . tried to kill me." Max now celebrates his dubious triumph with a drink and then another at a convenient restaurant, and after an encounter with the police and some infuriated citizens, he makes his way to the cemetery by cab. He goes to visit an old friend and enemy, John Ross, a man whom he had helped to bury and with whom he had attempted to inter his own last (and dismal) novel. Poor Max.

The American Civil War plays a major part in Sullivan's first novel and a lesser role in his second. It is the subject of a brilliant anthology that he has edited entitled *The War the Women Lived* (1995), a selection of lively and perspicuous essays and letters written by southern women who not only lived through the war but often participated in it, sometimes as spies. These pieces constitute a chronicle of war that occasionally has a fictive quality as well as a powerful autobiographical

impetus. Like many writers born in the South before World War II, Walter Sullivan has been fascinated by the Civil War, which continues to exercise a strong
pull. Think of *Cold Mountain* and *Jacob's Ladder*.

Walter Sullivan, being a real writer who is profoundly committed to that vocation, will continue creating fiction and forging criticism to the end of his days,
just as he will continue listening to classical music (particularly Beethoven), seeing the three children that he and Jane, his wife of fifty years, long ago produced,
and spoiling his grandchildren, all of whom live in Nashville. He will also watch
Vanderbilt sporting events, especially football, no matter how hapless the team,
and follow the fortunes of the resurgent Tennessee Titans. The Sullivans will also
continue to entertain their friends, including Louis D. Rubin Jr., Lewis P. Simpson, George Garrett, and Elizabeth Spencer. They have lost Tinkum and Cleanth
Brooks, Eleanor and Red Warren, and the Cheneys; but their numerous acquaintance still includes many persons, writers or not, whom they have long
loved and entertained. They are famous as hosts and conversationalists and racon-
teurs and are possessed of a grace and style rarely seen today.

Part

VI

Winter in the Mountains

David Middleton

Outside, unnumbered flakes unique
Yet one in common hexagon,
Build up against shut windows bleak
With restless flurries stilled and wan.

Within, huge hearth-logs fall in char,
Winged ash-flakes tinged by singeing fire
A flue-screen's meshings draw and bar,
Then drop like palls where flares expire.

And there, behind an iron grate
Some mountain Wayland made from ore
Running in deep-laid veins sedate,
A bolt-struck oak now burns before

This winter pioneer at last
To cabin bound though stream and wood
By title-deeds of our shared past
Are mine forever and for good.

Yet still my mind, unsettled, broods
On tares whose numbers dwarf the wheat
When these new minds whose lust exudes
Let flooded farms, split atoms meet

At Oak Ridge and the TVA,
Sappers of history's taproot truth,
Late stewards true to this false day,
Who never read the Book of Ruth.

Now I, like Ruth, am exiled home,
Our stories ones of love, not hate,
Though, unlike her, I could not comb
A yielding field, for I come late,

Too late to take the red man's path
Through those first-falls of frost and bloom,
Too soon for this sad aftermath
Of self-wed-self, both bride and groom.

And now from walls old frames come down
Of men long past such petty fate,
Great men our mountain laurels crown,
John Ransom, Davidson, and Tate.

Yet by this rocking chair, my hounds
Hunt on in dream the pigeon, quail
Through meadows where agrarian sounds
Still rise from memory's fading trail.

And I, till death, will brood on flames
Consumed by ash they cannot burn
Of laurel, oak, those ancient names
Souls yet unborn will come to learn.

About the Contributors

Robert Benson, professor of English at the University of the South and director of its program in medieval studies, has coedited books deriving from the university's annual colloquium on the Middle Ages, the latest of which is *New Readings of Chaucer's Poetry* (2003). He is completing a book of reminiscences provisionally entitled "Blood and Memory." These pieces have appeared in *Shenandoah, Southwest Review,* and elsewhere; one of his latest essays, "Charactered by Memory," won the Monroe Spears prize for the best essay published in the *Sewanee Review* during 2003.

Wendell Berry, who farms and writes in Port Royal, Kentucky, his hometown, is widely known as a novelist, a poet, a lecturer, and an essayist. His prose and poetry often concern the natural world and the agrarian economy of the small farm. Berry taught English at the University of Kentucky for many years before he quit to devote more time to farming and writing. Among his recent books are *Jayber Crow,* a novel; *Citizenship Papers,* a collection of essays; and *That Distant Land,* his collected stories. A new novel, *Hannah Coulter,* will be published in the fall of 2004.

Joseph Blotner, who lives in retirement in Charlottesville, taught principally at the University of Virginia, the University of North Carolina, and the University of Michigan. He is chiefly known for his durable biographies of William Faulkner and Robert Penn Warren. He coedited *Faulkner in the University* and edited Faulkner's stories and letters. Recently he has edited four volumes of Faulkner's novels with Noel Polk for the Library of America. His one-volume life of Faulkner is being reissued by the University Press of Mississippi. Next year Louisiana State University Press will publish his memoir, "Adventures of a Lucky Man," now in production.

Thomas Bontly did his Ph.D. work at Stanford and in the process, by a pleasant fortuity, studied writing under Wallace Stegner. Stegner placed Bontly's first novel, *The Competitor* (1966), at Scribner's. Since joining the faculty at the University of Wisconsin–Milwaukee (where he taught for thirty-five years), he published twenty-five short stories and three more novels: *The Adventures of a Young Outlaw, Celestial Chess,* and *The Giant's Shadow.* He has written critical essays on Henry James and William Allen White in addition to Stegner. Retired from teaching, he lives in Milwaukee and is at work on several new projects, including an academic autobiography.

Martha E. Cook studied under Walter Sullivan while doing her graduate work at Vanderbilt University. She has written on many southern authors, beginning with Allen Tate and Donald Davidson, the subject of an essay by her in *Southern Review.* She has also written about Ellen Glasgow, Evelyn Scott, Flannery O'Connor, and William Hoffman. She was coeditor of *Resources in American Literary Study* during 1980–1986 and held a Fulbright fellowship in New Zealand in 1988. For some years she has taught at Longwood University in Virginia, where she is professor of English.

George Core, who has edited *Sewanee Review* since 1973, was previously senior editor of the University of Georgia Press after having taught English at Davidson College. He has been a regular contributor to the American periodical press since the late 1960s and has edited various books, including *The Selected Letters of John Crowe Ransom,* with Thomas Daniel Young (1985), and *The Critics Who Made Us* (1993). He and Walter Sullivan wrote a textbook entitled *Writing from the Inside,* published by W. W. Norton. Since 1988 he and his wife, Susan, have sojourned in London in the late summer and have seen many plays, which they have occasionally reviewed for the *Hudson Review* and the *Sewanee Review.*

Scott Donaldson, who began his career as a newspaperman in his hometown, Minneapolis, taught American literature for many years at the College of William and Mary, where he was Cooley professor of English. He held two Fulbright appointments during his tenure there. His books include biographies of Winfield Townley Scott, Hemingway, Fitzgerald, Cheever, and MacLeish. He now lives most of the year in Scottsdale, Arizona, and the remainder in San Diego. He is writing a biography of Edwin Arlington Robinson. Donaldson has twice won prizes from *Sewanee Review* for his writing.

Denis Donoghue, a native of Ireland who taught for many years at University College, Dublin, before becoming Henry James professor of English at New York University, has lectured and written widely on many subjects in the United States, Great Britain, and Ireland. His books of criticism include *Connoisseurs of Chaos, Ferocious Alphabets, We Irish, The Practice of Reading* (which won the Cleanth Brooks prize in literary criticism), and, most recently, *Speaking of Beauty.* He writes regularly for the *New York Review of Books, New York Times Book Review, Times Literary Supplement,* and other periodicals. He is also the author of a memoir, *Warrenpoint,* which is devoted to his early life in Northern Ireland. He is writing a book tentatively entitled "Five in American Literature" on classic writers of the nineteenth century.

Charles East joined Louisiana State University Press as editor in 1962 after having worked at *Collier's* magazine and having been a newspaperman in Baton Rouge on the morning and afternoon papers. He became director of Louisiana State University Press in 1970 and remained in that position for five years. Later he returned to scholarly publishing at the University of Georgia Press (1980–1983), where under his direction the Flannery O'Connor Award for Short Fiction was established in 1981. East has published two collections of stories, *Where the Music Was* and *Distant Friends and Intimate Strangers,* and he edited *The Civil War Diary of Sarah Morgan.* His stories have appeared in the *Southern Review, Virginia Quarterly,* the *Yale Review,* and the *Sewanee Review.*

George Garrett, a man of letters who has written or edited some fifty books, is a novelist and short-story writer, a critic, and a poet who has received many honors. His career was celebrated at the University of Tennessee in Knoxville in October 2003. Among his latest books are *Southern Excursions* (a book of essays published in 2003) and *Double Vision* (a novel forthcoming in 2004). Garrett was for many years the Hoyns professor of English at the University of Virginia, where he ran the writing program. His most enduring work is his trilogy of novels on the Elizabethan period that begins with *The Death of the Fox* (1971).

Martha Lacy Hall worked for twenty years at Louisiana State University Press, beginning as an editor. For her last ten years there, she served as managing editor and as the acquiring editor for the press's fiction program. Her short stories have appeared in such magazines as *Southern Review, Virginia Quarterly, New Orleans Review,* and *Sewanee Review.* Her three collections of stories are *Call It Living, The Music Lesson* (in which "Privacy" appears), and *The Apple-Green Triumph.* She continues to write short fiction and to live in Baton Rouge.

Pat C. Hoy II, who has been directing the program in expository writing at New York University since 1993, previously taught English at his alma mater, West Point, and at Harvard University. He retired from the U.S. Army as a colonel after thirty years of service that included tours in Korea and Vietnam. He is author and editor of various textbooks and anthologies. Some of his essays have been collected in *Instinct for Survival* (1992); many of them appeared in *Virginia Quarterly* and *Sewanee Review.* In 2003 Hoy was awarded the Cecil Woods prize by the Fellowship of Southern Writers for distinguished achievement in nonfiction prose.

David Middleton is poet in residence, distinguished service professor, and Alcee Fortier distinguished professor at Nicholls State University in Thibodaux, Louisiana, where he has taught since 1977. He is poetry editor for *Classical Outlook* and *Anglican Theological Review.* His seven collections of verse include *The Burning Fields, As Far as Light Remains,* and *Beyond the Chandeleurs.* "The Habitual Peacefulness of Gruchy: Poems after Pictures by J.-F. Millet" is being released by Louisiana State University Press, his principal publisher, in 2005. Middleton's poems have appeared often in *Southern Review, Sewanee Review, Critical Quarterly,* and other periodicals.

William Pratt, professor of English, emeritus, at Miami University in Oxford, Ohio, has lectured widely, at home and abroad, and has presented papers at many international literary conferences, including the Yeats and Joyce summer schools. He has published poems, translations, and critical essays and reviews in various literary periodicals; and he is the editor of two durable anthologies now in revised editions: *The Imagist Poem* (1963, 2001) and *The Fugitive Poets* (1965, 1991). His latest book is *Ezra Pound, Nature and Myth,* which he coedited; and he is now working on another book about Pound.

Louis D. Rubin, Jr., a native of Charleston, South Carolina, is the author and editor of some fifty books, which include three novels. He is best known as a critic and editor. He has founded three literary magazines and Algonquin Books, a publishing house. His association and friendship with Walter Sullivan extend more than half a century and began when Sullivan published an essay in *Southern Renascence* (1953), which Rubin edited with Robert D. Jacobs. Rubin and Sullivan are founding members of the Fellowship of Southern Writers, and both have served as chancellor. *Writing in the South XVI* (*Southern Review,* autumn 2000) is a tribute to Rubin, whose latest book is a memoir, *My Father's People.*

Lewis P. Simpson, Boyd professor and William A. Read professor of English, emeritus, at Louisiana State University, coedited *Southern Review* from 1964 through 1987 and then served as consulting editor until 2004. His books include *The Man of Letters in New England and the South, The Dispossessed Garden, The Brazen Face of History, Mind and the American War* (which received the Craven award from the Organization of American Historians), and *The Fable of the Southern Writer* (which earned the Landry award and the Robert Penn Warren award). He has edited another five books, and he is the series editor of the Library of Southern Civilization (Louisiana State University Press). Simpson has held fellowships from the Guggenheim foundation and the National Endowment for the Humanities, and he is a founding member of the Fellowship of Southern Writers. He is completing a book entitled "Imagining Our Times: A Study in the Alienation of Memory in American Letters from Henry James to Walker Percy."

Elizabeth Spencer is a member of the American Academy of Arts and Letters and of the Fellowship of Southern Writers. She has regularly published fiction since 1948 when her first novel, *Fire in the Morning*, was released. Her novels include *The Voice at the Back Door, The Salt Line, The Night Travellers*, and *The Light in the Piazza* (of which a movie is now being produced). Her latest collection of stories is *The Southern Woman: New and Collected Fiction*, and her reminiscences appear in *Landscapes of the Heart*. Spencer has taught at many universities and colleges, chiefly the University of Mississippi, Concordia University (Montreal), and the University of North Carolina. She lives in Chapel Hill and is now writing a short novel.

H. L. Weatherby, who taught English for forty years at Vanderbilt University, began his career as a scholar and critic by writing on figures in the Victorian and modern periods, including Newman, Hopkins, Arnold, Hardy, and T. S. Eliot. That work resulted in two books: *Cardinal Newman in His Age* (1973) and *The Keen Delight: The Christian Poet in the Modern World* (1975). He also wrote on various modern southern writers for several periodicals. More recently he has given his attention to Edmund Spenser, and from this interest has sprung *Mirrors of Celestial Grace* (1994) as well as articles in a variety of scholarly journals. Weatherby lives and works in his hometown, Montgomery, Alabama.

Index